THE TROUBLED LIFE AND MYSTERIOUS DEATH OF JOHNNY RINGO

COLD WEST PUBLISHING

An imprint of Creative Texts Publishers, LLC
Barto, PA

The Troubled Life and Mysterious Death of Johnny Ringo
by Kevin Hogge
Copyright 2018 Kevin Hogge

Published by Cold West Publishing,
An imprint of Creative Texts Publishers, LLC
PO Box 50
Barto, PA 19504
www.coldwest.com

ISBN: 978-0-578-41767-7

THE TROUBLED LIFE AND MYSTERIOUS DEATH OF JOHNNY RINGO

BY KEVIN HOGGE

COLD WEST PUBLISHING

An imprint of Creative Texts Publishers, LLC
Barto, PA

ACKNOWLEDGEMENTS

Many thanks to Steve Sederwall of Cold West Detective Agency for his insight and contributions. Thank you for teaching me to approach history as an investigator and thank you for believing in me.

I would like to thank David Johnson, Gary Roberts, and Casey Teffertiller for their scholarship in this field. Any direct information gleaned from their bodies of work, as included in this project, have been properly credited within these pages. However, my attention to their works, as I've studied this field, have had a profound effect on my research ability and understanding of this topic. Their depth of commitment has been an inspiration to me, for which I am most grateful.

TABLE OF CONTENTS

History Is An Argument Without End
Pieter Geyl - 1949

This book is dedicated to our hard-working law enforcement officers.
From those who fought to tame the unsettled west,
to our current day police officers who risk their lives
each day to keep our communities safe.

Thank you!

CHAPTER ONE

THE MAN BEHIND THE MYTH

The Civil War changed America in many ways. We entered this devastating period of our history as "these" United States, and emerged as "the" United States. A distinction with little meaning to Twenty-First Century Americans, but clearly understood in May 1865 as a consequential defeat to personal freedoms. The sovereignty of the 'several' states, as protected under the Tenth Amendment of the Constitution, had been lost to the emerging power of a dominate federal government not intended by the founders. The animosity and bitterness which led to secession still existed at the end of the conflict, but now without remedy.

The war martialed in broad cultural and political changes, but it also accelerated the westward expansion of the nation. The south had little to offer after the war as her resources had been stolen or burned, which demoralized her citizens and destroyed the economy. Most Confederate soldiers returned to their homes with little hope of rebuilding their lives. The agrarian society of the south was buried in deep depression. Confederate currency was worthless, with U.S. dollars hard to find. Many were fortunate enough to find their families still intact, but even for them there were hard choices ahead. Many were not so lucky and returned to burned out homes and barns, some not knowing the whereabouts of loved ones.

It was a hard time, mentally as well as economically. Those who'd survived the physical maladies of war still returned with the trauma it had inflicted. Some possessed the fortitude to overcome the things they'd seen or done, while others suffered from 'Soldiers Heart' as it was described in those days. Today, the emotional aftermath of war is referred to as PTSD, (Post-traumatic stress disorder). For many who decided to leave the south and go west, this very syndrome separated the settler from the outlaw.

The Homestead Act of 1862 was one of the most important legislative acts of its day. Designed to enhance the westward growth of our nation, it offered 160 acres to those with a head of household at least 21 years of age. There were limited stipulations. Recipients had to vow not to take up arms against the United States, and to work the land for at least five years. This act opened up the vast area west of the Mississippi as never before. Eastern farmers with small parcels of land, immigrants, and ex-slaves were among the most interested parties. The west, with its many opportunities, offered hope for the hopeless. A place of promise for families to build a new life with only a dream and a few acres of dirt. For the young southern soldier who'd learned to kill, the west held a vast array of opportunities for him as well. It was a primitive time west of the Pecos, where man lived by his own law. Towns were few and far apart, with a lawman as hard to find as a preacher.

As dreams turned to reality, the new residents of the southwest found corn cribs harder to fill than they'd expected and harder to keep once they did. Rustlers, thieves, and Indians set upon the eastern tenderfoot until he learned the way of the west and began to shoot back. It was a new world, with the growing pains of a young nation, finding its way as the *Wild West* was born.

By the early 1870's, America was seeing the first wave of the industrial age. John D. Rockefeller incorporated Standard Oil in 1870, as the railroad was expanding westward with new towns growing from each water stop. On November 1, 1870, the National Weather Service issued its first weather report, and sixty years after the invention of the tin can, Connecticut resident William Lion invented the first efficient can opener. For his part, Johnny Ringo left San Jose at the age of twenty in late 1870, and headed south to begin life as a man. Industry was capturing the east, but to the newly settled heartland in the west, cattle would be the primary resource. As the eastern oil tycoons measured their wealth by the barrel, the Texas cattle barons counted theirs by the head.

The King Ranch, located in south Texas between Corpus Christi and Brownsville, is credited as having marked the beginning of what many would call the 'old west'. It was 1866. With a thriving market for beef back east and some five million head of cattle on the Texas range, ranching became her natural industry. It all began with their first cattle drive to the Kansas railheads that fall. The endeavor took better than a hundred days, and defined the drover as we know him today.

These were not the first cattle drives; the Mexican *vaqueros* had perfected that art many years prior. These were, however, the first under a new set of standards. The establishment of the Chisolm Trail, and the invention of the chuckwagon by Charles Goodnight brought a new discipline to a very difficult task.

By the mid 1870's, the cow-town was defined by places such as Abilene, Wichita, and the 'Queen of the Cow-Towns', Dodge City. With it came the presence of Wyatt Earp, a buffalo hunter and Earp friend Bat Masterson, and a gambler and a dentist named Doc Holliday.

Johnny Ringo

Wyatt Earp

As Earp and Masterson wore the badge of a deputy city marshal, Holliday applied his trade as a dentist in Room 24 of the Dodge House during the day and worked the gambling tables at night.

The Kansas cow-towns were the western point for the railroads at that time and thus became the final destination for the Texas ranchers driving their beef to market. With cattle drives originating in south Texas, a herd of two thousand head of cattle could take up to four months to deliver to the railhead. By the time they arrived in town, the drovers were ready to blow off steam and have a good time. Keeping them in line once they arrived was the task of men like Earp and Masterson. Their brand of law enforcement played a major role in taming the cattle towns.

With hundreds of young men off the trail, some as young as sixteen, it was the job of the lawman to keep them alive and out of jail. Dead or incarcerated men can't spend money and the gamblers, prostitutes, and saloon owners wanted to see as much of their money as possible placed on the bars, dressers, or poker tables of their establishments. Many of these careless drovers were separated from four month's pay in less than a week.

As the 1870's ended, a little-known section of the southern Arizona desert referred to as Goose Flats caught everyone's attention. A silver strike discovered by a Ft. Huachuca scout named Ed Schieffelin, unearthed some of the richest ore of its time. Prospectors, and fortune hunters came by the thousands. The community that grew there, would soon earn the name Tombstone. It will forever be known as the town "Too Tough to Die" and became the center of it all.

In November 1879, the Earp family and Johnny Ringo made their way into the Arizona Territory within days of one another. They came in from different directions and for different reasons, without realizing they were heading for a collision course. It was a clash of culture and ideals, as each struggled to stake their claim in a land yet undefined. The ill will which developed between the Earp supporters and those who favored the cowboy ways would soon begin to foment and neither side realized it was coming.

Ringo and Joe Hill, whose real name was Joseph Graves Olney, came to Arizona at the end of the Mason County War. Olney had ridden closely with Scott Cooley and Ringo during the Texas conflict, making him a target of "the mob", as law enforcement officers of Mason County were referred. In the aftermath, Olney moved his family to Silver City, New Mexico, while Ringo remained in Loyal Valley until leaving Texas along with Olney in November 1879.

Olney was wanted on a murder charge stemming from the September 7, 1876 shooting of Burnet County deputies S.B. Martin, and Wilson Roundtree as they attempted an arrest for the alleged theft of hogs and cattle. It was a charge Olney denied. This is but one of many battles of the Mason County War to be discussed later in greater detail.

Olney avoided capture at the time and stayed in the fight but he eventually left Texas for New Mexico. There, he established a ranch near Mimbres in the southwest portion of Grant County, but his stay there was short lived. In the midst of the Lincoln County War, Governor Lew Wallace issued papers for his arrest and extradition back to Texas, which he again avoided. By early June of 1879, Olney was back in Loyal Valley to enlist Ringo's help in getting his two brothers out of jail. He had a plan, and since they weren't exactly going through the front door, they also had a plan for leaving Texas once it was done. On June 11, 1879, he and Johnny Ringo left for El Paso on their way back to Silver City New Mexico, with the Arizona Territory as their intended destination.

Early writers and historians invested little research into why Ringo left Texas with Joseph Olney. His travels from Loyal Valley to Arizona have been widely overlooked until the exhaustive research by David Johnson for his 1996 novel; *John Ringo, King of the Cowboys*. In his research, Johnson concluded that Joe Olney came back to Loyal Valley to ask for Ringo's help. Olney had been instrumental in breaking Ringo out of the Lampasas jail in 1878, and Ringo by all accounts would go to great lengths to provide or repay a favor to a friend.

According to Joe Olney's grandson, his brothers Oscar and Ed had been arrested in Llano on a trumped-up charge to draw Joe back to Texas. With a plan to get them out, Joe Olney went to Johnny Ringo. Ed Olney recalled that he and his brother were sitting on a bunk when suddenly the back of the jail wall blew out. Next thing he knew, they were on horses fleeing to west Texas. Before reaching El Paso, Joseph Olney parted from his brothers, and sent them on their way as he and Ringo continued on.

In November '79, Ringo and Olney hooked up with Mr. John Parks and his wagon train in Ysleta, Texas (El Paso). Parks was moving his family and others, from Acton, Texas to New Mexico and had made camp near Ysleta to wait out an Apache dust-up. In Jane Parks Ringgold's reprint of her father's diary, *Frontier Days in the Southwest*,[1] she placed Ringo and Olney at their camp beginning in early November 1879. From there, they travelled along to help stave off Apache until they reached Silver City where Olney's wife Agnes Jane and their children were residing. With Arizona in mind, the two men set out for San Simon after a few days stay.

With any curiosity at all one has to ask why, or even how, Ringo rode into the Parks camp. As it turned out, John Parks' party stopped in Mason County in June of '79. Not much is recorded in his journal about their stay, except that they were there. It does, however, seem quite obvious that Mr. Parks and John Ringo crossed paths during that time. The encounter must have been pleasant, with Ringo leaving with the knowledge of the route Mr. Parks was undertaking. Parks in turn, must have left the conversation with an understanding of which side of the law John Ringo supported.

Jane Parks recalled that as Ringo and Olney rode into their camp in November, her father recognized Ringo right off. Marking Ringo's station in life, Parks referred to the two heavily armed men he saw approaching their camp as; "Johnny Ringo and another outlaw." Mr. Parks left Mason with a sense of respect for Ringo, referring to him as; "A man of many good traits." [2]

So why was Ringo set on heading to El Paso while in route to New Mexico? Very simple. He knew Parks was there, and also heading to New Mexico. What better place to hide from the law than riding along with a wagon train?

Ringo and Olney crossed into Arizona Territory within a few days' time, and settled near the San Simon Cienage, on the border of New Mexico, not far from Galeyville. Joseph Graves Olney had now become Joe Hill. By all accounts Ringo roomed at Hill's house and never established an actual residence. This would be the place where they spent

---

[1] Frontier Days in the Southwest; The Naylor Company 1952 Jane Parks Ringgold pg. 16-17

[2] Frontier Days in the Southwest; The Naylor Company 1952 Jane Parks Ringgold pg. 16-17

much of their time and soon became the default headquarters for the Texas cowboys – rustlers. It seems safe to conclude that, when he wasn't sleeping under a bed roll with his head on a saddle, Ringo bunked at Joe Hill's house. The census of 1882, shortly before Ringo's death, shows the occupants of the Hill home as Joe Hill, John Ringo, Phin Clanton, Ike Clanton, as well as Lula Belle Olney, age 7. Agnes Jane and Hill's four other children still resided in Silver City at the time.

Throwing in with the cow-boys seemed to be a natural for Ringo and Hill. Since their time in Texas they'd both run outside the law. Joining in as a part of the newly banded cow-boys was simply an extension of who they'd become. The cow-boy faction would play havoc on the Arizona landscape. They were a collection of Texas and New Mexico outlaws led by Curly Bill Brocius, and they would become known throughout the territory as cattle thieves and stage robbers. As a member of the cow-boys, Ringo would find himself further outside the law than he had ever been.

For Ringo, his Arizona experience started out with less than a warm welcome. Only a short time after his arrival, Ringo had his first scrape with the Arizona law. On December 14, 1879 the Arizona Daily Star and the Tucson Star reported an altercation between John Ringo and a man named Louis Hancock. On Tuesday afternoon December 9, 1879 in a Safford saloon, Ringo had offered the man a shot of whiskey, which he declined in favor of the beer he was drinking at the time. This angered Ringo and prompted him to shoot Hancock at point blank range.

This was reported on December 14th by the Arizona Daily Star as follows; [3]

Ringo struck him over the head with his pistol and then fired, the ball taking effect in the lower end of the left ear; and passed through the fleshy part of the neck, half an inch more in the neck would have killed him. Ringo is under arrest.

By the time he reached Arizona, John Ringo was very different from the man who arrived in Texas just a few years earlier. He'd become hard and quick-tempered. His experiences in Texas and Mason County had been only about survival, which changes a man and his view of life itself. No one knows how he saw the future at this point, but his memories of the past three years certainly must have played a role. Family was slipping further away. Whatever his purpose for returning to Liberty Missouri in

---

[3] Arizona Daily Star; December 14, 1879

1871, that, too, had obviously not been successful. His life was now in Texas and the Hill Country. That's who he had become.

JOHN RINGO AND THE MASON COUNTY WAR

The Mason County War is where the "Ringo" story begins in earnest. Looking back on the events of history, it's natural to ponder the 'what-ifs' and 'if-onlys'; those twists and turns that would have changed history but for that second in time that set the course of events. Johnny Ringo's decision to stake his future on Texas defined that moment for his life.

It was the late summer of 1870 when Ringo left his family and headed south. The census of that year includes John as a 20-year-old member of the Ringo family, still residing in Santa Clara County. As his sister Mattie Bell recalled, John left home late in 1870 and went south to work with a wheat harvesting crew in southern California. According to Walter Noble Burns in his 1929 title *Tombstone; An Iliad of the Southwest*, John Ringo left the family in a lurch in 1869. This, along with other information he'd gathered from Charles Ringo, turned out to be a self-serving pack of lies. According to Mattie Bell, Ringo's sister, Burns was wrong.

In the spring of 1993, David Johnson held a telephone interview with well-known historian Ed Bartholomew. In that conversation, Bartholomew said John Ringo and his cousin, Bruce Younger, traveled to Liberty Missouri in the spring of 1871.[4] This time line seems right. We know that Ringo traveled to southern California in the fall of 1870 to join a wheat cutting crew. That job would have played out at the end of the season, when Ringo apparently went back to San Jose. If he and Bruce did hook up, Ringo must have gone back to the Younger Ranch, where he'd worked since 1864 when the family arrived in California.

Why he went to Missouri in 1871 is as much a mystery as his 1881 Missouri trip. Ringo was of the age of majority in 1871, which gave him legal right of contracts. He could well have gone in search of any remaining holdings his father may have had, or even to find family with hopes of starting his adult life there. We really do not know for certain why he chose to go on this trip. Likewise, Bruce Younger's motive is as unclear as Ringo's. Sometimes, for as much as we try to give rational or nefarious explanations for everything people do, we simply have to conclude with; "he just did." This is one of those periods of time with no paper trail to confirm Ringo's purpose or travels and we must be satisfied with not knowing until something is found.

---

[4] John Ringo; King of the Cowboys. David Johnson pg.43

It was August 29, 1873, when Martin Albert Ringo, John's younger brother, died of consumption at only nineteen years old. Ringo knew of his brother's illness through family correspondence, but when he learned of his death is not known. Where Ringo himself was at this time is also a mystery. There is no certainty as to when he left Missouri, or if he went back to California before setting his sights on Texas. However, with Hopkins County, Texas located five hundred miles due south of Liberty Missouri, it is unlikely that Ringo made the journey back to California.

The lack of newspaper accounts or court documentation of any kind provide a good indication that things were quiet for Ringo during this period. The general curiosity of an investigator pushes the need to fill in the blanks, but at times the silence and lack of a trail can tell as much. Johnny Ringo was ambitious and motivated with the need to send money to his family. He knew cattle and he knew horses. At the time, there was no better place to apply his abilities than in Texas.

Peter Ringo, Martin Ringo's uncle, had obtained a 640-acre land grant in Red River County, Texas – just north of Hopkins – in the early 1840s. Peter was killed in a standoff with law enforcement in 1858, after which his son Benjamin, Martin Ringo's cousin, took over the now 5800-acre spread. Wheat was their major crop. This is where Johnny likely went first. Again, Johnny disappears from history until December 1874 where newspaper accounts report that he was arrested for discharging a firearm in the Burnet County town square on Christmas Day. He was charged a hefty $75.00 fine for his celebration.

GERMAN IMMIGRATION AND THE RUN UP TO CONFLICT

Thousands of Germans ascended on Texas in the early 1840's. Their homeland had become a place of oppression under a harsh government which had led to poor living conditions, excessive taxation, lack of jobs, and near starvation. Thus, under the guidance and advocacy of the German Immigration Company (the Adelsverein), those who'd registered were systematically brought to the Texas Hill Country under the Fisher-Miller Land Grant. On February 8, 1842 Henry Fisher and Burchard Miller petitioned the Republic of Texas for a grant to resettle one thousand families of German, Dutch, Swiss, Danish, and Norwegian descent. The grant, which covered 3,878,000 acres between Llano and the Colorado River, was approved on June 7, 1842.

Miller and Fisher had applied for the grant as representatives of the San Saba Colonization Company, with final approval as the Miller-Fisher Grant. After their efforts for colonization proved unsuccessful, they sold the grant to The Adelsverein. With a promise of free land and a new start,

Germans flocked to the open grasslands of the Texas Hill Country, but eventually favored Fredericksburg and New Braunfels, which lay outside the grant. This included Mason County.

Native Texans envisioned this same stretch of range as ideal for settling, and were enraged to find much of it owned by German immigrants, free of charge, and without restriction. Despite the German's effort to stay clear of American settlements, animosity toward these foreign land grabbers immediately emerged. After the Fisher-Miller Land Grant was annulled, the State Legislature still honored the agreement resulting in the population of Mason County becoming a majority German.

The pre-Civil War animosity between the American-born residents and the German immigrants was intensified by the German's support for the North. With their loyalty pledged to the Union for allowing them entry, they were further reviled in an otherwise Confederate environment. Their lack of support for the C.S.A. ran contrary to the Confederate Conscription Act of 1862. Under this law, as supported by Texas, all males, sixteen years of age and older, were ordered to register with the local provost marshal, and take an oath of allegiance to the Confederacy. Men between the ages of eighteen and thirty-five were liable for military service. There were exemptions for wealthy men, men in prominent positions, and those who owned twenty or more slaves.

Enforcing the law in heavily populated German communities proved impossible. Entire families were arrested and incarcerated. Young men who fled were tracked down and jailed under terrible conditions. With the word 'traitors' bandied about, some became the targets of violence. At an overnight camp in Gillespie County in late 1862, two men slipped away during the night, which resulted in the hanging of the remaining four Germans the following morning with their bodies thrown into the river. Due to the overwhelming German population, Gillespie and Kerr counties were placed under martial law.[5]

The Battle of Nueces, also known as the Nueces Massacre, took place on the morning of August 10, 1862. An encampment of German immigrants fleeing to Mexico was attacked on the banks of the Nueces River by ninety-four mounted Confederate soldiers led by Lt. C.D. McRae. Nineteen Germans were killed that morning with nine wounded, only to be executed a few hours later. In all, the battle ended with the deaths of thirty-seven German-Texans. The relationship between German immigrants and natural born Americans was at its lowest point.

By the end of the Civil War, Texas, as with most Confederate states, was in financial ruin. Reconstruction only made matters worse. At its

---

[5]The Mason County War; Glenn Hadeler.

conclusion in 1872, Reconstruction had brought devastation to the state's political and law enforcement apparatus. This took decades to repair. Duly elected officials finally replaced the political appointees who'd ravaged the state. Communities struggled to restore their Constitutional rights of self-governance, and with it came bloody battles of disagreement.

The focus once again was placed on commerce with cattle being the state's most abundant natural resource. Registered cattle at the end of the war was in excess of three million, with few experienced men to manage the herds. Mavericks, or unbranded cattle, added to that number substantially. Control and ownership of this vital resource sparked numerous feuds from the Sutton-Taylor disturbance in Dewitt and Gonzales Counties, to the Mason County War which spread into Burnett and Llano Counties. Each with their unique origins, these isolated battles across Texas perpetuated the loss of life and hindered their return to normalcy.

The election of December 1873 proved German dominance in Mason County. With John Clark, a man of German descent, elected as county sheriff, and Dan Hoerster as County Brand Inspector, the German immigrants now controlled the politics of Mason County for the first time. With political influence came the need for power. Corruption, which is fueled by power, didn't linger.

MASON COUNTY WAR

The causes for the Mason County War were many, but at its core was the long-held animosity between the Americans and the German immigrants, coupled with a range war over control of cattle and land. It was the foundation that provided the fuel, but other elements such as corrupt law enforcement and inadequate laws that played on hard working decent people fanned the flames. The Mason County Mob, which came into existence after the election of John Clark, was comprised of German residents – The Dutch were referred to as the "Law and Order" faction, although their activities were secretive, and largely illegal. The Americans were referred to as "Outlaws", although they made no secret of who they were, or their purpose.

The 1875 killing of Tim Williamson triggered an era of blood shed not previously seen in Mason County. Although he was the seventh man to be killed in the conflict, none brought such a retaliation against Sheriff John Clark and his mob. Clark's dislike for Williamson may have existed on two fronts, Williamson's friendship with rancher M.B. Thomas, and the fact that he'd worked for A.G. Roberts. Both adversaries of Sheriff Clark.

In April 1874, the opening salvo of the feud was sparked by Clark's arrest of Thomas and his men as they herded their cattle. Thomas immediately retaliated by filing charges against the sheriff and his German posse. On August 9th, drovers for A.G. Roberts, a non-resident stockman, were arrested by Sheriff Clark and his posse. Clark charged Robert's men with making a raid in Mason County and for being in possession of some 200 stolen cattle. Roberts responded by accusing the sheriff of intentionally filing a false charge and separating his herd. On August 13th, two of Robert's men were brought before the court where the charges were dismissed, but the cattle had already been scattered to the wind.

Sometime in May 1875, Clark and Williamson had a dispute over taxes levied on a lot owned by Williamson in Loyal Valley. Clark taxed Williamson's property at an assessed value of $1,200.00. This amount was more than a nearby business owned by German proprietor, John Meusebach, which was valued at $1,000.00, and far more than any of the surrounding properties. Williamson protested, but Clark pushed to collect the tax. Williamson refused to pay and was not at home when Clark showed up to collect the now past due tax. In his absence, Clark reportedly verbally abused Williamson's wife. In response, once he arrived home and learned of the exchange, Williamson went to Mason and confronted Sheriff Clark, trying to draw him into a fight, which Clark refused. In response, however, Sheriff Clark had Williamson arrested on a charge of stealing a yearling. It was an old charge that could never be proved, and very commonly used.

Williamson was a man well liked, with a good reputation. No one believed Clark, including Dan Hoerster, the cattle inspector, who posted his bond. With an obvious ulterior motive, Clark pressured Hoerster to rescind the bond, thereby giving Clark the authority to re-arrest Williamson. On May 13, 1875, Deputy Sheriff John [Johann] Wohrle was dispatched by Clark to arrest Williamson again – who was in Llano County at Karl Lehmberg's camp, outside Clark's jurisdiction. Upon his arrival, Lehmberg offered the bond to Wohrle, but he refused, prompting Lehmberg to follow along with the intention of posting Williamson's bond once they arrived in Mason.

They made it as far as Willow Creek, where they were ambushed by a band of armed men in an obvious set-up. When the men showed themselves, Williamson realized that he was their target, and pleaded with Wohrle to let him go. Wohrle refused, then shot Williamson's horse to prevent him from making an attempt to run. On foot and exposed, Tim Williamson was shot and killed by Peter Bader. The Sheriff's Office held no investigation into Williamson's ambush and murder. Little did Clark know, he'd opened a can of worms that he couldn't control.

It was the killing of Tim Williamson that brought Scott Cooley into the fight. Cooley was a Texas Ranger, who had been raised by Williamson after the murder of his family by the Comanche. Cooley broke down in tears at the word of Williamson's death, and immediately left his post to find the killer.

Scott Cooley

The day the news of Williamson's murder came to the Ranger camp, to which force Cooley at one time belonged, he sat down and cried at the loss of one he said was his best friend in the world and declared then that he would have revenge.[6]

Johnny Ringo would soon join Cooley's cause. Ringo didn't know Cooley previously, but he was friends with the Baird family in Burnett County. This is where Ringo was charged with disturbing the peace after firing his pistol into the air on Christmas Day 1874. It was the Baird family who posted Ringo's bond and where he and Moses formed a lasting friendship. Baird had become deeply involved in the conflict, and it would be the news of his death that would make the matter personal for Ringo.

Executing an investigation of his own, Cooley soon pieced together the facts which implicated Deputy Wohrle and Peter Bader as the responsible parties. On August 10 1875, Cooley rode into Mason County and entered a saloon where he began asking questions about Williamson's death. The men, probably assuming his inquiry to be in the capacity of a Texas Ranger, obliged, giving up the names of those involved. Karl Lehmberg is assumed to be the man who provided the information.

Later that day, Cooley rode to John Wohrle's home where, Wohrle, a man named Haircut, and a third man were digging a well. Cooley asked if he might bother him for a piece of leather to tie his rifle to the saddle. Wohrle complied, and soon returned with a length of *reita*. Wohrle walked away as he tied the strap, and proceeded to lower Haircut back into the well. Cooley then pulled his pistol and shot Wohrle in the back of the head with the bullet exiting through the nose. The third man, unarmed, ran, dropping the rope holding Haircut, plunging him some forty feet to the bottom of the well, where he was injured, but not killed. Cooley took his time, emptying his revolver into his dead body, then scalping Wohrle before he left, placing the bloody scalp in his pocket.

---

[6] San Antonio Herald, August 30, 1875

On August 19th, Cooley rode to the Bader farm in Llano County and mistakenly killed Karl Bader, confusing him for his older brother Peter. Cooley took his scalp as well. By now the secretive mob was caught off guard and Clark knew someone was on to them. Now frantic, Clark assumed the Bader killing was carried out by Moses Baird and George Gladden. On September 7, 1875, Clark sent James Cheyney, a local gambler, out to find Baird and Gladden to tell them they were wanted for some reason in Mason. Not suspecting anything of consequence, the men mounted up and unknowingly rode straight into an ambush at Hedwig's Hill, led by Sheriff John Clark. Both men were shot multiple times with Baird falling from his horse.

Though wounded and in a hail of gunfire, Gladden stopped to help Moses Baird back onto his horse before climbing on behind him. Both men took additional rounds and soon fell from the horse. Peter Bader and several members of the mob rode up to the men where Bader fired a mortal round into Moses Baird, killing him instantly. Bader then cut off his finger to steal his ring.[7] Charley Keller, a member of Clark's posse, was surprised by his action and threatened Bader's life if he killed Gladden. Bader relented, and Gladden was taken back to town and survived. Moses Baird had been a good friend to Johnny Ringo and now for him it was personal.

John Baird, Bill Farris, Sam Tanner, John Ringo, and Joseph Olney went to Hedwig's Hill to retrieve Moses's body. The men said he was so riddled and mutilated that none of them could eat on the way back to Burnett.

Gladden was taken to Mason and treated, but not arrested. Sheriff Clark had made a big enough blunder by killing a man as popular as Moses Baird. Arresting George Gladden without cause would serve only to make matters worse. Gladden was allowed to return home to mend. Two days later, Scott Cooley went to Gladden's house to find John Ringo, Gladden's brother John, and Jim Williams present.

Now with common interest, and personal vendettas, Cooley and Ringo became inseparable. To this point in his life, Ringo had been somewhat quiet. He was an honest man as told by many, who would go to any lengths to assist a friend. It was likely the influence of a hard man like Scott Cooley that turned Ringo's thinking and set him on the path of the man we would come to know in Arizona. Ringo followed Cooley's lead and for the next nine months was a major force in the Mason County War.

Cooley now had a posse of his own, a force of men undeterred and unwavering. Clark became aware of Cooley and his men and waited for retaliation. It soon came. On the morning of September 25, 1875, Jim

---

[7] Law and Disorder; J.T. Ringo ©2012 Booktango

Williams and Johnny Ringo rode to James Cheyney's house where he was preparing breakfast. Cheyney invited the men in, and suggested they wash their faces in the water bucket on the porch. Cheyney did so first, and was shot dead by Williams and Ringo while he dried his face. Ringo and Williams rode directly back to Mason, where they met Cooley for breakfast.

On September 29th, Cooley, Gladden, John Baird, and Bill Cook went to Mason to confront Sheriff Clark, but he had gone into hiding. On the way out of town, they spotted Dan Hoerster, along with Peter Jordan, and Henry Pluenneke, all suspected of being involved in the Williamson ambush. Cooley and his party confronted the men, leaving Hoester dead, with Jordan and Gladden wounded.

On October 4, 1875, a group of citizens from Loyal Valley, including the Rev. R.G. Stone, soon to be father-in-law to John Yoast, penned a letter to Governor Richard Cook, asking for a clarification of the raid on Loyal Valley the previous day, and pleading for help. In their description of events, they had unwittingly implicated Sheriff Clark and the mob, who had now lost control, and frantic to regain power.

Texas Rangers had now blanketed Mason County in search of Cooley and Ringo, but the pair had withdrawn to the hills. In an unusual move, Major John Jones offered an honorable discharge to any Ranger who felt he could not arrest Scott Cooley. Sometime in November, Ringo had a confrontation with a Ranger, but easily escaped. The Texas Rangers had little stomach for arresting Cooley or Ringo. On December 27, 1875, after a visit to Mason County, Cooley and Ringo were arrested in Burnett County following an altercation with Sheriff John Clymer and Deputy John J. Strickland.[8] Word of their arrests was reported throughout Texas.

Cooley and Ringo may have been off the trail, but the battle was not over. Peter Bader – the shooter – the man who'd killed both Tim Williamson and Moses Baird, was still alive and in hiding in Fredericksburg. John Wohrle was dead, as was Jim Cheyney, and Dan Hoerster. Clark had left Texas for a safer environment in Missouri, never to be seen again, but Bader was still breathing.

Sometime in late December, Bader asked an outsider, Max Krueger, to accompany him to Llano to meet with Karl Lehmberg to settle a debt. The fact that he'd asked Krueger was an indication that Bader had lost the support of the now powerless mob. John Baird and George Gladden were tracking Bader and ran into him and Krueger while in route, where a gun battle ensued. They made it back to safety at the home of Wilhelm Marschall, but Krueger wanted no part of it, and high-tailed it home. Bader

---

[8] The Mason County 'Hoo Doo War" David Johnson, pg. 143

stayed at the Marschall home until January 13th, thinking he was finally safe, but neither Baird nor Gladden had given up.

When he left that day, three men, Baird, Gladden, and a third man were waiting behind the rocks on the north side of the road. When Bader approached, John Baird stepped out with shotgun in hand and called out to Bader. He immediately blasted Bader, causing his horse to bolt some fifty feet down the road where Bader fell dead from his mount. Though not verified, the story of the day was that Baird took the opportunity to retrieve his brother's ring from Bader's finger before leaving.[9]

For their part, Cooley and Ringo were jailed in Burnett, then sent to Travis County where they stayed until late January when they were brought back to Burnett to appear before the grand jury. On February 3, 1876, Cooley and Ringo requested a change of venue, and were transferred to the Lampasas County jail in March 1876. Their arrival in Lampasas brought much fanfare:

"Quite an excitement was raised among our citizens last Sunday by the arrival in town of the notorious Mason County outlaws Scott Cooley and John Ringgold, who was brought here under heavy guard. These are the same men who killed and scalped the Deputy Sheriff of Mason County a few months ago." [10]

Despite the enthusiastic press, the men weren't incarcerated long. In May 1876, a number of men broke the pair out of jail. Scott Cooley was free, but died at the home of Dan Maddox in Blanco County on June 10, 1876. The cause of death was reported in the press as "brain fever", other theories include a cerebral hemorrhage, or perhaps metallic poisoning from a bottle of whiskey he'd purchased earlier in the day. With this unexpected twist of fate, the "Cooley Gang" had been broken, but so had Sheriff John Clark. In December 1875, he quietly fled Texas for the safety of Doniphan Missouri where he became a farmer and lived in hiding until his death in 1888. Ironically enough, Clark is buried in the Wohrle family cemetery in Doniphan.

Clark was no longer in the equation, but the feud was none the less raging. By September 1876, activities against the American 'outlaws' had moved away from Mason, and more directly into Llano and Burnet counties. On September 7th, Sheriff J.J. Strickland sent two deputies, Samuel Martin, and Wilson Roundtree to Joseph Olney's ranch on the Llano side of the Colorado River to make an arrest for stealing hogs in

---

[9] The Mason County 'Hoo Doo War" David Johnson, pg. 147
[10] The Daily Herald, March 18, 1876

Burnet, and for his involvement in the Cooley/Ringo jail break. The deputies went to Olney's house, but being unfamiliar with his appearance, they talked awhile, and asked the way to the ford so they might cross the river back to Burnet. Roundtree later admitted that they did not know exactly where Olney lived, or what he looked like. When they decided to head back to Burnet, it was only by chance that they landed at Olney's door.

Olney had been warned that he was a target, and to be on guard for increased 'mob' activity coming his way. To him it was an odd visit, and being on guard, he suspected it to be more than men looking for directions. He obliged, and directed them to the river, but distrusted their purpose. Gathering his sidearm and rifle, Olney mounted up and followed the men to make sure they had left. They soon realized they were being followed, and that the man they'd spoken with was the man they were pursuing. When they turned about, gunfire ensued. During the arrest attempt, both lawmen were shot, Roundtree in the left side, and Martin near the backbone, with the bullet passing upward to just below an artery in the neck. Roundtree survived, but Deputy Martin died from his wounds.

On October 31st, Ringo and George Gladden were arrested in Llano County by Sheriff J.J. Bozarth and Texas Rangers where Ringo was described as: "One of the most desperate men in the frontier counties." On November 7th, they were taken to Austin and placed in the Travis County jail. Gladden was brought back to Llano to stand trial on December 6, 1876 for the killing of Peter Bader, while Ringo was shuffled back and forth from Austin to Llano. A case against Ringo was becoming increasingly difficult to hold together. Joe Olney was still being pursued by Sheriff Strickland and the Texas Rangers with several close calls. Olney eventually took his family to Silver City, New Mexico. Jim Williams, the man who along with Johnny Ringo had killed James Cheyney, was killed near Cat Mountain in the pre-dawn hours of September 11th by a band of men. Williams attempted an escape, but was found later in the day face down in a thicket with seven gunshot wounds in his body.

George Gladden's trial in Llano lasted until mid-afternoon of December 7th, with the jury deliberating until dark before returning with a verdict of guilty. Gladden was given a life sentence, and transported to Austin on December 10th, where he was housed before entering Huntsville prison a year later on December 12, 1877. Gladden filed an appeal, which he lost, but a conditional pardon was issued on December 30, 1884 following a successful petition campaign by the residence of Llano County for his release. Gladden was freed on January 1, 1885, and moved to Apache County, Arizona.

Ringo was finally charged for his July participation in the attempted ambush of Sheriff Strickland to free John Redding as he was being transported from Llano to Austin. Redding was falsely accused of bank robbery in Comanche Texas, and for his role in securing the escape of Scott Cooley and John Ringo in Lampasas. Ringo was convicted of threatening the life of Sheriff Strickland, but it was later reversed on appeal.

While in the Travis County jail, Ringo was indicted by a Mason County grand jury for the murder of Jim Cheyney. On January 21, 1877, a fire destroyed the courthouse in Mason County along with its records. Ringo argued that without records, there was no case against him, but a new indictment was issued as Case #21 on May 18, 1877.

"On the names and by the authority of the State of Texas the Grand Jurors of Mason County in said State at the November Term A.D. 1876 . . on their oaths in said court present that John Ringo, George Gladden and others with force and arms in the County of Mason and state of Texas did heretofore to wit on the 25th day of September A.D. 1875 then and there willfully feloniously and with malice aforethought in and upon the body of James Chaney . . .make an assault and that they said Ringo, Gladden and others with certain guns and pistols then and there in there charged with gunpowder and leaden balls and then and there in their hands . . . shoot off and discharge . . . into the body of said Chaney . . . strike penetrate and wound . . . in the right side giving him the said Chaney one mortal wound . . . the said Ringo, Gladden and others . . . upon the said James Chaney did kill and murder against the peace and dignity of the state."[11]

On November 1, 1877, Ringo was taken back into custody and transported to Mason County where he was held until his court hearing on November 12th. The case was continued until the 19th, and Ringo was taken back to Travis County. In early December, Ringo's attorney filed a writ of Habeas Corpus, demanding that bond be set for his client. Ringo was released on December 20, 1877, and ordered to appear in court on May 10, 1878. Always the target, Ringo was arrested again by Texas Rangers in Junction City for disturbing the peace, where he posted bond and was released.

Ringo was back in Mason County on April 18th, were he filed a sworn affidavit stating that several men were needed as witnesses in his defense. On May 15, 1878, the District Attorney requested the case against John Ringo be dismissed as testimony to support his case could not be produced.

---

[11] District Court Clerk's Office, Mason County Texas.

 With this final legal maneuver, it was over. Ringo was finally clear of the law and went back to Loyal Valley. In November, he ran for Constable of Precinct #4 and won with a seventy percent majority. But as always with Ringo, he didn't stay long. In June, 1879, a familiar face came riding up, one he was glad to see. Joseph Graves Olney, now Joe Hill, had a proposition for him, and soon they were headed for Arizona.

CHAPTER TWO

SO, WHO WAS JOHNNY RINGO?
THE MYTH

"This is the west, sir. When the legend becomes fact, print the legend."

For no man does this famous line from *The Man Who Shot Liberty Valance* apply more accurately than it does to Johnny Ringo. Some may ask; "What's in a name?" For John Peters Ringo, it was the mystical ring of his moniker which gave him status as a formidable outlaw. Johnny Ringo, were his name not real, would surely have been contrived by Hollywood for such a character as he truly was. Although the silver screen reintroduced a number of real frontier names, it was not the focus of those early writers to introduce the personalities behind those names.

For sure, the names of many famous men were used. Doc Holliday, for one, now there's a name to reckon with. Likewise, the name Wyatt Earp, Bat Masterson and others were all portrayed as bigger than life. Although these men left a story to be told, the true nature of the men behind the events they experienced were woefully missing. The passage of time gave fodder to the early twentieth century writers who were eager to grant their brand of the old west a place in history.

The creation of the silver screen, and the public's interest in the old west, share a common place in history. For it was the silver screen, and the western writers of the early twentieth century who rekindled those previously all but forgotten names of the frontier. One unavoidable byproduct of co-mingling actors in a play with the lives of real people, however, is how viewers (or readers) lose sight of who is real and who is fictitious. Movies, more so than the written word, tend to give life to what is not real, and by nature diminish what is. Those behind the written word, however, are more inclined to take what was and turn it into what wasn't. Thus, was born the man we've come to know as Johnny Ringo.

Although Johnny Ringo was a real man, his story still remains largely untold. The authenticity of the historical Johnny Ringo has been obscured by the intertwined characters of Hollywood and the printing press. His name has spawned a variety of offspring not confined to American filmmaking. In 1965, screenwriter, Duccio Tessari released two spaghetti westerns for his Italian audience entitled; *"Una Pistola Per Ringo"* (A Pistol For Ringo) and *"Il Ritorno Di Ringo"* (The Return of Ringo). The role of Ringo in both projects was portrayed by a former stuntman named Giuliano Gemma, who was heralded for his success in mastering the American role. The character, unfortunately, was not written as a depiction of Johnny Ringo. He was instead an extension of John Wayne's role as the "Ringo Kid" in John Ford's 1939 movie *Stagecoach*. It seemed the Italian market was obsessed with the name during the 1960's with a number of movie projects borrowing the name. *Ringo; Face of Revenge*; *Ringo and Gringo Against All;* and *Ringo and His Golden Pistol*, were released in 1966 with success. As in Hollywood, no attempt was made to portray the man, but only to capitalize upon his name.

Ringo was also memorialized in music. In 1964, Bonanza star, Lorne Green released the song *Ringo*. Narrated in his unmistakable voice, he reminisces the days of a lawman in pursuit of this worthy outlaw. Green tells a story where only the name had any relevance to the person. It wasn't meant to be history in song, or a story of the man's life. In 1965, the song was released in French. Once again, the tale-tellers only borrowed his name, and included none of the man's substance.

As the nineteenth century came to a close, the old west began to fade with it. Coast to coast travel had become commonplace. Electric lights, telephones and even horseless carriages were no longer so farfetched. The solitude of the prairie was slipping, and territories were fast becoming states. The world was changing quickly. On December 1, 1903, the first full-length movie was released, *"The Great Train Robbery"*, and America's passion for westerns began.

As silent movies were taking hold, a flood of ex-drovers and 'cowboys' made their way to California to find work as extras, reenacting what they once were in real life. By this time, the term 'cowboy' had been condensed to one word, and no longer used as the intended pejorative as when first coined. In the 1880s, at the time John Peters Ringo lived in Arizona, the use of the term 'cow-boy' was one of disdain, and synonymous with rustler or thief. Splitting hairs, I suppose, but it seems the title bestowed upon Ringo as the "King of the Cowboys" would be more accurate were it written as "King of the Cow-Boys". Either way, it should hold that the use of the word "King" as a synonym for "leader", would not apply under either editing of the phrase.

The early twentieth century saw its share of less than credible writers, who carried grudges and agendas, making their one last stand to frame history as they wished it had occurred. Three such writers were Billy

Breckenridge, former deputy sheriff of Tombstone who wrote *Helldorado* in 1928; Walter Noble Burns, with his portrayal of events in *Tombstone; An Iliad of the Southwest* in 1929 and Eugene Cunningham's *Triggernometry* in 1947.

Each of these writers possessed a known dislike for the Earp family and it is quite easy to see their post-mortem attempts to create an anti-Earp hero. Antithetical to true historians, these less than plausible writers chose to exploit the lack of collected history and sparse documentation to create their respective myths from nothing more than a shadow. Hiding behind the ambiguity of Ringo's past, each found an open range to rewrite the past to their particular liking. For a man who was supposedly so well known, there was very little accuracy in the writings of those early old west authors.

One would think that historians would agree that a study of most historical figures should begin with what one gathers about the person from recorded documentation, photographs, family records, diaries, letters and eyewitness accounts. It seems that with Johnny Ringo, a search for the facts didn't begin until years after the first accounts of his life were written and accepted as fact. The myths and outright fallacies about his life have their origins in the early twentieth century, largely by those writers mentioned above. It is interesting that each of them attempted, with their own account and agenda, to accomplish with the pen what could not be accomplished with the gun. As a result, they introduced their readers to a man who did not exist.

FAMILY BACKGROUND

John Peters Ringo was born in Wayne County, Indiana on May 3, 1850 to Martin and Mary Peters Ringo. He was their first born, with his brother Martin Albert to follow on September 28, 1854; his sister Fannie Fern born July 7, 1857; his sister Mary Enna born May 2, 1860 and his sister Mattie Bell born April 18, 1862[12]. Later assertions that he was born in Texas, California, Missouri or even back east were either examples of a lack of research on the part of the writers, or an attempt to build the myth of a man who appeared without a past. Research would not have been difficult, since the Ringo family is traceable back to Henry Ringo 1724-1803.[13] This

---

[12] Mattie Bell Ringo Cushing's reference to her own age and to that of her brothers and sisters confirm the years of their birth. (*Journal of Mary Ringo "forward"*)

[13] David Lear Ringo *"Chart of the Ringo Family"*

would also debunk the Breckenridge story of his true surname being Ringgold; shortened to spare his wealthy southern family the shame of having an outlaw in the family.

Many say that nothing is known of Ringo in his youth. The fact that no court documents or newspaper accounts include his name, in itself, suggest he was a normal child and not given to trouble with the law. However, much is known about the family and many of the events which surrounded him during his early life. Johnny Ringo was first introduced through his mother's journal after the family joined a wagon train west in May 1864 in Liberty, Missouri. On that trail, Mary Ringo kept a journal which has become well known in western history. In it, she scribed the events of their journey, making very positive entries regarding John on numerous occasions.

Prior to that time, the family is very easy to follow, from Martin Ringo's business dealings to their relatives and home life. The life of Mary Peters Ringo, John's mother, is equally as transparent. From her childhood forward, she was known as an upstanding young lady, as were her four sisters. Martin's business dealings reveal a thoughtful, honest man who was not given to whims or careless attempts at unworthy fantasies. When gold was discovered near Fredericktown Missouri in 1860, many risked all they had in search of a few nuggets, hoping to strike it rich. Martin demonstrated a level head and wasn't tempted, holding fast to his business as a merchant.

Martin Ringo was surely a man of honor. When Mexico declared war on the United States in 1846, Martin quickly enlisted. He served until June 21, 1847 when he was honorably discharged and returned home to Liberty Missouri. On September 5, 1847, Martin and Mary were married in Clay County. On September 26, 1864, some two months after his death, The Liberty Tribune described him as a very mild, pleasant and unassuming gentleman who was highly esteemed by those who knew him.

By all accounts, the Ringo family led a very traditional life, with a strong belief in God. Both Martin and Mary came from family backgrounds which were held in high esteem. The former Mary Peters was the twin sister to Martha Peters, born on November 13, 1826. Their father, John R. Peters, was born in Woodford County Kentucky on February 15, 1797. Her mother, Frances Simms Peters was born August 24, 1796. Four years after their marriage in 1821, John and Frances moved to Liberty, Missouri. The family was well received in the community. John served on the Board of Trustees after the town was incorporated in May 1829. He later served as Sheriff of Clay County and justice of the peace.

Martin Ringo's family, as well as their personal interactions is easy to trace. Martin's father, Peter Ringo was born in Kentucky on June 29, 1791.

Peter married the former Margaret Henderson on October 6, 1813 at the age of twenty-two. Peter and Margaret had two children while in Kentucky, Joel on September 27, 1814 and Elvira on April 5, 1816. The Ringo's relocated to Wayne County Indiana in October 1817, where the birth of their son, William soon followed on November 24, 1817. Johnny's father, Martin was born there on October 1, 1819.

The Ringo and Peters families were very similar in their belief systems. Their ambitions and determinations, as well as their reverence for family and God were obvious. They each held family in high regard, providing Martin and Mary an array of relatives to view as role models. Morality and personal responsibility would have been measured by a high standard for Martin Ringo and for Mary Peters in their youth. Each family was well represented, with those who served as public officials including law enforcement, and county treasurer. Other family members studied law, or worked as honest merchants. In 1823 Martin's father, Peter was instrumental in the founding of the Centerville Methodist Episcopal Church. He also served as the Wayne County Treasurer that following year.

Upon their union, Martin and Mary Ringo were a good match. They were like minded, and obviously reared their children with the same morals instilled in them. Their marriage and home life have every indication of being harmonious. Their continued love for one another apparently prevailed until the day of Martin's untimely death in July 1864. This assertion can be made based on Mary's heart wrenching entry in her journal on the evening of his death.

Young John Ringo was surely raised in a proper home and in no way seemed to rebel. His participation on the trail west, as documented through his mother's journal, depicts a young boy who was obedient and willing to do his part. The assertions by writers, such as Walter Noble Burns who proclaimed him as a participant in the James Gang, and having ridden with Quantrill in 1864, were shamefully incorrect.[14] Besides, he was only fourteen at the time and on the Oregon Trail heading west with his family. During his formidable years, John was the protégé of a hard-working father, and apparently spent quite a bit of time at the family store in Gallatin.

The family's time in Missouri began in 1856, when they left Indiana for unknown reasons. It has been speculated they left due to the unrest following several skirmishes near their home, moving closer to other

---

[14] Walter Noble Burns *"Tombstone"* page 134-135

THE MYTH | 24

family members in Liberty, Missouri. They left Liberty in 1858, moving to Gallatin where Martin first rented space from John Sheets to open a mercantile. He later purchased one hundred twenty acres west of Jameson. There he became partner in a second dry goods store with a man named Adam Clendenen in Cravensville. The family remained there until they left for California in 1864.

The repetitive nature of the names John, Peter and Albert, makes for careful research when determining who was related to whom. John's maternal grandfather was John R. Peters; John's given name was John Peters Ringo. On his father's side, his grandfather was named Peter Ringo. Confusion has stirred over the identity of two Peter Ringo's. Some have written that John's grandfather, Peter had lived in Texas. Not true, the Peter Ringo who headed for Texas in 1839 was the son of Samuel Ringo, a cousin of John's grandfather. It was the family of this Peter Ringo who John would later spend time with in Texas. As for the Alberts, he had an uncle named Albert Ringo, his father's name was Martin Albert Ringo and his brother was named Albert Ringo. It requires a careful study to keep track.

Mary 'Peters' Ringo has been inaccurately recorded as Mary 'Simms' Ringo in at least one account. Mary Ringo's mother's maiden name was Simms. This is where some writers make the stretch to link Johnny Ringo with the James Brothers. The former Miss Frances Simms, Johnny's grandmother, was the sister of Benjamin Simms, born in Virginia in 1800. It was Benjamin who provided the link with the James Gang that so many have tried to exploit over the years. Benjamin was married to Zerelda James for a short time, thus linking Johnny Ringo to Frank and Jessie James through the Simms side of the family. Quite a stretch, as Benjamin and Zerelda were only married for a short while. As a result, Johnny was forever branded as being "kin" to the James Brothers, which he was not.

He had the same connection with the Younger Brothers. John's aunt Augusta, Mary's sister was married to the very prominent Col. Coleman Younger who happened to be the uncle of the Younger Brothers.[15] Coleman's half-sister, Adeline, was the mother of the Dalton Brothers. These notorious bands of outlaws were oddly enough tied together by marriage, but Johnny did not have "the blood of outlaws in his veins" as some have so proclaimed.

---

[15] Jack Barrows *"Johnny Ringo; The Gunfighter Who Never Was"* 1987 page 119

Life changed dramatically for fourteen-year-old John Ringo in May 1864. Along with his family, he left the only home he had really known and joined a wagon train west. Over the next few months, he would learn life on the prairie, and how to live off the land. At the time it was the price paid by those with the vision to journey west. For John, it was the beginning of a way of life which he never truly left.

His mother reports in her journal that Johnny was a good shot with a rifle. He came back with wild game for the family on a number of occasions, and was apparently proud of his accomplishments. The family traveled with two heavy wagons, one pulled by oxen, the other by mules. Johnny's task was to drive one of the teams. A big responsibility for a boy of his age, but one he obviously accomplished. He was close to his father. In her journal, Mary makes mention of Johnny heading out with his father on hunting expeditions with no indication of reluctance to do his part.

Tragically, on July 30, 1864 Johnny's father, Martin, was killed when his shotgun accidently discharged as he stepped down from their wagon. During that month, their party faced skirmishes with Indians on a number of occasions. This was likely Johnny's first brush with danger. On July 27th, Mary reports that they found a posting on a tree that six men had been killed by Indians, they knew there was a fight coming. A few days earlier, they came across the body of a man who had been scalped. Young John had now seen the face of death.

It is suspected that Martin was leaving to scout for Indians on the morning of his death. The event was best explained in the Liberty Tribune on August 26, 1864:

"Just after daybreak on the morning of the 30th July, Mr. Ringo stepped out of the wagon as, I suppose, for the purpose of looking around to see if Indians were in sight and his shotgun went off accidently in his own hands, the load entering at the right eye and coming out at the top of his head. At the report of his gun I saw his hat blow twenty feet in the air and his brains were scattered in all directions. I never saw a more heart rendering sight, and to see the distress and agony of his wife and children was painful to the extreme. Mr. Ringo's death cast a gloom over the whole company......[16]

---

[16] Letter from Mr. W. Davidson, a member of the wagon train, to Mr. R.H. Will---- in Liberty Missouri reported in the Liberty Tribune on August 24, 1864 and repeated on September 16, 1864. Reprinted in Jack Barrows *"Johnny Ringo; The Gunfighter Who Never Was"* 1987 page 113

Fourteen-year-old John Ringo witnessed his father's death. One can only imagine the unrelenting trauma this must have been for him. The security of their home was gone, but the family was unified in their journey. It must have been exciting for a boy to travel west, even with the responsibilities of their day to day travels. Now the family had been devastated and their future was in turmoil. The sight of his loving father's mangled face probably never left his mind.

Mary Peters Ringo

The account in Mary Ringo's Journal for July 30th was indeed heart wrenching. It tells the story of a loving, God fearing family, who was devastated in the loss of an obvious strong father figure, and dependable and loving husband. One can only imagine the confusion and devastation reeked upon the mental state of a fourteen-year-old boy as he watched his father die in such a manner. It appears obvious this was the beginning of the man we know as Johnny Ringo.

MARY RINGO'S JOURNAL, JULY 30, 1864:

"And now Oh God comes the saddest record for my life for this day my husband accidently shot himself and we buried him by the wayside and oh, my heart is breaking, if I had no children how gladly would I lay me down with my dead – but now Oh God I pray for strength to raise our precious children and oh – may no one ever suffer the anguish that is breaking my heart, my little children are crying all the time and I – oh what am I to do. Everyone in camp is kind to us but God alone can heal the broken heart. After burying my darling husband, we hitch up and drove some five miles. Mr. Davenport drove my mules for me and Oh, the agony of parting from that grave, to go and leave him on that hillside where I shall never see it more but thank God 'tis only the body lying there and may we meet in Heaven where there is no more death but only life eternally."

Martin was buried where he died with a small marker which simply read "Mr. Ringo." There were offers to take the family back to Missouri. The army offered assistance to get them on a stage east, but Mary decided to press on to their destination. Tragedy struck again in Austin Nevada when Mary fell ill and suffered a miscarriage. The last entry in her journal was on Saturday October 8th, where she simply entered; *"We remain in Austin Nev."* According to Mattie Bell, they likely stayed there for another week or ten days. Mary sold most of their possessions while there, and took a stage with the girls to San Jose. Young Johnny stepped up once again, and drove their remaining wagon and mules the distance to California alone.

This seems a good place to reiterate that this is the timeframe that Burns declares Johnny Ringo to be riding with Quantrill, the James brothers and the Younger's to whom he was related. Another myth we can dispose of here is "Johnny Ringo had outlaw blood being kin to the Younger's". The fact is that Coleman Younger was married to Mary Peters Ringo's sister, Augusta Peters. Johnny was related to the Younger's only by marriage.[17] Adding to the mix was Howard Monnett's *"General Jo Shelby"*, which has Johnny Ringo riding with Shelby in the Missouri Raid in 1864.[18] As one looks at the true facts of Johnny Ringo's life, the fabricated stories so carelessly woven in the past begin to quickly unravel.

Ironically, Nicholas and Virginia Earp pulled up stakes in Pella, Iowa in May 1864, and also headed west. In 1863, shortly after James returned home from the war, Nicholas set his sights on California. In 1851 Nicholas tried his hand at prospecting in California, and passed through the San Bernardino Valley on his way back to Iowa. It was a place of beauty that he never forgot. On May 12, 1864, four Pella, Iowa families including the Rousseaus, the Hamiltons, the Curtises, and the Earps headed west in a small wagon train of thirty people. In the Earp party were Nick, Virginia, James, Wyatt, Morgan, and Adelia. On the trail somewhere north of the Earps was the Ringo family bound for San Jose. With obviously no knowledge of one another, sixteen-year-old Wyatt Earp and fourteen-year-old Johnny Ringo travelled west under the same sky.

CALIFORNIA

The trail-worn Ringo family arrived in San Jose in late October or early November 1864. They initially made their home in a carriage house on the property of Colonel Coleman Younger. They lived there for the first

---

[17] Jack Barrows *"Johnny Ringo; The Gunfighter Who Never Was"* 1987 pg. 119

[18] Jack Barrows *"Johnny Ringo; The Gunfighter Who Never Was"* 1987 pg. 121

year before moving into a home on Second Street. As with his childhood, little is known about the time Johnny spent in San Jose. From the account of events which took place after his father's death, we can surmise that young Johnny had a difficult time. Upon reaching Austin Nevada, his mother gave birth to a still born boy, after which she was very weak, even after reaching San Jose. His brother Martin Albert soon after became ill with tuberculosis, which took much of his mother's time; Martin died on August 29, 1873. Caring for Martin and three young girls while trying to support the family alone, Mary Ringo obviously had very little time for her teenage son.

There is no indication that Johnny had any problems with the authorities, no record of him attending school or that he provided any meaningful help to the family. One can imagine the lingering trauma from his father's death, and the transition from a secure loving family in Liberty, Missouri. The feeling of being alone in San Jose surely helped to set the stage for who he became.

Frank Cushing, Ringo's nephew, supposedly told Charles Ringo; that *"Johnny had become a drunkard and left San Jose in 1869 at age 19, leaving the family in a lurch"*. This statement is suspicious, as much of what Charles S. Ringo told Jack Barrow has been called into question. It isn't likely that he left San Jose until late 1870 or early in 1871. He is listed in the 1870 census, along with the rest of the family. According to Mattie Bell, her mother said he left to join up with a wheat harvesting team later that year. The wheat crop was also a major industry in southern California at that time.

In an interview with Jack Barrow, Charles S. Ringo added that Johnny had no real education, having dropped out of grammar school, and this was probably true. It's possible that he had no formal education after they reached California. The family, however, was great on reading the classics and Ringo likely kept up the tradition in English, not Greek or Latin as portrayed by Breckenridge.

John Ringo left California at the age of twenty as a young man whose reputation would be of one who would go to any lengths to aid a friend. He carried with him the memory of a secure childhood in Missouri that was destroyed on a wagon trail west with the tragic death of his father. He struggled, I'm sure, as with any teenager learning to be a man. This he did under the influence of his uncle, Col. Coleman Younger, a good man, who without doubt set a good example. Paradoxically it was virtue, it was his desire to stand for good, and for others that led him in a very bad direction.

CHAPTER THREE

WE'RE HEADING FOR TOMBSTONE, BOYS; TO MAKE OUR FORTUNE

For Wyatt and Mattie Earp, their move from Dodge City, Kansas to the Arizona Territory began a bit less eventful than it did for John Ringo. Upon leaving Kansas, they first headed south to Las Vegas, New Mexico, arriving on September 9, 1879. Their sojourn there was just under a month, where Wyatt and Doc spent a majority of their time with the Dodge City Gang.

Wyatt Earp, c. 1886

Wyatt and Mattie arrived in Prescott in October 1879, where Virgil and Allie were beginning to settle in and make a name for themselves. With the added arrival of James and Bessie Earp, along with her seventeen-year-old daughter Hattie, the family was finally ready to make their mark on the newest silver town to the south; Tombstone. The 300-mile southeast ride from Prescott to Tombstone was mostly uneventful, with the exception of one encounter with a stage driver.

Just south of Benson, the Earp party was forced off the road by the driver of a mail hauling stage coach, who always enjoyed the right of way. Without apology, the driver cracked his whip, and shouted for the Earp's and their caravan of wagons to get out of the way. Nearly toppling Virgil's wagon in a ditch, the driver laughed as he roared by without a hint of care. Seeing that one of his horses was bleeding, Virgil made way behind the driver until he reined up at the next stage stop to change horses. By the time Allie climbed down from the wagon to follow her husband, Virgil had already knocked the man to the ground, with another punch following as soon as he came to his feet. According to Allie; *Virgil just thumped the pudding out of him, knocking him down as fast as he could get up.* [19]

At this same point in time, many others were making their way to this new mining camp in hopes of striking it rich. The number of people arriving in Tombstone during 1881 was overwhelming, enough so that new arrivals slept in their wagons, or whatever makeshift shelter they could assemble. By the beginning of 1882, the town had grown to a population of over 10,000 residents. It would, however, be the people who arrived in late 1879 and early 1880 who set the tenor of the town and the events yet to follow.

Two of the earliest arrivals were Frank and Simpson Stillwell who showed up in Prescott, Arizona in October 1877. As brothers, the two were very different. Simpson, who would later become better known as "Comanche Jack", was an Indian fighter, Deputy U.S. Marshal, U.S. Commissioner, and Police Judge. Jack left Arizona in 1878 and headed to Ft. Davis, Texas, while Frank stayed to try his luck at mining.

Comanche Jack

Frank Stillwell wasn't long in making a name for himself. In October 1877, while working at the Miller Ranch near Prescott, he shot and killed Jesus Bega. Bega angered Stillwell after serving him hot tea instead of coffee, which led to a heated argument. Stillwell shot Bega in the chest, he died moments later. Stillwell claimed it was self-defense, and was acquitted.

Less than a month later on November 9, 1877, Stillwell got into an argument with Col. John Van Houten at the Brunkow Silver Mine near Tombstone over a mining claim in Mojave County. As the disagreement intensified, Houten was beaten in the face with a rock until he was dead. Stillwell and James Cassidy were charged, but the grand jury could find

---

[19] Wyatt Earp Explorers – John D Rose

no evidence to hold them over for trial. Frank Stillwell was off to a roaring start. Today, the cabin where Houten died is considered one of the most haunted places in America.

Among those arriving in November of 1879 was John Clum. Clum was an easterner who had become a renowned Indian Agent, scout, and blood brother to the Chiricahua Apache, who named him *Nantan-betunnykahyeh*, which means; "Boss with-the-high-forehead." Clum had been bald since his early twenties, and had earned the name. His role as mayor of Tombstone became pivotal during the turbulent time which laid ahead.

Big Nose Kate

As Jonny Ringo was facing his first scrape with the law in Safford, AZ in December 1879, another, and perhaps the most colorful character to make his mark on this new town, was working his way into history. John Henry (Doc) Holliday and his companion Mary Katherine Horony, aka Big Nose Kate, had sojourned in Las Vegas, New Mexico after leaving Dodge City in the spring of 1879. There, Holliday held a partnership with Jordan L. Webb in the Holliday Webb Saloon on Center Street. Las Vegas was a hard town with its share of vagabonds and cutthroats. This soon included a man named Mike Gordon.

On the night of July 19, 1879, Gordon was drunk, as he had been for days, causing a ruckus in Holliday's saloon where he was unsuccessful in convincing a young lady to accompany him to another drinking establishment on Railroad Street. To put this in perspective, Gordon was not exactly a handsome man. Still in his late twenties, he carried a disfigured face as the result of an earlier confrontation with an opponent who decided to bite off a large portion of his nose. One can imagine how this might

Doc Holliday

have played a role in the young lady's decision. Angered by her rejection,

Gordon retreated into the street and fired his revolver into the saloon. Return gunfire was heard, but no witnesses were willing to name the shooter. Some said three shots rang out, others numbered it at five.

Gordon disappeared into the night, but was later found with a gunshot in the chest below the right clavicle, exiting through the right shoulder. He died at 6:00am the next morning. The coroner ruled it an excusable homicide without naming a shooter. It wasn't until two years later in the midst of Doc's exploits in Tombstone that Russell Kistler, editor of the *Optic*, named Holliday as the man who killed Gordon. [20]

I would be remiss not to point out some of the notable individuals Holliday interacted with during his time in Las Vegas. Sometime during the days between July 26th and 29th, 1879, Doc Holliday sat across the poker table from Jessie James and Billy the Kid at the newly completed Las Vegas Hotel.[21] In town at that same time was Hyman G. Neil, and the Dodge City Gang. Hoodoo Brown, as Neil was known, was at the time the coroner of San Miguel County. This probably explains why Doc was not indicted for the shooting of Mike Gordon. Other acquaintances of Doc's such as Bat Masterson and Jim Pierce were also in town at the time.

On or about October 1, 1879, Doc and Kate left Las Vegas for Prescott, Arizona. Upon arrival they took a hotel room before meeting up with Wyatt Earp, who was still looking for Virgil. Doc had foregone his dentistry career and taken on a full-time vocation as a 'sporting man' or professional gambler. Soon finding his place on Whiskey Row, the gambling region of Prescott, Doc set up shop where he applied his trade throughout the winter. In early 1880, Doc received a letter from Wyatt urging him to come to Tombstone. Disillusioned by the thought of Doc throwing in with the Earps, Kate decided to make her way to Globe instead. Undeterred by their separation, Doc agreed and travelled along with Kate to Gillette, where they went their separate ways. Doc arrived in Tombstone sometime in September.

With the presence of the Earp Brothers, Johnny Ringo, Doc Holliday, John Clum, Curley Bill Brocius, the McLaury, and Clanton families, who were longtime residents of the area, the cast of characters for what was to come was almost complete.

Tombstone would not have come into existence had it not been for a man named Ed Schieffelin. Schieffelin was an adventurer and prospector,

---

[20] Doc Holliday; The Life and Times Gary Roberts pg.110-111

[21] Doc Holliday; The Life and Times Gary Roberts pg.113

born in Tioga, Pennsylvania in 1847. Born to a prominent family, life in an eastern city was certain to be much easier and more predictable than his chosen profession. Still, at the age of seventeen, Schieffelin set out for the Pacific Northwest and assumed the life of a prospector. By 1875 he had worked his way into the Arizona Territory, searching for riches around the Grand Canyon area. In 1877, Schieffelin was in southern Arizona, prospecting and working as a guard for the Brunckow Mine and part-time scout at Camp Huachuca.

It was the spring of 1879 when Schieffelin made his first strike in the area known as Goose Flats. When he announced his intention to prospect for silver in the Indian country, those at the camp told him the only thing he would find there would be his tombstone. Remembering their words, Ed named his first claim "Tombstone". With the discovery of more silver and the boom which followed, the area began to see an influx of miners, thus forming the new town in the desert aptly named Tombstone.

George Parsons

George Parsons, who arrived in Tombstone on Tuesday February 17, 1880, ran into Schieffelin the next day in town and noted the encounter in his diary; "Saw Schieffelin, the original discoverer of Tombstone today. Rough looking customer."[22] Fate must surely have placed Parsons in Tombstone. He was an avid diarist, and stranger to no one. With more conviction and accuracy than any reporter of his day, Parsons recorded events, both good and bad, with such description as to provide an open window into this new town.

November 1879. Tombstone was a town of makeshift structures, tents, and camp sites. For those who were there, and beginning to make a life for themselves, the sight of new arrivals must have been something to behold. There was no stage road into town. At first, it was basically a trail which spurred off the Benson to Bisbee stage road approximately three miles to the west of the new town. The dust and dirt that surely covered the wagons

---

[22] A Tenderfoot in Tombstone; The private journal of George Whitfield Parsons pg.19

and livestock gave witness to the harshness of the trail, while the wind and sunburned faces of those sitting on the hard, wooden seats offered proof of the persistence and determination of those in search of a better life. Still, by February 1880, Tombstone's population was greater than that of Dodge City.

On January 6, 1880 Frederick G. White was elected as the first marshal of the town of Tombstone. Only a few months into the town's official charter, there were still less than 1,000 residents. White was a New Yorker, born in 1849. Fred White was a man who was liked by all. He had no political, or economic ties which make people choose sides. He was a friend of the Earps as well as the Clantons and Curly Bill Brocius. He was a man with no agenda, and lived off the pay of a lawman. After Wyatt Earp was appointed deputy sheriff of Pima County in July, he and Marshal White formed a pact to keep their new town safe.

John Behan

Melding and mixing like a fine recipe, each newcomer played a role in the flavor of this new town. Enter John Behan. As Undersheriff of Pima County, John Behan was soon thrust upon the scene. At the time of its inception in 1879, Tombstone was located in the south-east section of Pima County, and thus under the jurisdiction of Sheriff Charles Shibell and eventually Undersheriff John Behan. It wasn't until February 1881 that Cochise County was carved from Pima. John Behan was appointed as its first sheriff. Behan and his son Albert arrived in Tombstone on September 14, 1880 and made their home there.

Virgil Earp

Virgil Earp became City Marshal of Tombstone on October 28, 1880 after the shooting of Marshal Fred White by Curly Bill Brocius. Virgil recruited his brothers, Warren and Wyatt as deputy city policemen. This wasn't the life Wyatt had expected when he left Kansas. To use his words, he was: "done with lawing". His plan at the time was to open a freight line, which in modern terms would be the equivalent of a trucking company, but that plan was doomed before it started. By the time he arrived, there were already two freight companies in town fiercely fighting for the available business. Enough so that each was accused of poisoning the livestock of the other. As an alternative, Wyatt took a job riding shotgun for Wells Fargo, investing in mining strikes, water lines, and gambling tables. By this time, friendships and loyalties had been forming for more than a year, placing Behan and the Earps on opposite sides of numerous coming conflicts.

The Earps did not ride into town as welcomed heroes, quite the opposite. They were law and order "Yankee" sympathizers, who held a hard line on the rowdiness of those like Johnny Ringo, Curly Bill Brocius, the McLaury brothers, and the Clantons - just to name a few. Their position didn't set well with most of the town, who were southern Democrat "Confederates" who enjoyed the low cost of rustled Mexican beef, as well as the money they spent in town. John Behan saw the cow-boy faction as good for business. To many, the Earps brought trouble when everything would have been just fine without them. This mindset held true even years later. Bob Boze Bell, editor of *True West* Magazine, once told the author of the anti-Earp stories he'd heard as a child. Seventy or even eighty years after their short stay in Arizona, the Earps were still disliked in southern Arizona, and considered by many as the catalyst for the trouble for which Tombstone is so famously remembered.[23]

Political affiliations and, more directly, the philosophy of each, played a major role in town. Newcomers from Texas and the south were predominately Democrat. Those from the North and back east were surely Republican. In his diary entry of September 1, 1880, George Parsons wrote the following regarding the upcoming Presidential election;

---

[23] Author's conversation with Bob Boze Bell.

Garfield, I hope, is the coming man because in my judgement he represents the best interest of the country. The Republican Party saved it and must perpetuate it. It is too soon to trust it to the hands of the party seeking its destruction 17 years ago.[24]

Parsons was from Washington D.C. Behan was an opportunist whose love for the sheriff's badge was primarily for the money that came with it. As county sheriff, he was also the tax collector, which entitled him to a ten per-cent cut. In 1881, when most drovers and laborers made thirty dollars a month, three hundred sixty dollars a year, Behan is said to have made forty thousand dollars that year. No doubt that he benefited from looking the other way, thereby allowing the cow-boys a free hand in the county. The politics of the town drove many of Tombstone's problems, a trait which many will say hasn't changed much over the years.

Within the city limits of Tombstone, the cowboys didn't have such an easy time, nor did the Earps. This group of rowdies brought a challenge quite different from the Dodge City Saturday night dust ups. In Kansas, the task was in keeping the cattle drovers out of jail, and in the saloons. After all, men who are incarcerated or dead can't spend money. For the most part, these were young men who had never left Texas and who were now finding themselves in Dodge City with more money in their pockets than they had ever seen. This group in Arizona didn't come with such humble backgrounds. The make-up of the cowboys were ex-Confederate soldiers, criminals, and drifters. With numbers at times nearing 200, the cowboy faction roamed the countryside and brought a serious and dangerous challenge that neither the Earps, nor Marshall Fred White had ever faced.

At this point in time, Tombstone was not a primary gathering place for the cowboys, as some may think. In fact, in October 1880 when Curly Bill Brocius shot Marshal White, he was hardly known in town. Instead, Charleston to the south, and Galeyville to the east at the foot of the Chiricahua Mountains served as their primary haunts. Having a free hand elsewhere, they didn't take the law and order pushback in Tombstone so kindly. This was a pot that began to simmer in the fall of 1880 and reached its boiling point by mid-1881.

---

[24] A Tenderfoot in Tombstone; The private journal of George Whitfield Parsons pg. 82

1880 saw the growth of a town now replacing its canvas living quarters with more permanent structures. Business ventures and investment in shops, large and small, were changing the landscape of the hilly countryside. On Allen, Fremont, and Toughnut Streets, the growth of commerce was advancing at a record pace. Mercantiles, restaurants, blacksmith shops, saloons, dry goods stores, and the like were raising their signs and proclaiming that they were ready for business. A gathering of folks who started out as low skill prospectors searching for a vein of silver were now expanding to include a more educated demographic. The mines needed engineers, the town needed doctors, and the business owners needed bankers.

Frank Leslie

In spite of its struggles, Tombstone was morphing into a real town. In the midst of those flocking to Tombstone was "Buckskin" Frank Leslie. The thirty-eight-year-old Texas native arrived in the spring of 1880. According to a job application he submitted on March 10, 1886, Nashville Franklyn Leslie was born in San Antonio, Texas on March 18, 1842. Leslie's personal account of his life prior to reaching town seems a bit too self-serving to be believed. A new journal, Arizona Quarterly Illustrated, published a highly imaginative account of his early life in June 1880. Leslie told the journal he was a Texas native who joined the Army in 1861 and stayed until he, a first lieutenant, surrendered on April 9, 1865, with the 10th Texas Cavalry. He then worked as an Indian scout, known as "Buckskin Frank." From 1871-73, he served as a deputy sheriff in Kansas. First in Abilene, and then Ellsworth under James Butler "Wild Bill" Hickok. He played cowboy and Rough Rider in Australia, piloted a ship around the Fiji Islands, and performed exhibitions as a rifle shootist all around the world. [25]

A more plausible account of Leslie's whereabouts come from the 1878 San Francisco city directory which list him as tending bar at Thomas Boland's saloon. Leslie wasted no time in becoming known in Tombstone. Shortly after his arrival, Leslie and William Knapp opened the Cosmopolitan Saloon, next door to the Cosmopolitan Hotel. On April 23,

---

[25] True West Magazine October 9, 2016

1880, Leslie was present at the wedding of Michael Killeen and a hotel employee by the name of Mary Jane Evans. Their marital bliss, however, had a short run. Only weeks later, Killeen accused Leslie of spending too much time with his now estranged wife.

On the evening of June 22, 1880, Killeen decided to look for Frank Leslie, finding him and Mary Jane sitting on the porch of the Cosmopolitan Hotel. As Killeen approached, Leslie was warned by George Perine of his presence. The warning was almost too late, as Mike Killeen immediately fired two shots which barely missed Frank Leslie's head. Killeen kept coming, and began hitting the surprised Leslie in the head with his sidearm. Leslie fired one shot which proved fatal to the angry Mike Killeen. On July 6, 1880, just eight days after her husband's death, the widowed Mary Jane Killeen married Frank Leslie, her second wedding in ninety days.[26]

Two first impression accounts of what one would have seen if present come from highly credible sources. The first is adventurer, miner, and diarist, George Whitfield Parsons, who arrived in Tombstone on Tuesday February 17, 1880. Following a day's journey that began in Tucson at approximately 7:00am, Parson's stage finally arrived in Tombstone eleven and one-half hours later at 6:30pm. Parson's first description of the town was recorded in his diary as; *"One street of shanties, some with canvas roofs. Hard crowd."*[27]

In June 1880, Clara Brown came to Tombstone with her husband, Theodore. In the dual role of correspondent for the San Diego Union and keeping house for her husband, Clara found this new mining camp to be quite different from southern California. The writings of newcomers like Clara Brown and George Parsons give cold case investigators, such as Cold West Detective Agency, of which this author is a member, access to credible witnesses who have insight, and no reason to lie. Mrs. Brown promised her readers a "woman's view" of this new town. She instead, found herself reporting on gunfights and bloodstained streets.

On July 7, 1880, Clara Brown provided for her readers, and by extension for us, a very descriptive picture of the new town of Tombstone;

---

[26] True West Magazine October 9, 2016

[27] A Tenderfoot in Tombstone; The private journal of George Whitfield Parsons pg.18

*"We behold an embryo city of canvas, frame and adobe, scattered
over a slope...It is a place more pretentious than I had imagined, and full
of activity, notwithstanding the hundreds of loungers seen upon the streets.
The only attractive places visible are the liquor and gambling saloons,
which are everywhere present and are carpeted and comfortably
furnished.*

*The ladies of Tombstone are not so liberally provided with
entertainment, and find little enjoyment aside from a stroll about town
after sunset, the only comfortable time of the day. The camp is one of the
dirtiest places in the world... and one is never sure of having a clean face,
despite repeated ablutions. It is time to talk about dirt. The sod lies loose
upon the surface, and is whirled into the air every day by a wind which
almost amounts to a gale; it makes the eyes smart like the cinders from an
engine; it penetrates into houses, and covers everything with dust. I do not
believe the famous Nebraska breeze can go ahead of the Tombstone
zephyr.*

*The mercury gallivants around in the nineties, with altogether too
high-minded ideas. One could stand two or three days of that sort of thing
with tolerable grace, but it taxes one's endurance to receive no quarter at
all... We cannot obtain desirable food for hot weather, fresh vegetables
are scarce, and the few fruits in the market require a very large
purse...The camp is considered a remarkably quiet one – only one murder
since my arrival...Religious services are held in a furniture store, and
attended by the few who know when Sunday comes around; in about two
months, an adobe church will be completed. As far as I can ascertain,
everyone from San Diego is doing well and making the best of everything.
All feel that this is a place to stay for a while; not a desired spot for a
permanent home."* [28]

On Friday July 16, 1880, George Parsons made the following entry in
his diary;

*"Rain tonight. Remained in town and (staid) with George Houghton.
Major Morgan and Mead were also guests. M went to the ball tonight. We
three took it in from the outside. A grand mixture. All sorts. Some of the
tough ones present, in fact, plenty of them including one Lucretia Borgia.
This place holds some of the most depraved – entirely and apparently
totally so that were ever known. I have seen hard cases before in a frontier
oil town where but one or two women were thought respectable but have
never come across several such cases as are here. It would be impossible*

---

[28] San Diego Union; July 7, 1880

to speak here of some or one form of depravity I am sorry to know of – for bad as one can be and low as woman can fall – there is one form of sin here fortunately confined to two persons which would I almost believe bring a blush of shame to a prostitute's cheek. Such persons, if the facts were generally known, it seems to me, would be run out of town. One of the two I saw tonight in the ball room. Also, other depraved women and men, of course. Others wore the garb and appearance of gentility. Good manners and good was but there was a sad mixture.

The rain coming down pretty well, went home and had some guitar music before retiring. How men of good family and connections east can come here and marry prostitutes, then take them out to a dance house, I can't see.[29] "

In case you missed it, there were lesbians in Tombstone, at least one couple. Clara Brown wrote of them as well without specifics, but enough for her San Diego readers to get the message. Yes, Tombstone was a hard and dangerous place. But as the hotels, social halls, reading rooms, and upscale restaurants grew, the canvas tents, and garbage lines streets began to fade away.

Tombstone was in fact a mining camp comprised of sojourners, there for the taking, for however long that might last. Civic pride wasn't even an afterthought. Dirty wind-blown streets cut from wagon paths, lined with garbage and refuge would morph only a block away into opulent establishments fitting for the upper crust of Chicago or San Francisco. On September 9, 1880 the Grand Hotel opened with lavish elegance one would not expect in a mining town. The following article from the Epitaph provides a window into the level of sophistication beginning to develop in town.

SEPTEMBER 9, 1880
THE GRAND HOTEL

Through the courtesy of Mr. H.V. Sturm, an Epitaph reporter, who yesterday paid a visit to and made a brief inspection of the new hotel christened the Grand which will be formally open for dinner this evening at five o'clock. The general size and character of the structure have been

---

[29] A Tenderfoot in Tombstone; The private journal of George Whitfield Parsons pg. 63

mentioned so often during the course of construction that further mention would be superfluous and we will confine ourselves to a description of the interior appointments of it. Passing into the building by the front entrance the first thing that strikes the eye is a wide and handsome staircase covered by an elegant carpet and supporting a heavy black walnut banister. Thence upstairs to the main hall, and turning to the right we are ushered into a perfect little bijou of costly furniture and elegant carpeting known as the bridal chamber. This room occupies half of the main front and is connected with the parlor by folding doors through which the reporter passed, and entering the parlor was more than astonished by the luxurious appointments. A heavy Brussels carpet of the most elegant style and finish graces the floor, the walls are adorned with rare and costly oil paintings; the furniture is of walnut cushioned with the most expensive silk and rep, and nothing lacks, save the piano which will be placed in the position shortly. On down through the main corridor peeping now and then into the bedrooms, sixteen in number, each of them fitted with walnut furniture and carpeted to match: spring mattresses that would tempt even a sybarite, toilet stands and fixtures of the most approved pattern, the walls papered, and to crown all, each room having windows. All are outside rooms thus obviating the many comforts in close and ill-ventilated apartments. Returning we pass down the broad staircase and turning to the left are in the office and reading room. Here we met Mr. R.J. Pryke, the polite and affable clerk, so well-known to Yosemite tourists in California. The office fixtures are as is common in first class hotels and fully in keeping with the general character of the house. The dining room adjoining next invites inspection. Here we find the same evidence of good taste in selection and arrangement that is so marked a feature of the whole interior. Three elegant chandeliers are pendant from the handsome centerpieces, walnut tables, extension and plain, covered with cut glass, china, silver castors and the latest style of cutlery are among the many attractions of this branch of the cuisine.

Thence into the kitchen where we find the same evidence before mentioned; an elegant Montagin range, 12 feet in length, with patent heater, hot and cold faucets, in fact, all the appliances necessary to feed five hundred persons at a few hours notice are present. The bar occupies the east half of the main front and is in keeping with the general furnishings. Want of space prevents more than this cursory glance at the Grand and its appliances for the comfort and convenience of guests. A Grand (no pun intended) invitation ball will take place this evening. [30]

---

[30] Tombstone Epitaph September 10, 1880

1880 was indeed a time for establishing the direction of this shanty town. If she were to grow, or simply remain a support mechanism for the laborers and profit takers, was a question yet to be answered. Men who came for the work had for the most part come alone. Wives and children were yet to become a common sight on the boardwalks in town. However, establishments such as the Grand Hotel were beginning to line the boardwalks, drawing those with the means to indulge in its opulence. An enigma of sorts, the engineer of higher education, accustomed to a moral society, was now living in social conflict with reprobates, counter balancing the scale of good manners.

It was mid-July 1880 when Morgan Earp arrived, immediately taking on the job of a lawman. At the time, the Earps – Wyatt, Virgil, and James – lived with their families in three houses on Fremont Street, near First. James, who made his living as a bartender, never wore a badge. He chose instead to take on work at Vogan's Saloon & Bowling Alley. Wyatt, whose initial desire was to open a stage line, found the Kinnear, and the Ohnesorgen & Walker lines competing for passengers, charging only $4.00 for a seat on the Benson – Tombstone run. With the pricing not worth the cost, Wyatt chose instead to work as a shotgun messenger for Wells-Fargo for the next eight months. Virgil still wore the badge of a deputy U.S. Marshal.

KILLED OVER AN UGLY SHIRT

It would be funny if not so serious, but a man named Tom Waters bought a new shirt, and within hours got himself killed over it. In mid-July, Waters purchased a blue & black checkered shirt, which he proudly wore about town. When he entered a saloon, Waters soon became the center of attention. Angered by the ridicule, and fueled by whiskey, he vowed to; "knock the son-of-a-bitch down that says anything about my shirt again". A short time later, E. L. Bradshaw, a close friend of Waters, saw the shirt and made the mistake of mocking his friend's choice in attire. Without hesitation, Waters cold-cocked Bradshaw. So angered by the exchange, the normally quiet Bradshaw left to place a bandage above his eye, then returned with his revolver. He fired four shots into Waters, killing him where he stood.

DOC MAKES HIMSELF KNOWN IN TOWN

Lines were further defined on the evening of October 11, 1880. In his first dust-up since arriving in Tombstone, Doc Holliday had a heated exchange with Johnny Tyler over a card game in the Oriental Saloon. Once the disturbance was quieted, Milt Joyce accused Holliday of starting the affair, and threw him out of the saloon after Tyler had left on his own accord. Angered by Joyce's actions, Holliday soon returned and demanded his firearm, which was behind the bar. When Joyce refused, Holiday left, only to return moments later with another pistol. As he approached Joyce, Holliday fired the revolver wildly, striking Milt Joyce in the hand. Joyce rushed Holiday and hit him in the head with a pistol. John Holiday was charged in Judge James Reilly's court with assault with a deadly weapon, which he pled down to assault and battery, earning a fine of $20.00 and $11.30 in court costs. It was a run in that affected more than just Holliday. From that day forward, the relationship between Doc Holiday and Milt Joyce became very strained. Joyce's political influences in Tombstone would eventually have a negative effect on the Earps as well.

MARSHAL FRED WHITE

Just after midnight on October 28, 1880, Marshal Fred White responded to a disturbance on Allen Street near the corner of Sixth. Curly Bill Brocius and others were having a jolly old time firing random shots at the moon with their sidearms, scaring the awakened townsfolk half to death. Upon hearing the shots, Wyatt Earp, who was currently in a card game at the Bank Exchange Saloon, quickly made his way to the scene. As he approached, he ran up on his brother Morgan and Fred Dodge. Being unarmed, he asked Dodge for his sidearm, and arrived just as the marshal was attempting to unarm Brocius. In the marshal's attempt to remove the firearm from Brocius's hand, it discharged, striking Marshal White in the groin. Earp immediately hit Brocius in the back of the head with a pistol, knocking him to the ground, then placing him under arrest. With the wounded young marshal lying on his death bed, Virgil Earp received a temporary appointment as town marshal later that day.

The question is why? What brought on the mid-night celebration, and the need for Brocius and others to unload their sidearms in the night sky? What had started as a group of pseudo-cattlemen making a deal in the Alhambra Saloon, ended up in the street with a number of drunken cowboys causing their usual ruckus. The list reads as a San Simon Who's Who, with Frank Patterson, Johnny Tyler, Pete Spence, and Dick Lloyd leading the disturbance. Wyatt Earp and the 'law and order' element in town were beginning to see the cow-boys as a real problem. With no regard for the law, they would force confrontation and make the outlaw faction known as loyalties and friendships grew on each side. The death of Marshal White, and particularly Wyatt's rough treatment of Curly Bill marked the beginning of hard-feelings and animosities that never healed. Although Wyatt Earp protected Brocius on the ride to Tucson and stood up for him at trial, the chasm between them grew. Marshal White died two days later.

November was election season throughout the country. James Garfield was elected President of the United States, and Charles Shibell was re-elected as Sheriff of Pima County. Johnny Ringo and Joe Hill were Democrat delegates for the San Simon district. In the November 12, 1880 special election for town marshal, Ben Sippy beat Virgil Earp by a comfortable margin. As 1880 came to an end, the effects of each sunrise, and the assemblage of personalities created the catalyst for 1881. It would be a year no one expected.

CHAPTER FOUR

WHERE WAS RINGO?

In 1880, Tombstone wasn't a place of interest to John Ringo and the recently formed coalition of rustlers and so-called cattlemen. Galeyville, Charleston, and the border canyons provided the resources and anonymity needed to exercise their new business venture with great success.

GALEYVILLE

Cochise County deputy, Billy Breakenridge described Galeyville in his 1929 novel as follows;

The outlaws that made Galeyville their headquarters were most of them cattle rustlers. A party of them would make a raid into Old Mexico where cattle were plentiful, run off a large heard, bring them up through Guadeloupe and Skeleton Canyons, and through the San Simon Valley near Galeyville. They had squatted on every gulch and canyon near there where there was water, and had built a corral on each of their claims. Here they would divide up the stolen stock, and placing their different brands on them, have them ready for market. The men were nearly all Texas cowboys, whose feeling toward Mexicans were so bitter that they had no compunction about stealing from them, or shooting and robbing them whenever they got the opportunity.

One of their men did a thriving commission business acting as the banker, and disposing of the stolen stock. Then, while another bunch of rustlers were off making a raid, those left behind would turn themselves loose on Galeyville, having a good time drinking and gambling until they were broke. After the Mexicans found out what they were doing, there were many of them killed. There was no killing among themselves while they were drinking, and they confined their crimes to stealing stock and robbing Mexican smugglers who were bringing Mexican silver across the line to buy goods. They generally killed the smugglers. Their leaders were John Ringo and William Brocius, better known as Curly Bill.[31]

Unfortunately, the new town didn't turnout as planned by its founder, John Galey, who formed his new hamlet as a mining town. An eastern entrepreneur from Pennsylvania, Galey arrived in Arizona in 1880 with hopes of developing a silver mining empire at the base of the Chiricahua Mountains, sixty miles east of Tombstone.

His silver mining effort, however, played out in less than a year, leaving ten saloons and thirty other small business efforts with no resource. As the town died a slow death, Curly Bill Brocius saw it as the perfect base for his rustling enterprise and took up residence there.

Justice Jim

CHARLESTON

Charleston was a more traditional town than Galeyville, but still offered the protection a man living outside the law would need. Founded by Amos Stowe on the west bank of the San Pedro River, Charleston came into existence in April 1879, basically as a support town for the new stamping mills, and mining ventures beginning to spring up in nearby Tombstone and Contention City. Although the economy of Charleston was based almost entirely on the surrounding silver mines, all effort was made by town officials to stand out on its own.

Perhaps the most colorful character in town was James Burnett, better known in Charleston as "Justice Jim". He was born in New York in 1832, but unlike the new comers, Burnett had lived in the area around Ft. Huachuca for twenty-five years. Burnett assumed the position of Justice of the Peace on November 4, 1880 when the election ended in a tie vote of 107 each for him and his Republican opponent.

Burnett soon became the only law in town, and used his position strictly for personal gain. With no official courthouse in town, Justice Jim held impromptu hearings on street corners and saloons. With the aid of Constable Sam Starr, he tried and convicted his defendants on the spot, pocketing the fines he imposed. There were no appeals. In a twist of irony, Justice Jim met his fate near the O.K. Corral in Tombstone on July 1, 1897.

---

[31] William Breakenridge; Helldorado; Houghton Mifflin Co. 1928

Jim was shot and killed on Allen Street close to the O.K. Corral by his neighbor William Greene. Greene, who was well liked by all, was the opposite of Burnett whose reputation was less than perfect. The two men had neighboring farms, but never liked one another. In early 1897, Greene built a small dam on the San Pedro River, which didn't impede the flow of water, but Burnett wanted it gone. On the evening of June 24th, Burnett had three Chinese workers to blast the small canal dam. Greene's two daughters and a friend took an evening dip to cool off on the night of June 27th to find themselves in deep rushing water, where shallow water had been. Eve made it to shore, but ten-year-old Ella and her friend Kate Corcoran were caught in the rushing water and died. Greene swore retribution. When he spotted Burnett in Tombstone on July 1st, he shot him three times. Greene was not convicted for the killing.

"Old Man" Newman Clanton's ranch was located five miles to the south. He and his sons, Phin, Ike, and Billy, made a living off of stolen Mexican cattle, and worked closely with the likes of Pete Spence, Frank Stillwell, The McLaury's, Johnny Ringo, Curly Bill, and others who frequented Charleston. The inception of Charleston and Tombstone go almost hand in hand, while Galeyville, some seventy miles to the east, would be 1880 before it had a name. Throughout most of 1880, Tombstone was only a stopping place between Charleston and the San Simon Valley for the cowboys. As the population grew, and more eating establishments were opened, Tombstone businesses provided a wider customer base for Mexican cattle. By early 1881, their presence in town was routine.

Ringo and Joe Hill settled in the San Simon Valley in late 1879. Around the same time, Curly Bill Brocius was taking his place in southern Arizona, rustling cattle and building a coalition with the Clanton's and McLaury brothers. Little is known about Curly Bill's travels before he reached Arizona, though much is speculated. The one exception was his 1878 conviction for waylaying a government ambulance coach in May of that year, where one man was killed, and another wounded in El Paso, Texas.

According to Steve Gatto, Curly Bill Bresnaham, and Robert Martin, an associate of John Kinney, were arrested by Mexican authorities a few days later, and turned over to Military officials. They were later tried, with both men convicted and sentenced to five years in prison. After filing an appeal, the two men were held in Ysleta under the custody of Texas Rangers. On November 2, 1878, Curly Bill, Robert Martin, and three Mexican prisoners escaped and high-tailed it to Arizona. In early 1879, Curly Bill showed up at the San Carlos Reservation with a herd of cattle.

He had apparently used an alias in Texas and was convicted under the name of William "Curly Bill" Bresnaham. His real name has always been in question. If it was Brocius, Graham, Bresnaham, or something entirely different is unclear. His relationship with Robert Martin, one of John Kinney's top men during the Lincoln County War, leaves the question of Curly Bill's whereabouts at that time. Some have concluded, without evidence, that he was a participant there under a different name, and perhaps with ties to Jessie Evans. All speculation, but it makes one wonder.[32]

In a conversation he had with Wyatt Earp, Curly Bill confirmed that he was the man convicted in El Paso. Wyatt later reported to the Tombstone Epitaph that as Curly Bill was being transported to Tucson for the killing of Marshal Fred White, he asked him where he could get a good lawyer. Earp suggested the firm of Hereford and Zebriskie in Tucson, but Curly Bill said he could not because James Zebriskie had prosecuted him in El Paso, Texas.[33]

In early 1880, Ringo's focus was on cattle, and making money. He'd started to run with Curly Bill and his crew, as well as running stolen stock for Old Man Clanton, but he still battled the effects of the Mason County War. It played heavily on Ringo, as it did on many who'd participated in that disturbance. Ringo needed to put all that behind him. Joseph Olney, now Joe Hill, had provided him with the motivation, and the timing to do just that. When he settled into Arizona, Ringo intended to stay to himself, and away from people. He was carrying brutal memories of things most men will never see, which accounts for the increased drinking and his violent outbursts.

Real life is very different from Hollywood's depictions of the old west gunfight. When a man is fighting for his life he looks for every edge. There is no such animal as a fair fight. The heart races, the mind is addled, and the senses are at a heightened state. With each report of a firearm, you immediately wonder if that bullet just tore a hole in your body, as you anticipate excruciating pain at any second. Some men shake, puke, and piss their pants. It is not the cool, heroic, 'good guy wins the day' carefully scripted scene for a Saturday Matinée. For those who survive, the memories and 'what ifs' haunt them for the rest of their days.

For a man like Ringo, the experience and muscle memory of repeating such a process kicks in at the time of 'fight or flight'. Tunnel vision, instinctively takes over as the heart rate exceeds 140 bpm. The focus now is entirely on the threat. Life itself is isolated, and you are the only person there. There are no conscious decisions. It's all muscle memory, as the mind decelerates every movement to slow motion, focuses only on the

---

[32] From Steve Gatto's web site www.curlybill.com
[33] Wyatt Earp; The Life behind the Legend; Casey Tefertiller pg. 52

threat, and relies on experience for survival. The mind is in command of the body – there is work to be done. The fear and analyses will surely come, but there is no time for it now.[34]

Ringo, however, carried a burden that others didn't have to bare. At the age of fourteen, he witnessed the death of his father in the most violent and unexpected manner. I would suggest, the combination of which, accounts for his depression and alcohol dependency in Arizona. Ringo was more of a follower than a leader, and re-active in many instances. Although he was given the title "King of the Cowboys", the nefarious events in which he was associated, show him riding in the pack. I know of no instance where he was riding lead. He rode with Curly Bill, and probable second in command. He seemed to be a part of, but never in control of the events around him.

Regardless of his intentions, it didn't take long for Ringo to make a splash in Arizona. After the December 9th shooting of Louis Hancock, John Ringo was arrested, and released on bond. He was to appear before the Pima County Grand Jury in March 1880, but did not show up. Instead, he wrote an advance letter to Sheriff Charles Shibell on March 3, 1880 explaining why he could not appear.

> *Dear Sir, being under bond for my appearance before the Grand Jury of Pima Co., I write to let you know why I cannot appear – I got shot through the foot and it is impossible for me to travel for a while.* (An apparent reference for his inability to ride a horse) *If you get any papers for me, and will let me know, I will attend to them at once. As I wish to live here, I do not wish to put you to any unnecessary trouble, nor do I wish to bring extra trouble on myself. Please let the Dist. – Att. Know why I do not appear, for I am anxious that there is no forfeiture on the Bond.*

Pima County District Attorney Hugh Farley did not accept Ringo's explanation as sufficient, and requested that his bond be revoked. On March 11th, a capias warrant was issued for his arrest. The disposition of the case is unclear to history. There are no remaining records of the case, but the common acceptance of fact is that the case was pled down to drunk in public, with a fine of $50.00. This seems plausible since he spent no jail time, and continued to live in the area. The circumstance surrounding his injury is also unclear, but the common conclusion at the time was that he shot himself in the foot. This, too, is plausible with the absence of any report of gun-play by him or those around him at the time.

---

[34] Author's conversation with Steve Sederwall.

Around this time, in March of 1880, several things were coming together at once. Ringo, had started to run with Curly Bill, and working some for "Old Man" Newton Clanton, running cattle from the south up to his ranch. The Clanton Ranch was a short southeast ride from Charleston, and a straight shot south into Mexico and their choice of herds. Near the San Pedro River, among the cottonwoods just south of the ranch, were corrals and holding pens to drive the stolen cattle as they came north. From Charleston, less than ten miles from a growing beef market in Tombstone, the cowboys had a free hand, which had not yet come into question. As business grew, the seventy-mile run between the two outlaw hamlets of Galeyville and Charleston was becoming routine.

The cowboys had clear access to Mexican cattle in Sonora, just south of the eastern border of Arizona. From the Cienega south to the Valley, and Galeyville, to Skeleton Canyon just west of the New Mexico border, then south to Guadeloupe Canyon, their access in and out was unchecked. They had water, and gamma grass tall enough to clean your boots in the stirrups. There were corrals at each of their claims, and enough open range to hold the stolen herds before they were branded and moved out.

It was a long ride from Charleston to the San Simon Valley, but these guys lived in the saddle. Called the Barfoot Trail, they would start out from Charleston, up the San Pedro River, cut northeast past Tombstone, through the South Pass of the Dragoon Mountains, across Sulphur Springs Valley to the Chiricahuas, then down into Galeyville. That was a seventy-mile ride. Johnny Ringo spent the last two days of his life riding the portion of that trail east of Tombstone.

By mid-1880, Ringo and the cowboys had formed a well-managed organized

Ike Clanton

crime operation. On November 26, 1880, Ringo and Ike Clanton filed notice for a "squatters claim" with Grant County New Mexico for 320 acres of unoccupied Government land in Animas Valley. The stated purpose was for farming and grazing, but the strategic location of the claim said something very different. Twenty-eight miles north-northeast of Guadalupe Canyon, and only a short run into Sonora, Mexico, the new location would take those herds out of the jurisdiction of the Arizona Territory.

They had their own highway system. Skeleton Canyon, called Canon Bonita by the Mexicans, was thirty miles northeast of Douglas, and almost a straight shot north from Guadalupe Canyon. They were connected in New Mexico from the Animas Valley, south to Cloverdale, then west across the Arizona border to Guadalupe Canyon. From there it was a straight run into and out of Sonora and all the beef they could drive. In San Simon they had holding pins, corrals, and all the grass they needed. Total investment---Zero. They were covered at every angle. Even if followed out of Old Mexico, there were a number of directions they could go once back in the Territory. Hiding, branding, feeding, or watering a fresh herd was of no worry to these guys.

The trail is still there, it is now called Guadalupe Canyon Road. It runs from Geronimo Trail, east of Douglas, Az., to Animas Valley, N.M., passing just north of Guadalupe Canyon. This isn't surprising. Most of our current secondary roads are nothing more than wagon roads, widened for cars, and mapped in the early twentieth century. Cow trails, turned into horse trails, then widened for freight wagons and stage coaches. They were the beginning of our current highway system. Most folks give it little thought, but a great number of the current twists and turns in secondary country roads were simply there to avoid a tree.

Ringo's first venture into New Mexico real estate, raises a lot of questions. On April 2, 1880, John Ringo and a man names M.C. Blakely sold a mining property to John E. Price. Price was at the time a partner in Smyth, Long & Price; dealers in general merchandise, and mining supplies. Price however, was removed from that firm in November 1880.[35] Record of how Ringo acquired ownership in this property is unclear, as well as his relationship with either Blakely or Price. Shares of their ownership in the one-thousand-dollar sale price is also under question.

A week later on April 7th, John Ringo executed a Power of Attorney to James B. Price of St. Louis, Missouri. The POA granted Price six month to sell a different mine, one owned by John Ringo, located in the San Simon mining district, for $2,000.00, the equivalent of $43,600.00 in today's economy. Price's commission for the sale was any amount that he could secure above the two thousand dollar asking price. James B. Price of Missouri appears to have no connection with John E. Price, who resided in New Mexico.

---

[35] Arizona Daily Star November 16, 1880

James B. Price was a postal route contractor who on April 17, 1880 came under federal indictment for bribing postal inspector, Thomas J. Brady, who was a Northern Civil War General. The bribe was five thousand dollars for the Star Route postal contract from Socorro to Silver City, New Mexico. Brady had been appointed by President Grant as Assistant Post Master General.

William Pitt Kellogg

In the indictment, Louisiana Senator William Pitt Kellogg, and Thomas J. Brady, were charged with conspiracy on April 17, 1880 along with James B. Price, to defraud the United States by means of false oaths, fraudulent allowances for expenditures, and false and fraudulent claims to be made for increased pay for expedition on post roads from Monroe to Shreveport in Louisiana, and San Antonio to Corpus Christi in Texas, the said routes then being in the name of James B. Price as contractor.

The charges against William Pitt Kellogg, as set forth that on April 17, 1880, stated that; "whilst Senator from Louisiana, he did unlawfully receive from James B. Price, contractor, a sum of money, post office drafts, and promissory notes, together for the value of twenty thousand dollars."[36]

The case against Brady covered the period of 1878, 1879, and 1880. The total amount in question was over $4,000,000.00 transferred from the United States Treasury to the Postal Department. Brady was found Not Guilty in June 1883. The fact, however, that he was a man of little means when he entered the postal position, and was worth in excess of $1,000,000.00 at the time of his acquittal remained in question. William Kellogg avoided trial by claiming Senatorial Privilege. May 18, 1883 the

---

[36] The St. Joseph Herald; March 28, 1883. Las Vegas Gazette (NM) March 28, 1883

Holt County Sentinel in Missouri listed James B. Price as now living in Grant County New Mexico. Apparently, they all made a lot of money and got away with it.

At some point in 1880, logically during the summer, John Ringo made a trip to San Jose to reunite with his family. It is suspected that the only known photo of Ringo was taken while he was in California. His visit has been written about for a century, with most describing Ringo as leaving depressed and dejected after he was rebuked and turned away. As with much of what people do not know about Ringo, that was a falsehood first broadcast by Walter Noble Burns in his 1929 version of the truth *"Tombstone; An Iliad of the Southwest"*. Perhaps misled by Charles Ringo, who seemed to have a greater interest in having his name in print than in presenting the truth, Burns asserted a number of fallacies in this regard.

In 1934 members of the Ringo extended family formed a research group in Valrico, Florida. The family's heritage extends back to 1700, with much to celebrate. However, for their first family newsletter, they chose to write a monolog about John Peters Ringo, primarily based on information from Burns. Advanced copies were sent to Mattie Bell and Mary Enna for review, they went ballistic. In a response letter to Minerva Letton, dated October 5, 1934, they threatened to sue anyone who published the article. On November 5, 1934 the sisters sent a follow up apology letter stating that they had read Burns novel, and that he was "full of s...." In their October letter, the sisters confirmed that Ringo had visited them in 1880, and was a fine upright gentleman.

Ringo was for the most part a quiet and obscure figure. With exception of the crowd he ran with, he kept to himself, only popping up in a newspaper or before a judge on occasion. He was good with cattle, making his association with the cowboy faction a natural move for him when he settled in Arizona. Back in Texas, prior to his involvement with Scott Cooley and the Mason County War, Ringo made his money in cattle. He and a couple of his friends mavericked, which was a common occupation for a freewheeling spirit in those days. They would round up mavericks, (unbranded cattle) and sell them to ranchers for $5.00 a head. Five or six unbranded cows per day, and these boys were making pretty good money, when most drovers were making $30.00 per month. The problem with that line of work was their honesty. It wasn't uncommon for guys to sell mavericks to a rancher in the afternoon, and just steal them back after dark, before they felt the branding iron.

November 2, 1880 was Election Day around the country. Republican Presidential candidate James A. Garfield beat Democrat candidate William Scott Hancock with a total of 214 electoral votes to Hancock's

155. They each carried 19 states. For Pima County it was an important day as well. Democrat incumbent Charles Shibell was facing Republican challenger Robert H. Paul for the office of Sheriff. Paul, who had experience as Undersheriff, then as sheriff of Calaveras, California, stood a head taller than Shibell. At six foot six inches, and two hundred forty pounds, Paul had a commanding presence, and was expected to win the election, but Shibell was suspiciously reelected by a 46-vote margin.

A week later, Bob Paul challenged the results, accusing Shibell and the election officers of the San Simon Precinct of ballot stuffing. Joe Hill's house in San Simon was first selected as the polling place, but it wasn't clear if the house was actually in Arizona, or the New Mexico Territory. It was finally moved to the home of J. Magill. Ringo had attended the Democrat County Convention in August, where he and James Speedy were selected as delegates for the San Simon Cienga District, Precinct 27. James Hayes, brother-in-law to Louis Hancock was also in attendance. Objections to Ringo's appointment were raised when he could not provide a residence. In the end, he was approved.

The Pima County Board of Supervisors, who had approved Ringo as a delegate in October, later removed him as a polling official, stating his inability to prove himself as a resident of Arizona. Curly Bill Brocius, Ike Clanton, and Frank McLaury did remain. Shibell received 103 votes in San Simon, from a precinct with 15 eligible voters. In addition, it seemed that these same 'voters' elected Ike Clanton as Justice of the Piece, and Joe Hill as constable. No chance of fraud there!

Shibell remained in office pending the court case, while Bob Paul went back to work for Wells Fargo as a shotgun messenger. On November 9th, Wyatt Earp, resigned his position as undersheriff of the eastern section of Pima County, a job he'd held since July 29, 1880. As a supporter of Bob Paul, he cited a 'conflict of interest' as the reason for his resignation. Shibell immediately chose John Behan to fill that position.

It was in the cow-boy's best business interest for Shibell to stay in office with the friendly face of Johnny Behan wearing the badge of a Pima County lawman. The election of Bob Paul would have seen Wyatt Earp in that position, and they knew it. Thus far, Shibell was still in charge, but with the pending court case, and accusation of voter fraud, the future seemed very uncertain.

The case became quite drawn out, with the Arizona Supreme Court ruling in Paul's favor in February, which prompted an appeal by Shibell. Shibell stayed in office until April when the appeal was ruled in Bob Paul's favor. By then the final election result had become a moot point for the San Simon cow-boys. On February 1, 1881, Cochise County was founded, saving Ringo and his crew from the new Pima Sheriff. When the new county was founded in February, Democrat John Behan, who had served two terms in the Arizona Legislature, was appointed by the Territorial Governor as its first Sheriff. His appointment served as a testament to how well Behan was liked. Governor John Fremont was a Republican.

CHAPTER FIVE

THE BENSON STAGE ROBBERY

T he future of Tombstone was altered when the Kinnear & Company stage rolled out of town on that cold March afternoon. For within an hour of departure, her scheduled destination of Benson was unexpectantly derailed at Drew's Station. Perhaps to be more accurate, it was the Sheriff's failure to capture the 'would be robbers' that set Tombstone's unfortunate wheels of fate in motion. On Tuesday evening March 15, 1881, George Parsons wrote of the beauty of a lite morning snowfall, but as with many things, beauty soon turned to tragedy.

> *Tuesday March 15, 1881: A strange and pretty sight this A.M. Just enough snow had fallen to whiten everything around and it looked very pretty. Would like to see a good snowstorm once more. Didn't last long. Excitement tonight. Outgoing stage attacked by robbers and driver and one passenger killed.*[37]

On the box that night was Bud Philpot, a well-known, and top-rated driver from California. By his side was Bob Paul, Wells Fargo shotgun messenger, and Calaveras California lawman. On board the Kinnear & Company stage were nine passengers, and $26,000.00 in silver. It was a normal run, as the Sandy Bob Stage left Tombstone, and rolled along in the cold air. About eight miles north of Contention, and some two hundred yards from Drew's Station, the stage slowed, as the horses pulled their cargo up a small incline. Suddenly a man stepped out into the road and called "Hold!" Bud Philpot and Bob Paul were now facing an attempted robbery. Two other men immediately stepped to either side of the road as a shot was fired. Bob Paul returned the call with a loud; "By God, I hold for no one!" He immediately returned fire, almost simultaneously emptying two barrels at the robbers. Bud Philpot fell dead from his seat, tumbling to the ground between the wheelers. (Wheelers are the two rear horses nearest the hitch.) One passenger, who was riding topside, was also hit, and bleeding badly. Peter Roerig (or as named in the March 20, 1881

---

[37] George Parsons: A Tenderfoot in Tombstone, pg. 134

Arizona Weekly Citizen "O.E. Oertig"), a miner, was mortally wounded, and later died.

The sudden excitement, and unexpected reports of gunfire spooked the horses, sending the stage into a hard ride. Bob Paul quickly took the driver's seat. With the stage now out of control, he pulled the brake to slow the horses, then grappled for the lines, which had fallen around the tongue. He eventually took hold, regaining control of the team. The run had been nearly a mile before Paul slowed the stage, and brought it to a stop. It's unlikely that he knew it at the moment, but the sudden action by the horses probably saved the stage and its passengers from further peril.

Once back in control, Paul continued on to Benson at a fast pace, safely arriving with his passengers and cargo. It wasn't until he arrived that Roerig's condition became clear. Sitting topside in the 'dicky seat', he was in a direct line of fire, and caught the blast intended for Bob Paul. Roerig didn't survive. Before returning to the scene, Paul quickly wired Wells Fargo agent, Marshal Williams in Tombstone to apprize him of the incident, and the condition of his wounded passenger. Time was of great importance, and a fast response from Tombstone was imperative.

Arriving back at the scene, Bob Paul, found the station agent and employees of Drew's Station out by the road with Bud's body. Their best guess at the time was of three men executing the hold up, with one man holding the horses. Their assessment turned out to be accurate. Marshal Williams, (Wells Fargo agent,) John Behan, Bat Masterson, Virgil, Wyatt, and Morgan Earp saddled up and headed for the scene as soon as they got word. A number of men volunteered to ride along, but Sheriff John Behan selected only the Earp Brothers, Bob Paul, and Bat Masterson to join the chase.

Upon hearing of the situation, George Parsons wrote in his diary on the evening of the 15th:

> Excitement tonight. Outgoing stage attacked by robbers and driver and one man killed.

With more information, his entry for the 16th, was very different.

> Wednesday, March 16, 1881: A most terrible affair of last evening. First intimation I had was when Doc. Goodfellow burst into room and asked for a rifle. Abbott finally let him have his upon Doc's assurance he didn't want to kill any one. I stopped our chess, got revolver and followed him up, not wishing him to get hurt if I could help it. Men and horses were flying about in different directions, and I soon ascertained the cause. A large posse in pursuit - $26,000 specie reported on stage. Bob Paul went

as shotgun messenger and emptied both barrels of his gun at the robbers, probably wounding one. "I hold for no one," he said and let drive. Some 20 shots fired – close call for Paul. Capt. Colby wished me to form one of another posse, to head the robbers off at San Simon if we could get necessary information upon arrival of stage, and we worked the thing up. Got rifle and horses, I got Clum and Abbott to go with us. Probably six in all. Information didn't come as we expected, so delayed, and several of us shadowed several desperate characters in town, one known as an ex-stage robber. Couldn't fix anything. Bud Philpot, the driver, was shot and almost through the heart and the passenger, a miner, through the back. Doc showed me the bullet that killed him – an ugly .45 caliber. Some more tracking tonight. Our birds have flown...[38]

LUTHER KING'S ARREST AND ESCAPE

Three days into their search, the posse rode up on the Redfield Ranch, where brothers Len and Hank were known to have ties to the outlaw faction. Luther King was there, and apparently tried to hide when he saw the posse coming. Morgan Earp saw him, and quickly made the capture. As standard practice for an investigation, Wyatt had John Behan to secure King, and separate him from the others, and not be allowed to talk to either Len, or Hank Redfield. As Wyatt and Bob Paul conferred, Behan had given King free access to both Redfield brothers. What was said seemed to be of no interest to Sheriff Behan. The information exchanged was enough for Hank Redfield to immediately mount up and ride off, no doubt to warn the others. What could have been the break they needed, was just intentionally sabotaged by the highest-ranking jurisdictional officer on the scene.

Furious at Behan's actions, Wyatt grabbed King and quickly began an aggressive interrogation, where he gave up the names, and admitted to holding the horses, and being a part of the attempted robbery. He also told them where the others were camped, but it now seemed that Wyatt and Bob Paul were the last to know. They had witnessed the exchange between King and the Redfield brothers - permitted by Sheriff Behan – and also realized that any chance of surprising the three remaining bandits had just ridden off to warn them. At this point, the Earps, Masterson, and Paul decided the best course of action was to send the prisoner back to Tombstone while they continued on with what they had. Marshal Williams accompanied Behan back to town with the prisoner as a precaution to

[38] A Tenderfoot in Tombstone; George Parsons. Pg. 134

make sure he got there, and didn't 'escape' before reaching town. They arrived in town on March 21st, and placed King in custody.

The balance of the posse continued unsuccessfully for six more grueling days. They did find the campsite, now cold, but with signs of recent activity. They also knew the men were on fresh horses from the Redfield Ranch, where their mounts had played out. With information about the posse, and riding fresh mounts, Leonard, Head, and Crane had the edge, and the Earps knew it. Virgil later telegraphed Behan for fresh horses, which he never delivered. Virgil Earp later said; "That night, Bob Paul's horse laid down and died." Wyatt Earp, and Bat Masterson's horses were so used up, that they walked eighteen miles back to Tombstone.[39]

Behan's motives in law enforcement were never clear. His friendships, and involvement with Ringo and the cow-boy faction was often enough for him to look the other way. But, in circumstances like the stage robbery, it seemed that his interest was better served by creating an unwinnable situation for Wyatt Earp. Behan was the sheriff, and lead law enforcement officer on the case, but Wyatt Earp had the spotlight and would be heralded as the hero in a successful capture of the perpetrators. With an election looming, John Behan couldn't have that.

When Wyatt returned to Tombstone, empty handed, he learned of news that made his day even worse. Harry Woods had been named Undersheriff, probably while he was on the chase. There had been an agreement between John Behan and Wyatt Earp, that if Wyatt did not contest his appointment as Sheriff of Cochise County, that he, Behan, would appoint Earp with the high paying job as Undersheriff of the new county. Being the calculated man that he was, Wyatt put that aside to concentrate on the more pressing matter of a stage robbery and two dead men.

Wells Fargo man, Jim Hume arrived in town on the 28th, posting a reward of $300.00 for the capture of each robber. All the while hell was brewing. "Wyatt told Hume there were about seventy-five cowboys in town who would try to release King." Virgil later said. "Hume got Wyatt to go with him to the sheriff's office to notify them, and they asked a favor of the Under Sheriff to put King in irons. He promised to do so, and fifteen minutes afterwards King escaped, going on a horse that was tied back of the sheriff's office."[40] Luther King was never heard from again.

---

[39] Casey Tefertiller; Wyatt Earp pg. 77
[40] Ibid. page 78

Parsons' entry March 28, 1881

"[Luther] King, the stage robber, escaped tonight early from H. [Harry] Woods [Sheriff John Behan's undersheriff] who had been previously notified of an attempt at release to be made. Some of our officials should be hanged. They're a bad lot.[41]"

When Behan returned to town, he promptly billed the county for $796.48 for horses and supplies. The Earps didn't see a dime. It wasn't until Wells Fargo learned of the situation that they were paid. Virgil received $32.00 since he was a Deputy U.S. Marshal, and receiving pay, Wyatt and Morgan each received $72.00 for their part in the chase.

In both the apprehension and escape of Luther King, as well as heated accusations of others accused of being involved, the once quiet differences between men, were now growing louder. While the search was on for the three robbers, who were later known to be in New Mexico, speculation regarding Doc Holliday's whereabouts and actions of that evening was gaining attention.

SO, WHERE WAS DOC?

The Benson Stage robbery would soon be realized as the most significant event in Tombstone's young history. The accusations, intrigue, and political finger pointing that emanated from this situation lit a slow burning fuse that led directly to October 26th. Many people have speculated, including Bob Paul himself that it may have been an assassination attempt disguised as a robbery. Threats had been made, and the timing seemed quite suspicious. Then, to make things really interesting, another question quickly arose. Where was Doc Holliday?

A pale thin man, who was gray at thirty, J.H. 'Doc' Holliday, was a 'lunger' with many acquaintances, but few friends. He held an unwavering loyalty to Wyatt Earp, which rarely worked in Wyatt's favor, yet their friendship was mutual. As a man who promoted law and order, Doc Holliday's presence caused unnecessary friction for Wyatt on a number of occasions, but Wyatt always felt he owed a debt to his Dodge City friend. Prior to August 1878, Wyatt Earp and Doc Holliday were little more than acquaintances. Doc and Kate had arrived in Dodge City in the spring of that year, when Doc set up a dental practice in Room 24 of the Dodge House.

---

[41] George Parsons; A Tenderfoot in Tombstone. Pg.137

It was a hot August night when Wyatt approached the Comique Theater, where Tobe Driskill, a Texas cowhand known by Earp in Wichita, and Ed Morrison were drunk and causing a ruckus. Wyatt Earp had served as a peace officer in Wichita from 1875-1876 before coming to Dodge. As the drover's numbers increased, Wyatt and another officer began 'buffaloing' the law breakers to re-gain control of the situation. Foolishly not watching his surroundings, Wyatt soon found himself on the short end when a drover stuck a revolver in his back. Holliday, who observed the fracas saw the drover, and called for Wyatt to watch his back. Holliday then fired a shot that distracted the Texan long enough for Earp to take control of the situation. Wyatt Earp from that day forward credited Doc Holliday with saving his life.

This event was but a month after Wyatt Earp had an encounter with another Texas drover, who decided to get even after things didn't go his way. Returning with several of his friends, the drovers lit up the Comique, where Eddie Foy was calling a square dance, while Doc Holliday was focused on the cards at Bat Masterson's Spanish Monte table. As a barrage of lead tore through the windows and walls of the theater, those inside hugged the floor until it ended. Outside, Wyatt and Jim Masterson tried unsuccessfully to pull one of the men from his horse as they rode away. Their returning gun fire, however, did manage to take George Hoy out of the saddle with a bullet to the shoulder that cost the young man's life just over a month later. No one was sure whose bullet killed Hoy, but Wyatt Earp believed it was his, and always felt bad about the possibility that he'd killed that young man.

Another friend to Doc Holliday was William Leonard, one of the suspected bandits involved in the Benson Stage robbery. He and Doc met in Las Vegas, New Mexico, where Leonard applied his talent as a jeweler, and was considered a respectable citizen. Both men suffered from consumption (tuberculosis; TB), with Leonard's disease progressing faster than Doc's. After reaching Tombstone in early 1880, he fell in with Harry Head, Jim Crane, and Luther King. The four men shared a house at the Wells, a couple of miles north of Tombstone, where Doc Holliday would visit his friend from time to time. By the time of the stage robbery, Leonard had become frail, and weighed 120 lbs.

At approximately 4:00 pm on the day of the robbery, Doc rented a horse from Dunbar's Stables, stating his destination as Charleston, where he planned to join a high-stakes poker game. By his account, the game had broken up before he arrived. Doc was soon back in town, but speculation grew as to his true whereabouts. Rumor was soon around town that he had gone to the Wells, and was somehow involved in the robbery.

In an interview with Walter Noble Burns on March 15, 1927, Wyatt remembered the timing of the event a bit differently:

"Holliday went to the livery stable on this day, hired a saddle horse which he did quite often to visit Leonard at the Wells. The horse came from Dunbar Stables...Holliday remained there until 4:00 pm. Old man Fuller was hauling water to Tombstone at that time and leaving the Wells with a load of water Holliday tied his horse behind the wagon and rode into town with Fuller and which many people knew. After Holliday ate his dinner, he went to playing faro. And he was still playing when the word came to Tombstone from Bob Paul to me that there had been a hold up." [42]

When Wyatt returned to Tombstone on March 23rd, his first task was to inform Doc of Bill Leonard's involvement in the robbery. Doc knew that once the information became public, he'd have trouble.

The next day, March 24, 1881, The Tucson Star reported;

"The names of the three who are traveling are Bill Leonard, Jim Crane, and Harry Hickey [sic]. The fourth is at Tombstone and is well known and has been shadowed ever since his return. The party is suspected for the reasons that on the afternoon of the attack he engaged a horse at 4 o'clock, stating he might be gone seven or eight days [or] he might return that night. He left about 4 o'clock, armed with a henry rifle and a six shooter, he started toward Charleston, and about a mile below Tombstone he cut across to Contention, and when next seen it was between 10 and 11 o'clock, riding into the livery stable in Tombstone, his horse fagged out. He at once called for another horse, which he hitched in the streets. Statements attributed to him, if true, look very bad indeed, and which, if proven, are more conclusive as to his guilt either as a principal actor or an accessory before the fact.[43]"

Doc's name is not used in the article. He was the man who rented the horse that afternoon, although the report is far different from Doc's account of the evening. A fourth man was in Tombstone, Luther King, who was under arrest at the time. The article sites no source, has errors, and is skewed with poetic liberties. Its printing, though, was enough to bring Doc's concerns to fruition.

It seemed that Doc was everywhere that night. He said he left that afternoon bound for Charleston and a poker game. The Tucson Star on

---

[42] Doc Holliday; A Family Portrait. Karen Holliday Tanner pg.148
[43] Doc Holliday; Gary L. Roberts pg.143

March 24th had him leaving Tombstone, then cutting across to Contention. Rumor in town was that he high tailed it to the Wells, then on March 26, 1882, the Arizona Daily Star reported Doc to be in Charleston at 8:30pm that evening, looking for Billy Clanton.

The gossip and wild speculation fueled Doc's contrived involvement in the stage robbery, which John Behan and Milt Joyce used to their advantage. With the escape of Luther King, whether aided by the sheriff's office or enabled by their incompetency, John Behan suffered an embarrassing public confidence problem. He needed to change the subject and give folks something else to focus on and Doc Holliday was his scape goat.

Dislike between Wyatt Earp and John Behan intensified. Behan's betrayal in appointing Harry Woods as undersheriff played on Wyatt, as well as his decision not to pay them for their time riding with the posse. Rumors against Doc were intensifying, fueled by Milt Joyce, who was now on the Board of Supervisors and backing Behan's every move. Doc was now the target of the stage robbery and everyone in town knew it.

CHAPTER SIX

ORDINANCE #9
TO PROVIDE AGAINST CARRYING OF
DEADLY WEAPONS

April 9, 1881, the implementation of Ordinance #9 caused a stir in Tombstone. Passed with good intentions, it created more problems than it solved. The ordinance was highly unpopular and compliance was difficult to prove. Most men slid their pistol to the back of their waist band or gun belt, if they had one, or concealed it in their pocket. Enforcement of the law was also highly selective. Although it was classified as a misdemeanor, this town regulation was the given cause for Virgil Earp's decision to disarm the Clantons and McLaury brothers on October 26, 1881.

ORDINANCE #9

SECTION 1. It is hereby declared UNLAWFUL for a person to carry a DEADLY WEAPON concealed or otherwise (except the same be carried openly in sight and in the hand) within the limits of the City of Tombstone.

SECTION 2: This prohibition does not extend to persons immediately leaving or entering the city, who, with good faith, and within reasonable time are proceeding to deposit, or take from the place of deposit such deadly weapon.

SECTION 3: All officers of the law and their deputies are not bound by this decree in the execution of their duties.

SECTION 4: Any person or persons violating this ordinance shall be found guilty of a misdemeanor and shall be fined a sum of TWO HUNDRED and FIFTY dollars or shall be imprisoned in the city jail for 30 days or both. Bear in mind, $250.00 in 1881 is the equivalent of $5,325.00 in today's dollars.

On April 13, 1881, Doc was in court before Justice Wallace, facing a charge of "threats against life" stemming from an argument he'd had with Milt Joyce in the Oriental Saloon a few days earlier. When Doc entered the room, Joyce said; "Well, here comes the stage robber." Words were had, and Doc was immediately arrested by Behan. He was indicted again on May 29, 1881 by a Grand Jury on charges that stemmed from an altercation between him and Milt Joyce the previous fall. He posted bond and was released pending trial. As county supervisor, Joyce had the pull to get an indictment, but the charges were later dropped by Justice Wallace.

June of '81 was a busy month for Tombstone residents. On June 8th, Al Schieffelin, brother of Tombstone founder Ed Schieffelin, opened the new theater and opera house carrying the family name; *Schieffelin Hall.*

With a seating capacity of 575, it was the largest entertainment venue of its kind in the territory. It was designed as the center of Tombstone's societal events and would host recitals, town meetings, theater, and opera. With its large stage, and hand-painted curtain, Schieffelin Hall was the shining jewel of this up and coming town.

As folks were basking in the growth of their town, an undercurrent of trouble was continuing to build. Doc Holliday was still trying to shake the rumors of involvement in the Benson Stage robbery.

On June 6th, City Marshal Ben Sippy decided to take a leave of absence, with Virgil Earp being appointed temporary city marshal. Sippy was less than honest to say the least. His decision to release three prisoners in May without explanation, as well as his repeated absence for days at a time, drew an admonishment from the Mayor's Office. When Sippy bugged out of town, he had approximately two hundred dollars of city money, with unsettled debt all across town. It seemed that Ben Sippy could hear the hounds at the door.

Wyatt Earp was seething over John Behan's decision to back out on his promise to appoint him as Undersheriff and on June 1st, began a deadly deal with Ike Clanton. Wyatt had given the matter much thought since returning from the unsuccessful chase for the Benson Stage robbers. Talk of the attempted robbery had calmed, as folks went on to other issues. For Wyatt, getting even with Behan was still high on the agenda.

The District Attorney's Office was in turmoil. Both Littleton Price and John Miller claimed title to the position, with neither willing to give up his claim. Price, a Republican, had been appointed by Governor Fremont but blocked by the Democrat controlled Board of Supervisors. In turn, they approved Democrat John Miller, who appointed James Southard as Deputy D.A. to run the day to day operations of the office. In July, the chaos would work in Doc Holliday's favor.

Wyatt's solution for getting even with Behan was to challenge him for the sheriff's job in the fall elections. It was a battle he felt he could win. Wyatt had a good reputation with the law and order group in town, but he knew that wouldn't be enough. If he could be the one who brought in the bandits who were now in New Mexico, he knew that would seal the deal. Knowing that Ike Clanton would have knowledge of the whereabouts of Leonard, Head, and Crane, he made an offer of $6,000.00 if he, Clanton, would flush them out so Wyatt could apprehend the men. Ike knew they would make a fight, and didn't suspect they could be taken alive. He asked Wyatt for his assurance that the reward money would be paid dead or alive. Wyatt obliged, and went to Marshal Williams, the Wells Fargo agent, and asked that he telegraph Wells Fargo in San Francisco to verify the reward as payable 'dead-or-alive'. Wyatt relayed the information to Clanton that it was. The only problem now, was Marshal Williams had figured out Wyatt's deal.

It was a dangerous proposition for Ike. He knew if Curly Bill, or any of the others knew of his deal with Wyatt, that he was a dead man. To his knowledge, Joe Hill and Frank McLaury were the only ones that knew.

They were in the conversation with Wyatt and would help Ike set up the operation and split the money. According to Wyatt, Joe Hill would go to Eureka, New Mexico to lure the three men back to the McLaury Ranch, where they would plan to rob the paymaster going from Tombstone to Bisbee. Once there, it was up to Wyatt to do the rest without implicating either of the cow-boys. By the Earp's account, Joe Hill immediately left for New Mexico, but got there one day too late.

"Oh, what a tangled web we weave."

As Wyatt Earp and Ike Clanton were planning the capture of the Benson Stage robbers, they – Harry Head, Bill Leonard, and Jim Crane – were making plans of their own. They had plans to take the Haslett Brothers ranch.

The other "Ike and Billy", William and Isaac Haslett, had acquired land in Animas Valley, just south of Eureka, New Mexico. It was a prime location for cattle, with the following description by John Pleasant Gray;

"Going east from Tombstone you cross the Dragoon Mountains into the Sulphur Spring Valley, thence through the Chiricahua Mountains into the San Simon Valley of New Mexico and right there under the shadow of the Animas Peak was a big green meadow about a thousand acres which was at the time covered with red top clover and watered by numerous springs."

In this area was the 320 acres that Ringo and Ike Clanton had laid claim to in November 1880. The land was never owned by Ringo and Clanton, they only held what was known as a squatter's claim. Former Tombstone judge Mike Gray wanted the section owned by the Haslett Brothers and by many accounts would go to any length to get it.

Head, Leonard, and Crane, who had occupied a shack in The Wells, were now controlling a ranch in Animas Valley, New Mexico. Conflicting stories suggest the three men devised a plan to kill Ike and Bill Haslett at their store in Eureka, then take over the vacant property. An anonymous letter dated June 12, 1881 to the Tombstone Epitaph suggest they were doing the bidding of Mike Gray. To thicken the plot a bit more, one of the key motivations for Ike Clanton in flushing out the stage robbers for Wyatt Earp, was to free up that land so he could again take control. Ownership of the land didn't leave the Federal Government until March 16, 1884 when it was purchased by the Gray family.[44]

The unnamed source reported that; *"On Friday June 10th Bill Leonard and three more cowboys or "rustlers", as they call them came to camp to*

---

[44] Western Outlaw. December 23, 2009

a store about one-quarter mile from the mine...Well the rustlers went in there and got drunk and said they were coming up to the mine to kill the Haslett boys, so some fellow came up and told Ike, which put him on the lookout.

Yesterday I went down to the store, getting there at noon, so I went in and ate my dinner. Bill Leonard and the others were at the table with their six shooters alongside their plates and their rifles lying in their laps, and a fellow outside guarding. I tell you it looked tough. Well, Bill said he was going to shoot the Haslett boys on sight, and we looked for them last night, but they did not come, so Ike thought that the best thing that he could do was to catch them himself, so this morning at day break he went to the store and laid in wait for them.

Back of the store is a corral, and Ike and his brother got in there. The fence is about three and a-half feet high. Bill Leonard and the one they call Harry the "Kid" [Head] had to come down the road past the corral, so when they got within fifty yards Ike and his brother Bill jumped up and opened fire on them. The "Kid" was on foot and Leonard on horseback. Ike let drive and got Leonard just below the heart, when he dropped to one side of his horse, when Bill thought that he would get away so he plugged the horse and he fell. The "Kid" pulled his gun when Ike pulled on him and told him to stop, but he was going to pull when Bill Haslett gave it to him in the abdomen, and he started to run when both Bill and Ike commenced to pop it with him. They put six balls in him. When they picked Leonard up he was breathing his last breath. "Kid" is still alive, but they think he will die soon. Bill Leonard said last night that he wished someone would shoot him through the heart and put him out of his misery, as he had two big holes in his belly that he got the time he tried to rob the stage at Tombstone. He was put out of sight at sundown this evening.[45]

Within days, before the boys could collect the $2,400.00 reward coming their way, they were killed, ostensibly by Jim Crane and a number of men. Several accounts of the gun fight that ended in the death of the Haslett brothers were initially printed.

---

[45] Wyatt Earp; Casey Tefertiller. pgs. 84-85

On Thursday June 21, 1881, The Arizona Star printed;

"The killing of Bill Leonard and 'Harry the Kid' at Eureka, N.M. by the Haslett brothers, a full account of which appeared in the Star on Sunday morning, had been summarily avenged. It appears that a cowboy named Crane organized and got a band of congenial spirits in the work of vengeance. They followed the Haslett boys for some twenty-five miles from Eureka before they overtook them, and as soon as they came up with them the fight to the death commenced. The Haslett boys were game and made a brave fight killing two and wounding three of the Crane party but being overpowered, were finally killed."

The day earlier, The Tombstone Nugget had a slightly different version of events;

The [Haslett] boys were playing cards in West McFadden's saloon when about fifteen or twenty men came down on them by surprise, and they did not have a chance to protect themselves.

On Tuesday June 21, 1881, The Tombstone Epitaph ran a much different, and probably more accurate account of the event;

MORE MURDER IN SAN SIMON

As we go to press the report is current, said to be reliable, that friends for Leonard and Harry the "Kid" have killed both the Haslett boys. They were attacked and slaughtered at their own home. The circumstances of the first killing appeared in the Epitaph on Saturday morning last. These events all transpired on the San Simon, that seat of the cowboy troubles. It is asserted that the Hasletts killed Leonard and Harry Head (that being the Kid's real name) for the sake of the reward offered for the capture of Leonard for his participation in the Contention stage robbery. Two or three of the cowboys are reported wounded in the fight. At this rate the gang will soon be exterminated much to the joy of all law-abiding citizens.

The stronger message was the resolve of the cowboy organization to hold together, and exact revenge where needed. It was obvious now that from Cochise County, Arizona to Grant County, New Mexico, that no one was safe.

Besides Jim Crane, the list of men who attacked the Hasletts is unclear. Ringo was allegedly in Liberty, Missouri at the time of the killings, and could not have been involved here. Curly Bill was also excluded from the fight. He was in Galeyville, still recovering from a near fatal gunshot wound after being shot in the face by Jim Wallace. On May 21, 1881, Curly Bill and a group of men, including Wallace who had fought in the Lincoln County War, were drinking heavily and playing cards. Billy Breakenridge was present as well when a drunken Wallace decided to hurl an insult his way. Curly Bill took offence, and demanded that Wallace apologize. He complied and did so, but that didn't seem to be enough for Curly Bill, who laid a few insults back at Wallace, ending with "You damned Lincoln County son of a bitch, I'll kill you anyway." With that. Wallace left only to find Curly Bill following him. Afraid that he was aiming to make good on the threat, Wallace pulled his .44 and shot him in the face. The bullet entered through Curly Bill's cheek, and exited near his neck, taking a few teeth with it. He almost died. A picture, passed down as that of Curly Bill, shows a large indention in his right jaw.

When Joe Hill returned with the news of the two dead stage robbers, Ike Clanton knew the deal was off. His plans for a quick payday was now replaced with Wyatt having the proof that he would betray his friends. He knew if Curly Bill ever found out, he was a dead man. This wasn't information Ike wanted in Wyatt's hands for fear that he would tell or use it to get over on him. It ate at Ike all summer. With two dead outlaws and no reward money, it was too late now to change his mind, and Ike felt he was more exposed than ever.

It seemed that nothing Wyatt had tried worked out as planned. His glory for capturing the stage robbers was gone, Ike's reward was gone, only to be replaced with his prior animosity. John Behan was still hell-bent on destroying Doc Holliday, and Wyatt Earp in the process. And little did they know, a fire would rip through Tombstone in a week's time, leaving a third of the town in ruins.

Tragedy struck on the afternoon of June 22nd, beginning at the Arcade Saloon:

Missrs Alexander and Thompson, proprietors of the Arcade Saloon, three doors above the Oriental Saloon on the corner of Allen and Fifth, had a barrel of liquor that had been condemned by them for a long time, which they had intended to re-ship, and as fate would have it, they had a team ready to take it away at this time. They rolled it out in front of the bar and knocked out the bung for the purpose of measuring the quantity in the package. Mr. Alexander in pitting the gauge rod into the barrel, accidently let it slip from his fingers into the same. His bartender got a wire to fish it out, and came to the front with a lighted cigar in his mouth, one report says, and another that he lighted a match for some purpose, when the escaping gas caught fire and communicated with the liquor which caused an instantaneous explosion, scattering the burning content in all directions...In less than three minutes the flames had communicated with the adjoining buildings and spread with a velocity equal only to a burning prairie in a gale.[46]

Fire was the greatest fear of a small southwestern town. With little rain and low humidity, the wooden structures built side by side were a tinder box. In all, sixty-six buildings covering four blocks burned before sundown.

The July 4th festivities did little to raise the collective spirits about town.

- The expense of a great celebration with music, fireworks, and speeches, had taken a back seat to the needs of the newly formed Hook and Ladder Society, who insisted on the purchase of hoses and fire wagons.
- There was sad word from Washington that President James Garfield had been shot by Charles J. Guiteau on the morning of July 2nd, and not expected to survive.
- Rain poured most of the day, with thunder storms reminding folks of things to come.
- Virgil Earp, who had been appointed as City Marshal on June 28th, was officially sworn in that afternoon.
- Later in the day, a drunken Kate Elder made John Behan's wishes come true.

Things would not soon improve for the Earps or Doc Holliday. After a drunken argument with Doc, Kate swore out a warrant implicating him in the Benson Stage robbery. On July 5th, Behan arrested Holliday, charging him with involvement in both the attempted robbery of the U.S. Mail, and the murder of Bud Philpot. He was taken before Judge Wells Spicer, and released on $5,000.00 bond, secured by Wyatt Earp, John Meagher, and J.L. Melgren. When the case against Holliday was brought before Judge Spicer, it was summarily dismissed at the request of Littleton Price for lack of credible evidence. With that, the matter of Doc Holliday having any involvement in the stage robbery was gone.

On July 6th, Kate was arrested by Virgil Earp on a complaint made by Doc Holliday for drunk and disorderly behavior. Virgil held her in jail until she sobered up, then took her before Andrew Felter's court. There she was found guilty and charge $12.50 before being released.

---

[46] Los Angeles Herald; June 28, 1881

On the 7th, the very next day, Marshal Earp re-arrested Kate, this time for threats against life, a charge entered by Doc Holliday. Kate hired Judge Wells Spicer to represent her in a habeas corpus before Commissioner T.J. Drum, where the charges were dismissed due to the defendant being "enraged and intoxicated." Kate found it was time to leave, and boarded a stage the next day for Globe. Some years later she credited Johnny Ringo for giving her the money for the trip home.

Ringo didn't seem to be involved in anything west of the San Simon Valley during this period of time. He was mentioned only twice in March, and kept a very low profile, with his focus primarily on cattle between Animas Valley and San Simon. He was in Jack O'Neil's, Maxey Saloon, on the 8th of March to witness the death of Dick Lloyd. For an event of such little consequence to world affairs, word of Lloyd's death graced newspapers from New York to California. If only a line, word of his death spread from coast to coast. Lloyd, who was reportedly upset over a card game, shot ex-Justice of the Peace, Ed Mann, and threatened to kills others in the saloon. Lloyd in turn was shot and killed by Jack O'Neil when he attempted to ride a horse, presumably Joe Hill's, into the saloon. The jury in the case exonerated O'Neil by a verdict of justifiable homicide. "It is expected that Mann will recover."

On March 27, 1881, The Arizona Weekly Citizen listed the pending Tucson District Court cases. For Friday March 25th, there was a posting on the docket for "Territory vs. John Ringo and Ben Schuster. Nolle Pros. entered." The nature of the charges against Ringo and Schuster are not clear, as well as the relationship between the two men. The most interesting two words of this short notice, however, are "Nolle Pros", which is Latin for "will no longer prosecute". It amounts to a request for dismissal of the charges by the prosecutor. In the U.S., judges will usually sign a dismissal order prepared by the prosecution or make a docket entry indicating the disposition of the case to be *nolle prosse* after a declaration, or motion by the prosecution. This short entry would lead one to conclude that whatever the charges, they received little attention, and were dropped.

Territory vs. John Ringo and Ben, Schuster—Nolle pros. entered.

Sometime around April 1881, John Ringo left Arizona. He was reported as being at Austin, Texas on May 2, 1881, apparently in route to Liberty, Missouri.

After spending some time in a house in the "jungles" (whore house?) late into the morning hours he began to make his way to his hotel room.

While doing this he discovered that he had misplaced his money. Thinking that three young men who were seated in the hallway may have his money he pulled out his gun and commanded them to hold their hands up. He then searched them. Not finding his money he smiled at the men and left to retire to his room. The three men ran to the marshal's office and told him what had happened. Marshal Ben Thompson, a notorious Texas gunman, personally went to Ringo's room. When he got there Ringo refused to open the door. Thompson kicked in the door and arrested Ringo for disturbing the peace and carrying a pistol. Ringo paid a $25 fine plus costs and was released. John Ringo left Texas and at some point traveled to Missouri. On July 12, 1881, the *Tombstone Nugget* indicated that Ringo was staying at the Grand Hotel and that he just returned from Liberty, Missouri.[47]

Ringo's purpose for traveling to his home state, if he did, is a mystery. The Austin Daily Statesman on May 3rd, verify that he was in Texas, and had been arrested by City Marshal Ben Thompson, but that's where the trail ends. Where did he board the train? He surely didn't ride a horse. Its 870 miles from Tombstone, Arizona to Austin, Texas. Liberty, Missouri is another 750 miles almost dead north of Austin, Texas. Why he travelled that distance, if he in fact did, has always been up for debate. Ringo had family in both Missouri and Indiana, but none he'd seen since he was fourteen.

If one is to speculate, let's look at 'who' in Missouri might be of interest to a man like Ringo. An investigator would begin with a list of potential contacts who could be of like mind, or have something to offer. Missouri, at the time was probably the 'outlaw' headquarters of the mid and south west. The Younger Brothers, the James Brothers, and the Dalton Gang come to mind. Ringo was not directly related to either, although early writers on the topic liked to boast that he was.

John Ringo's aunt, Augusta (his mother's sister), was married to Col. Coleman Younger, who was an uncle to the Younger Brothers. In addition, Coleman Younger's half-sister, Adeline Lee, was the mother of the Dalton Brothers. Ringo was no more related to the James family than the others, but…Benjamin Simms, Mary Ringo's uncle was married for a short time to Zerelda James. You guessed it, Frank and Jessie James's mother. Small world.

Regardless of where he'd been, Ringo returned to Arizona in July to a near border war between the cow-boys and Mexican vigilantes. On May 13, 1881, George Turner along with Galeyville butcher Alfred McAllister, and two drovers named Oliver, and Garcia were killed while resisting arrest by a group of Mexican citizens. Turner had recently acquired a

---

[47] Johnny Ringo History Page. www.johnnyringo.com

contract from Fort Bowie to provide beef for the command, and quickly decided to fill the order by taking a little trip across the border. After a raid on his Sonora ranch, Jose Juan Vasquez, and a band of vaqueros followed the outlaws north of Fronteras where they were camped along with four hundred head of Vasquez's cattle. Vasquez and his men surrounded the bandits with hope of making an arrest, but the men responded with a hail of gunfire, resulting in the death of all four Americans, as well as Vasquez.

The near border war that followed became tense for both Mexican and American officials. Sonora Governor Luis Torres directed Commander Filipe Neri to assemble a force of two hundred soldiers at the border to keep the cowboys out of Mexico. Rumor in Tombstone was that the cowboys were banding together for a raid on Fronteras that would clean the place out. On the American side, General Orlando Wilcox was in communication with U.S. Army headquarters in San Francisco seeking permission to intervene. Permission was denied as illegal with Wilcox ordered to stand down. It was ruled a civil matter.

Even with the involvement of the American authorities, the Mexican Army, and vigilantes from Sonora, the cowboys persisted in their border raids. On July 27, 1881, at Cajon de Sarampion, the cowboys attacked a band of sixteen Mexican smugglers as they entered the United States through the Peloncillo Mountains at the Arizona, New Mexico border. The party of approximately twenty outlaws initially killed four Mexican men, and made off with $2,500.00 in cash and bullion, as well as $1,500.00 in mescal, and livestock. There were reports of up to nineteen members of the Mexican party listed as either dead or missing. Joseph Bowyer, manager of the Consolidated Mining and Smelting Company in Galeyville, later heard the cowboy raiders as they told of their attack:

> *"One of the cowboys in relating to me the circumstances said that it was the d-----st lot of truck he ever saw; he showed me a piece of bullion, I should judge it to be one-half gold. Upon my telling him that trouble would likely arise from this, he replied that it was a smugglers train and they wouldn't dare say much."* [48]

Wyatt Earp later testified at the inquest that he was satisfied that Tom and Frank McLaury, as well as Curly Bill, and the Clantons were involved. Jim Hancock reported that three other men, Milt Hicks, Jim Hughes, and Jack McKenzie were also involved. It was reported that mint condition

[48] Arizona Weekly Citizen; December 11, 1881, pg.4 / Wyatt Earp; The Life Behind the Legend; Casey Tefertiller pg. 92

coins soon found their way into the saloons, and other establishments of Galeyville.

On August 11, 1881, the cowboys were back in Charleston, were they made a hit on three of General Pesqueira's Mexican soldiers driving a pack train south after purchasing goods in Tombstone. They left with approximately $1,000.00 in goods and bullion. The August 13, 1881 Tombstone Epitaph wrote the following:

THE MURDERING COWBOYS

When the latter party got above Hereford, and half way to Ochoaville, they were set upon by a party of five cow-boys, who fired mortally wounding one of the Mexicans and killing one of the horses. They took a rifle and one package of goods and it is supposed killed the one who had the money, as he has not up to last evening been seen or heard from since the encounter. It is said that the Mexicans who escaped recognized one of the bandits having seen him in Tombstone the day before.

Grown bold with the deeds of crime they have committed between here and Deming, and their merciless murders at Fronteras, these outlaws, having no fear of the civil authorities, have taken up the San Pedro valley as their headquarters, knowing there is a large travel between Benson, Contention, Tombstone, Charleston, and Bisbee, besides the Mexican travel from Sonora to these points. It will be seen from the foregoing that they have made a good beginning and unless immediate steps are taken by the citizens to rid the county of these outlaws there will be no more protections to life and property between Benson and the Sonora line than there have been in the San Simon and eastward for the last year. When the civil authorities are insufficient or unwilling to protect a community, the people are justified in taking the law in their own hands and ridding themselves of the dangerous characters who make murder and robbery their business. It remains to be seen how much longer such damnable acts as Fronteras massacre and the San Pedro murders shall go unpunished. [49]

On August 13, 1881, a group of cowboys pushed a hundred head of beef cattle off Bill Lang's New Mexico ranch at Cloverdale, and straight into Mexican retaliation. Heading for market in Tombstone, the men were driving stolen Mexican cattle purchased from American rustlers. In the group with Lang, were Dick Gray (Mike Gray's son), Old Man Clanton, who was driving the chuck wagon, Charlie Snow, Bill Byers, and Harry

---

[49] Tombstone Epitaph August 13, 1881 / Wyatt Earp; The Life Behind the Legend; Casey Tefertiller pg. 92

Earnshaw. Jim Crane, last of the Benson stage robbers, would arrive later in the evening. During the night, a band of Mexicans, who many have long presumed, but cannot confirm, to be military, took up position just outside the cowboy camp, and lie in wait until first light.

At dawn, Charlie Snow rode out to check on the herd, which prompted the Mexicans to take action. Riding straight into the hidden guns, Storms was the first to be killed. Once the fight commenced, four other Americans, Old Man Clanton, Dick Gray, Billy Lang, and Jim Crane quickly followed. Bill Byers was hit, but hugged the ground and played dead until the thing was over. Harry Earnshaw managed to get away, and hid in the brush until he could make his way to John Pleasant's ranch with the news.

Tempers flared as word spread to the ranchers and townsfolk of southeast Arizona. Retaliation was imminent. Rumors soon circulated, including names and numbers of men ready to strike back within the heart of Sonora. The Tombstone Nugget declared a war with Mexico would be justified. Others saw the Mexican reprisal as warranted, and declared the cow-boys to be of greater danger than the Apache. George Parsons wrote on August 17, 1881;

"Bad trouble on the border, and this time looks more serious than anything yet. Dick Gray – the lame one – killed by some Mexicans, along with several others, among them the notorious Crane, and revenge seems the order of the day, a gang having started out the day to make trouble. The killing business by the Mexicans in my mind, was perfectly justifiable as it was retaliation for killing of several of them and their robbery by cowboys recently, this same Crane being one of the number. Am glad they killed him, as for the others, if not guilty of cattle stealing – they had no business to be found on such bad company."

Townsfolk were taking sides, and federal authorities were not taking chances. Federal troops were ordered to "intercept all armed parties raiding into Mexico with hostile intent and disarm them, or if found returning, to aid the civil authorities to arrest them.[50] In reality, it was the possibility that Mexican troops had planned and executed the assault within the United States caused the most angst. More prevalent along the Rio Grande in search of Apache, the American troops had no deference in crossing the Mexican border, but never reciprocated or encouraged Mexican authorities to do the same in pursuit of hostiles or outlaws. [51]

---

[50] Doc Holiday; Gary Roberts pg. 173
[51] New York Times, December 18, 1881 pg.8

Mexican troops north of Sonora, and into Guadalupe Canyon was not acceptable.

In his never-ending campaign to discredit the Earps, Milt Joyce tried to link Wyatt Earp and Doc Holliday to the Guadalupe Canyon Massacre. Claiming that Jim Crain was the last of those who could implicate Doc in the Benson stage robbery, Joyce accused Doc and Wyatt of staging the incident to murder Crain before he tied them to the incident.

Pulled further into his insecurity after the death of Jim Crain, Ike Clanton's anxiety level was rising quickly, only now without guidance from his father, who was killed in the same incident. Ike Clanton was now a ticking time bomb.

The tension between Wyatt Earp and Ike Clanton was rising. With three of the stage robbers dead, and Luther King long gone, Ike had no one left to claim any portion of the reward. There was no up-side left for him. All he had now was a cloud of apprehension, and constant fear that others would learn of his deal with Wyatt. The plan was over as far as Wyatt was concerned, but throughout the remainder of the summer, and into the fall, Ike became increasingly paranoid over the possibility of being outed by Wyatt, or whomever he may have told. Unable to let it go, Ike's angst was compounded by a flurry of activity during September and early October.

On September 9, 1881, Sheriff Bob Paul finally arrested Pony Deal on the charge of robbing the Globe stage back

Sherm McMasters

in February. Deal, along with Sherm McMasters, an ex-Texas Ranger, had been the primary suspects in the robbery, but had thus far evaded capture.

Paul immediately sent a telegram to Tombstone for City Marshal Virgil Earp to be on the lookout for McMasters. Virgil soon wired back, informing Sheriff Paul that McMasters was in Tombstone, and asked if he should make an arrest. While waiting for a reply, Virgil kept an eye on McMasters, and soon witnessed Johnny Ringo ride up with his horse in a lather. Ringo was coming in after a hard ride from Galeyville, where he and David Estes had robbed a poker game at around mid-night, just nine hours earlier. This event is discussed later in further detail.

With a second matter soon to occupy Virgil's time, word came to Tombstone around 9:30 a.m. that the Tombstone to Bisbee stage had been robbed the prior evening as it passed through Mule Mountain. A mail sack, a Wells Fargo box containing $2,500.00, and passenger valuables totaling $600.00 had been stolen. With Virgil finally getting word from Sheriff Paul, after the telegram was mistakenly delivered to the Wells Fargo office, he attempted to apprehend McMasters. After a spirited search for McMasters, aided by his brother James, Virgil finally gave in. McMasters and Ringo had escaped on foot to Contention where they were provided with horses and rode off.

To illustrate the fluidity of events culminating that morning, there were now three issues to occupy law enforcement.

- Sherm McMasters, who was wanted for a stage robbery in February, had shown up in town.
- Johnny Ringo was there in plain view of the marshal. He had ridden in on a lathering horse only hours after robbing the participants of $400.00 during a card game the night before.
- Now there was word of the Benson stage being robbed in Mule Mountain.

This also demonstrates the callousness of the cow-boy faction, and their disregard for a frustrated city marshal.

With Virgil tied up chasing McMasters, a posse consisting of Wyatt and Morgan Earp, and Deputy Billy Breakenridge headed to Mule Mountain, soon to be joined by Fred Dodge and Marshal Williams. Reports from passengers on the stage said that one of the robbers referred to money as "sugar". "Maybe you got some sugar", he said. Frank Stillwell was known for use of that term, and may as well have left them his name.

Wyatt and Dodge took the lead in tracking the robbers, and soon found a narrow boot heal that matched the foot prints seen around the stage. When he questioned the boot maker in Bisbee, he told Wyatt that he had replaced a heel for Frank Stillwell that morning. Dodge had split off, and was searching for Stillwell, suspecting he would find him with Pete Spence. Dodge found Stillwell with a new boot heel. He and Wyatt arrested Stillwell there, and found Pete Spence later in the day.

On the way back to Tombstone, both men became angry, and openly told Wyatt and Morgan to their face that they would get them. It was this statement more than any other that flagged Stillwell as a participant, if not the shooter, the moment Morgan was shot. In the aftermath of the October 26th shootout, primarily the shootings of Virgil and Morgan Earp, too many writers have connected the motives of those events to the still lingering animosity over the deaths of Billy Clanton, and the McLaury brothers. It ran much deeper. With the Benson stage robbery obviously being a motive for Stillwell, earlier events including Wyatt's failed deal with Ike Clanton, his hard-handed arrest of Curly Bill a year earlier following the shooting of Marshal Fred White, not to mention tougher laws in town that made 'commerce' a little harder for the cow-boys, there was enough hatred to go around.

Pete Spence

Stillwell and Spence were brought to Tombstone, where they appeared before Justice Wells Spicer, and released on $2,000.00 bond each. With dubious alibis, however, the charges were dropped for lack of evidence, and sworn statements that they were elsewhere at the time of the robbery. With Frank Stillwell serving on occasion as deputy sheriff, his arrest came as a personal embarrassment to John Behan.

Elsewhere in town, John Behan kept up the façade of a fun-loving servant of the people. Amidst the broken promises, and an unholy alliance with outlaws, Behan still enjoyed the support of many Tombstone residents, but his divide with the Earps was growing deeper. Behan added to his treasure by sporting around with a young lady said by many to be the prettiest girl in town. According to Josephine Sarah Marcus, she met John Behan in Prescott, Az. in 1879 while there with the Pauline Markham Theater Company performing their version of Gilbert and Sullivan's H.M.S. Pinafore. When their tour was over, Josephine returned to San Francisco along with her friend, Dora Hirsh. As she explained later in life, Behan stayed in touch, and eventually followed her to San

Josephine Marcus

Francisco, asking on a promise of marriage, that she return to Arizona to be with him.

In the spring of 1881, she traveled to Tombstone, and moved in with Behan and his son, Albert. This is where Josephine's (Sadie's) story deviates a bit. According to her, she moved in with a lawyer and his wife, while caring for Albert Behan and keeping house for John during the day. While in fact, she referred to herself as "Mrs. Behan", it is generally accepted that she did indeed move in with John upon arrival in town. As she waited for the marriage proposal he'd promised, Behan enjoyed the money her family had sent, presumably for the purpose of building a house. Sadie reportedly went home to California in early July, and upon her return later in the month, found that Behan had already taken up with a married woman. She later referred to her time in Tombstone as a bad dream.

Sadie kicked John out of the house, but still cared for Albert, with whom she maintained a life-long friendship. Her friendship with Wyatt apparently grew at that time, although there's no evidence of them having an affair during her stay there. They were seen together enough for word to spread that Wyatt had taken Behan's wife. Behan became furious, I'm sure much to Wyatt's delight. Sadie returned to San Francisco in early October, but Wyatt's interest in her grew.

~

The Tombstone lumber business came to a near halt in September '81. The wagon owners who hauled lumber from the mountains to town refused to put their teams on the road for fear of attack. With security on the Mexican border becoming tighter, the operations of the cow-boys turned inward. Reports increased during September of horse and livestock theft being on the rise in the remote parts of Cochise County. Stage robberies, and highwaymen had become commonplace. Freighters and wagon owners refused to operate outside the city limits, with lumber now being purchased from California. Virtually all trade on the roadways soon came to a stop. The Nugget editorialized;

"The scarcity of hemp and rope factories is a serious drawback to all new and unsettled countries."

Although a bit vailed, it was an angry call for the hanging of those who threatened their society.[52]

With never a dull day, October 5th brought the scare of an Apache uprising. Amidst the routine false alarms, and unverified newspaper accounts, this time Apache renegades were actually seen near Cachise's stronghold in the Dragoon Pass. An Apache attack on Tombstone was always a lingering fear in the minds of local residents, but this time it seemed more than possible. Mayor John Clum, who had served as the Indian Agent for the San Carlos Reservation, spoke the language and

---

[52] Wyatt Earp; The Life Behind the Legend; Casey Tefertiller. pg. 99

helped to assemble a posse. He, Sheriff Behan, and Virgil Earp gathered forty men willing to make a stand, and headed toward the Dragoons. Behan served as the captain, with Virgil as his lieutenant while Wyatt rode as a regular. At the prospect of what might lie ahead, Behan and the Earps put their differences aside, likely for the last time, and moved forward as a unit.

George Parsons, who joined the posse later in the day, described the event in his journal under Wednesday October 5, 1881:

"Later that night Bulford informed me that Indians and solders were fighting in Dragoon Pass, north of town, and having a regular battle. The Indian scare spread in town, although Nick and I slept tranquilly through it last night. Being on the edge of town, I did not hear the whistles blowing and the general commotion and was surprised at the excitement existing this a.m. and all last night. Armed squads went out and reconnoitered and it seems that after their fight, the Indians started for my mountains, the Huachucas. But the noise drove them back and they started ostensibly for Mule Mountains, passing near Turquois.

I was only staying to ascertain their true direction, having promised several going back yesterday to do so, and have thought of returning this A.M., but Mayor Clum advised my waiting over another day. If going my way, I should, of course, tried to get ahead and notify my folks in the mountains. Well about noon a large party formed meaning business, at the head of which were Mayor, Sheriff, and Chief of Police – and I joined it, Milton letting me have a new Winchester bought for bank and belt cartridges. I wanted to discover trail and probable direction for my people. Couldn't depend on rumors with which the air was thick. I had "Billy" and 20 odd of us dashed through town thoroughly armed and equipped, and on the outskirts, chose Behan (Sheriff) Captain and Earp First Lieut. When then called off by fours, every fourth man to hold horses in engagement, and quickly went for the trail, which we followed some time; and then thinking to cut it, struck across Sulphur Springs Valley. Hay ranches deserted. At one place, food left as parties were eating, they not having stopped for anything, not certainly on the order of their going, but went at once....A terrible rain storm set in after leaving road and it seemed to me as though it never rained harder, and such a continuous heavy rain I never knew before in Arizona."[53]

With the rain and hard ride, coupled with the lack of contact with the Apache, a number of Behan's posse broke off and headed home. By the

---

[53] George Parsons; A Tenderfoot in Tombstone. Pg. 180

afternoon of October 6th, they were down to seventeen riders, but what remained stood ready for a fight, including George Parsons. In his diary for Thursday October 6th, Parsons wrote of a conversation he had with an old Indian scout who advised him to join up with the military's effort or turn back. Given the situation, and the distance they'd come, he knew they could not, and would not turn back.

It must have come as quite an awakening, but after the men had fed the horses and themselves, they re-crossed Sulphur Springs Valley, toward the McLaury Ranch. Frink, a friend of Parsons, remained behind to hunt for game, who shortly after their arrival came in at a dead run. Once alone, the Indians began firing at him, but he made an escape unscathed. No one in the posse had seen an Apache since they left Tombstone, but it now became apparent that they'd been watching them the entire time.

By the time they'd reached Sulphur Springs, the threat had subsided, and the military was wrapping up their mission. When they reached the McLaury Ranch, Curly Bill was there, where he and Virgil Earp shook hands in a cordial manner, but he and Wyatt weren't so eager to exchange pleasantries.

It was October 7th when the men disbanded the posse, and returned to Tombstone. As it was never in the cards for the law to have any downtime, another stage robbery took place near Charleston the following morning.

October 8, 1881 marked Cochise County's fifth stage robbery since February. Five highwaymen attempted to stop the Sandy Bob Stage near Charleston as she made her daily run from Benson to Tombstone. When the masked highwaymen stepped out onto the road, the driver wanted nothing to do with it. In an unexpected move, he dropped the lines, and bailed from the seat, hitting the ground running. With the lines loose, the team barreled down the road until the stage crashed, rattling the passengers, and freeing the horses. Eleven passengers made their way out of a shattered coach to find five men holding them at gunpoint, and relieving them of their valuables. In an effort to not appear cold hearted, they kindly returned five dollars each to the shaken passengers.

Virgil Earp suspected Stillwell and Spence to be involved, but with the lack of evidence, he couldn't make an arrest. Several days later, however, Virgil was able to get a federal warrant for the September 9th robbery of the Bisbee stage. The stage was carrying the U.S. mail, which made that incident a federal matter. Frank Stillwell was quickly re-arrested in Tombstone, Pete Spence was picked up in Charleston later in the day. On October 13th, Virgil took Stillwell and Spence to Tucson to await their appearance before Commissioner Stiles on the 20th. Virgil returned to Tombstone the next day, but returned to Tucson on the 19th along with Johnny Behan and Marshal Williams for the hearing. Ike Clanton, and a number of Stillwell's friends also traveled to Tucson, and were there for the hearing. In his ruling, Commissioner Stiles released Pete Spence, but held Frank Stillwell over for trial.

Ike Clanton and Frank McLaury took this second arrest of Stillwell and Spence as abuse by the Earps. With the help of both town newspapers, the Epitaph, and the Nugget, who wrongfully reported the nature of their arrests, the cow-boys were left to believe they'd been jailed for the Contention stage robbery. Such outrage would lead one to consider the possibility that Stillwell and Spence actually had no involvement in that crime. The inference in their minds could only have been that the Earps used the incident as an excuse to harass them.

Frank McLaury became increasingly vocal. A few days after Spence was released, McLaury confronted Virgil Earp on the street, asking if he and his brother were a target of some vigilance committee. Earp said they were not, but McLaury was not satisfied, and issued a warning to Earp: "Now I tell you, it makes no difference what I do, I will never surrender my arms to you…I'd rather die fighting than be strangled." Obviously, a reference to Ordinance #9.

Later, in the presence of Johnny Ringo, McLaury confronted Morgan Earp in front of the Alhambra Saloon. McLaury told Earp: "If you ever come after me, you will never take me." Morgan informed McLaury that if circumstances required it, he would arrest him. Frank McLaury was irate. "I have threatened you boys' lives and a few days later I had taken it back, but since this arrest, it now goes."[54]

---

[54] Doc Holliday; The Life and Legend. Gary L. Roberts pg. 178

CHAPTER SEVEN

THE FUSE HAD BEEN LIT, AND THEY ALL HELD THE MATCH

The march to a confrontation picked up speed when a drunken Marshal Williams approached Ike Clanton and told him that he knew of the deal between him and Wyatt. It was more speculation than fact on Williams' part, but having read the Wells Fargo wire concerning a reward, he knew Wyatt was leaning on someone, with Ike being the most likely party. In a fit of anger, Ike found Wyatt and accused him of breaking their deal. Wyatt assured him that he had not, but Ike was certain that Doc Holliday, who had been a known friend to Bill Leonard, knew of the scheme.

With Doc in Tucson, Wyatt assured Ike that he would prove it to him once Doc returned to town. Ike still contended that he didn't believe it, and would only be satisfied if he talked to Holliday. Wyatt sent Morgan to Tucson on October 21st to fetch Doc. On the afternoon of the 23rd, Morgan, Doc and Kate were back in Tombstone. By that time, Ike was back at his father's ranch in Charleston. Wyatt didn't tell Doc about the deal, only that Ike suspected that he, Doc, thought there was one, and might tell it around town. Doc denied any knowledge of such a deal, and said he would straighten it out with Ike as soon as he saw him in town.

On the same day, Deputy Billy Breakenridge arrested Milt Hicks on a charge of possessing stolen cattle. On October 24th, Hicks, Charles Thompson, and Jim Sharp, overpowered the jailer as he opened the cell door to serve the men dinner. After a struggle, they locked Charles Mason in the cell, and made their escape. The timing of which could not have been worse. Once Mason was able to summons for help, Sheriff Behan, Billy Breakenridge, Wyatt, Virgil, and Morgan Earp took chase, but the three were long gone. Behan instructed Breakenridge and David Neagle to continue the search. With Deputy Harry Woods in El Paso awaiting the extradition of cattle thieves, and two men now on the chase, the available lawmen in Tombstone was getting thin.

The morning of October 25, 1881 was cold and windy, with a lite snow. Ike Clanton was heading toward Tombstone when he met up with Tom and Frank McLaury just past the Dragoons, they naturally rode into town together. With some business to square up before leaving for Iowa for their sister's wedding, the McLaury's went their own way after leaving their horses and weapons at the West End Corral. Ike, who was driving a wagon did the same, and set his sights on whatever saloon was closest.

At approximately 1:00 am, Doc went to A.D. Walsh's Can Lunch and Eatery Counter located in the front of the Alhambra Saloon, where he spotted Ike Clanton. Wyatt had been intentionally vague in his request, with Doc not understanding the importance of what he was asked to accomplish. As he had promised Wyatt, he confronted Ike about the rumor. However, in Doc's usual fashion, it wasn't so subtle. "I understand you say the Earp brothers have given you away to me, and that you have been talking bad about me." [55] Doc told Ike that he knew nothing of what he was talking about, and to stop talking about him. Already drunk, Ike fired back, telling Doc that he didn't believe him. Doc in turn called Ike a liar for what he'd said to Wyatt, again saying that he knew nothing of what he was talking about.

By this time, Doc obviously knew that Ike had indeed intended to set up his friend Bill Leonard, along with Jim Crane and Harry Head. That surely didn't set well. The language and tone of voice was now at a fever pitch, and getting out of hand, which prompted Morgan Earp to step in and break it up. Wyatt, who was at the lunch counter, wisely chose to leave it to Morgan, and to stay clear of the argument. Morgan took Doc by the arm, and led him outside as Ike followed. The argument became so loud that Virgil heard it from next door, and came out. The confrontation broke up when Virgil threatened to arrest them both.

Arizona Weekly Citizen; October 30, 1881

Tuesday night Ike Clanton and Doc Holliday had some difficulty in the Alhambra Saloon. Hard words passed between them, and when they parted it was generally understood that the feeling between the two men was that of intense hatred.[56]

After the situation quieted, Wyatt went to the Eagle Brewery, where he had a game open. According to Wyatt, Ike followed him and said he wasn't fixed right before, but now he was armed. Ike wouldn't give it up,

---

[55] Doc Holliday; Gary L Roberts pg. 185
[56] Arizona Weekly Citizen; October 30, 1881

and later asked Wyatt to take a walk, said he wanted to talk to him. Wyatt agreed, but said he had little time. "You must not think I won't be after you all in the morning." Ike threatened.[57] He once again threatened Doc, to which Wyatt assured him that Doc did not wish to make a fight, only that he, Ike, understand that he knew nothing of any deal, and wanted him to stop talking about it. After Wyatt closed his game he went home. Doc had already returned to Fly's Boarding House. Ike proceeded to the Oriental, where he joined in a card game with Virgil Earp, John Behan, and Tom McLaury, which lasted until sun up. In hind sight, that evening must have been quite surreal for Virgil Earp.

Still drinking, and probably unsure of where he was, or who was at the table, Ike continued to gamble and lose, although he still had money for whiskey. The game went on until nearly 7:00 am, when Virgil left for home, but not until he laid down a full house to take more of Ike's and Tom McLaury's money. As he was leaving, Ike was still fuming over Holliday's comments, and told Virgil to inform Doc that he was ready to make a fight. Virgil reportedly advised him that he was an officer of the law, and he shouldn't be making such threats.

Ike didn't let up. By 8:00 am on the 26th, he was back on the street near the telegraph office, where he ran into Ned Boyle, a bartender at the Oriental, and friend of the Earps. Ike pulled him into the conversation by vowing that "the ball would open" as soon as the Earps and Holliday showed up on the street. Boyle tried to convince him to go sleep it off, but Clanton wouldn't hear of it. Ike continued his rant from one saloon to another. Around 11:00 am, near the Capital Saloon, Ike spouted off about how he was going to kill Holliday and the Earps. Only this time, he was within ear shot of a city police officer who went straight to Virgil and got him out of bed. Ned Boyle meanwhile went to Wyatt's house to warn him of Ike's threats.

As his drunken rage continued, Ike made threats at Kelly's Wine House, then to Hafford's where he repeated his intent for making a fight with the Earps and Holliday. R.F. Hafford also tried to talk Ike down, but he simply upped the wager by going to Mollie Fly's Boarding House in search of Doc. Mrs. Fly informed Kate that Clanton had been there, and to warn Doc. When Kate woke him with the news, Doc replied; "If God lets me live long enough to get my clothes on, he shall see me."

October 26, 1881 was a cold and snowy day in Tombstone. The temperature was unusually bitter which hadn't let up for days. As the shops opened, and folks began to stir, it became obvious around town that a confrontation was coming soon. The dark skies and cold wind gave an

---

[57] Doc Holliday; Gary Roberts pg. 185

eerie feeling as rumors of a coming fight was broadcast by those who'd heard Ike's threats. Virgil didn't take Ike's threats seriously, and took his time about getting on the street. Morgan and James were already aware of the situation by the time Virgil arrived, which should have convinced him to see the matter as a bit more precarious. Wyatt had also taken Ike's pronouncement as bluster, and paid it little mind. As he entered the Oriental Saloon, Harry Jones informed him that Ike was looking for him. Wyatt thought little of it, but said he would walk out to find him and see what he wanted.

As Wyatt stepped onto the boardwalk, he ran into Virgil and Morgan where they put their stories together, then split up to search for Ike. Around noon, Mayor John Clum and Charles Shibell, who had just passed Ike on Fourth Street, saw Virgil and Morgan, armed and approaching Clanton, Clum knew it wasn't good. Virgil found Ike walking up Fourth Street between Allen and Fremont with a Winchester in hand and a pistol showing from his waist band. Wyatt soon rounded the corner from Allen Street. Virgil later recalled:

> "I found Ike Clanton on Fourth Street between Fremont and Allen with a Winchester rifle in his hand and a six-shooter stuck down in his breeches. I walked up and grabbed the rifle in my left hand. He let loose and started to draw his six-shooter. I hit him over the head with mine and knocked him to his knees and took his six-shooter from him. I asked him if he was hunting for me. He said he was and if he had seen me a second sooner he would have killed me. I arrested Ike for carrying firearms, I believe was the charge, inside the city limits."[58]

At the recorders court, Ike took a seat, then turned his attention to his bleeding head while Morgan stood against the wall with Ike's firearms as evidence of the charge. Virgil at this time was in search of Judge Albert O. Wallace, who was not in the court. Wyatt soon arrived, along with Deputy Sheriff Rezin J. Campbell, and the court's clerk. Wyatt testified at the November hearing that Ike Clanton looked over to him and said; "I will get even with all of you for this. If I had a six shooter I would make a fight with all of you." Morgan then said to him, "If you want to make a fight right bad I will give you this one." At the same time offering Ike Clanton his (Ike's) own six-shooter. Ike Clanton started to get up to take it, when Deputy Sheriff Campbell pushed him back on his seat, saying he

---

[58] Tombstone Daily Epitaph; November 20, 1881

wouldn't allow any fuss. I never had Ike Clanton's arms at any time as he has stated."[59]

In the November hearing before Judge Wells Spicer, Mr. Ruben F. Coleman, a miner, testified that he witnessed the exchange.

"I saw the arrest of Ike Clanton before the shooting commenced. I saw the City Marshal go up to Ike Clanton from behind or partially toward his side. Marshal Earp spoke to him but I did not hear what he said. The Marshal made a grab and took a rifle out of Clanton's hand. There then seemed to be a little scuffle by both of them when Clanton fell. I did not see the Marshal strike him but I saw Clanton fall and they took his revolver from him and took him into the Police Court. Earp had a revolver in his hand but whether he took it from Clanton or not I could not say."

Arresting Ike Clanton for a single charge of carrying a gun in town was a mistake that Virgil Earp would soon regret. Had he jailed Ike for threatening a police officer, or being drunk in public, he couldn't have instigated a fight. As a U.S. Marshal, a position Virgil still held, he could have charged Ike with a felony for threats against a federal officer. Had he done so, Frank and Tom McLaury would, in all probability, gone about their business, and been alive to attend their sister's wedding. As it stood, Judge Wallace fined Ike $25.00 plus $2.50 court cost. Ike paid the fine of $27.50, but continued his threats.

According to Mr. Coleman, Morgan Earp offered the return of Ike's pistol if he was man enough to use it, which he refused. They continued to have words, which the inquisitive Mr. Coleman said he could not hear. He did, however, clearly hear Ike challenge Wyatt, proclaiming that all he needed was "four feet of ground." [60] A clear threat for gun play. According to Wyatt, he was tired of their lives being threatened so he initiated that part of the confrontation by firing back at Ike; "You damn dirty cur thief. You have been threatening our lives, and I know it. I think I should be justified shooting you down any place I should meet you, but if you are anxious to make a fight, I will go anywhere on earth to make a fight with you, even over to the San Simon among your own crowd." Ike replied, "all right, I will see you after I get through here. I only want four feet of ground to fight on." [61]

Although Wyatt had fed Ike's anger, Marshal Virgil Earp missed another clean opportunity to jail Ike Clanton until he was sober. Given the decisions Marshal Earp had made thus far in the day, he was yet to take Ike seriously. It was about 1:00 pm when the parties left the hearing. Ike's

---

[59] Testimony of Wyatt Earp; November 17, 1881
[60] Mr. R.F. Coleman's testimony November 1881.
[61] Ibid

rifle and revolver were taken to the bar at the Grand Hotel for him to retrieve before leaving town

When Ike left the court, he went to P.W. Smith's store, which is where Mr. Coleman lost sight of him for a while. This was about the time Billy Claiborne showed up and assisted Ike to Dr. Gillingham's office to get his head dressed. Mr. Coleman next saw Ike when he met up with his brother, Billy Clanton, on Allen Street where they proceeded together to Dunbar's Corral. Coleman stood in front of the O.K. Corral, where he could see the two Clantons, and two McLaurys in conversation at Dunbar's. None of the day's events had taken place quietly. By this time, the whole town was aware of the ever-increasing tension on the street. Mr. Coleman happened to be on Fourth Street at the time of Ike's confrontation with Virgil, and obviously followed along to see how things would play out in police court. His curiosity didn't end there, and turned out to be a valuable asset in documenting the chain of events.

As the hearing closed, and the parties left the building, Wyatt came face to face with Tom McLaury, who was looking for Ike. Already agitated, Wyatt barked at Tom, who stood his ground, replying to Wyatt; "If you want a fight, I'll fight you anywhere". Wyatt replied; "Alright make a fight right here." At that moment he slapped McLaury across the face with his left hand and drew his pistol with his right. Wyatt saw McLaury's pistol on his right hip, and taunted him to use it; "Jerk your gun and use it," Wyatt challenged. McLaury stood his ground without reply. Wyatt then hit him on the head with his six-shooter, and calmly walked toward Hafford's for a cigar. According to eyewitnesses, Wyatt struck the normally quiet Tom McLaury several times before striking him with his pistol. McLaury stumbled, then picked up his hat and relented, choosing instead to make his way to the Capital Saloon to check his firearm.

Wyatt, had the need to regain his composure, and walked unchallenged to Hafford's where he bought a cigar and stood out by the door then lit up. Billy Clanton and both McLaury's soon passed by on Fourth Street where Wyatt saw them enter George Spangenberg's gun shop. He followed along to see what they were up to, when he saw Frank McLaury's horse on the boardwalk with his head in the gun shop doorway. Wyatt said; "I took the horse by the bit, as I was deputy city marshal, and commenced to back him off the sidewalk. Frank and Tom McLaury and Billy Clanton came to the door, Billy Clanton had his hand on his six shooter. Frank McLaury took hold of the horse's bridle. I said; "you will have to get this horse off the sidewalk." He backed him off on the street. Ike Clanton came up about that time, and they all walked into the gunsmith's shop. I saw them in the shop changing cartridges into their belts. They came out of the shop and walked along Fourth Street to the corner of Allen Street. I followed them as far as the corner of Fourth and Allen Streets, and then they went down Allen Street and over to Dunbar's corral.[62]

Sheriff John Behan had arrived on the street around 1:30 pm, and stopped at Barron's Barber Shop for a shave. There he heard someone in the shop say there was about to be trouble between the Earps and Clantons. Behan was yet unaware of the situation, but all conversation in the barber shop seemed to be focused on that one topic. After leaving Barron's, Behan saw Virgil on Hafford's corner, and inquired about the situation. Virgil quickly let him know there were; "a lot of sons of bitches in town looking for a fight." Behan demanded that Virgil disarm the men, but he would not comply. Virgil was more of a mind at that time to let it play, and give them a chance to make a fight if that's what they wanted. Behan, who was alone with no deputies in town said he would disarm them, but that put him in a compromised situation, given the nature of his relationship with the cow-boys at large.

As Virgil was leaving Hafford's, he was approached by H.F. Sills, a railroad man who had arrived in Tombstone the day before. Mr. Sills had been standing on the street near the O.K. Corral where he overheard the McLaurys and Clantons. He told Virgil that he saw four men standing in front of the O.K. Corral talking of some trouble they had with Virgil Earp, and they made threats at that time, that on meeting him they would kill him on sight. Someone of the party spoke up at that time and said they would kill the whole party of Earps when they met them. Mr. Sill knew no one involved, and had no stake in the situation, and asked a man in passing on the street about where to find Earp.[63]

Wyatt soon met Virgil, Morgan, and Doc at the corner of Allen & Fourth where several people alerted them that "there's going to be trouble with those fellows." Wyatt said Mr. Coleman told Virgil; "They mean trouble. They have just gone from Dunbar's Corral into the O. K. Corral, all armed. I think you had better go and disarm them." Virgil turned around to Doc Holliday, Morgan Earp and myself and told us to come and assist him in disarming them. Morgan said to me, "they have horses; had we not better get some horses ourselves, so that if they make a running fight we can catch them?" I said, "No, if they try to make a running fight we can kill their horses, and then capture them."

The Earps had no idea of what level this thing could go. Someone claimed to have seem Ike go into the telegraph office, inferring that he had

[62] Testimony of Wyatt Earp; November 17, 1881
[63] Wyatt Earp; The Life Behind the Legend; Casey Tefertiller pg120

wired for help. The presence of Claiborne, Billy Clanton, and both McLaurys appeared to be only the start of what could come. From San Simon, Johnny Ringo and Curly Bill could have brought an army.

The Earp party began a slow walk up Fourth Street, then turning left on Fremont. From there, the cow-boy group could be seen from the corner, standing at the edge of the vacant lot next to Fly's Photography Studio. Wyatt could see Tom and Frank McLaury, Billy Clanton, and Sheriff John Behan standing together. As they closed in, Ike Clanton, Billy Claiborne, and a third man (Wes Fuller) came into view to the left. When Behan saw the Earp party coming toward them, he broke away and headed toward Virgil, looking back every few steps like a man caught in the middle.

As the minutes ticked by, the tension in town grew deeper. Folks peered out of store windows, and listened intently for the next move, expecting more men to arrive at any time. The wind was cold, as the light flurries continued, but those on the street and boardwalk seemed to have little concern for the weather. Mr. C.H. Light had stopped by the barber shop for a shave, but all eyes were on the Earp party as they began their walk down Allen Street toward Fourth. The scene was ominous enough for Mr. Light to forego the shave and head home.

Mrs. Martha J. King was making her way to Baur's Meat Market. Baur's was on Fremont Street, just past the post office, and before Fly's Photography Studio. She was fortuitously in the Earp's line of travel. Mrs. Brown recalled the tension in the air;

> *"I was coming from my home to Baur's Meat Market to get some meat for dinner I saw quite a number of men standing by the door of the market and I passed on into the shop and to get what I went for and the parties in the shop were excited and did not seem to want to wait upon me. I inquired what was the matter and they said there was about to be a fuss between the Earp boys and the cow-boys."[64]*

Further in her testimony, Mrs. King said that she saw Doc Holliday's long gray coat blow open in the wind, exposing a gun, which she proclaimed to have clearly seen. Her thoughts, as she continued, were to run toward the back of the store, but gun fire broke out before she was half way there.

With all the pondering and speculation of historians and writers, the best source of information is research gathered from the time of the event. It's always best to question the individuals who were at the scene. I refer to them as post mortem interviews. Quotes from locals, diaries, pictures,

---

[64] Testimony of Mrs. M.J. King November 1881

and newspaper accounts have a way of removing personal bias, or preconceived conclusions for which a writer may be working to justify. The recorded recollections from Mr. Ruben Coleman, and those who testified at the November hearing provide a wealth of information.

Behan met up with them about a hundred feet from the vacant lot next to Fly's where the cow-boys had gathered. According to Wyatt he approached Virgil and said; "For God's sake, don't go down there or you will get murdered." Virgil replied; "I'm going down there to disarm them." When Wyatt and Morgan came up to Behan, he told them that he had disarmed them. Behan's version of their exchange wasn't much different. In his testimony, Behan said; "I saw Marshal Earp, Doc Holliday, Wyatt, and Morgan Earp a coming down the street. Expecting that there would be trouble if they met, I walked up the street toward them and ordered them back. Told them not to go down, that I was there for the purpose of disarming this party, they paid no attention to what I said. I appealed to them several times not to go any farther. They passed me, said something, I forgot what it was, but it was to the effect that they would not go back."[65] In his testimony, Behan claimed that he didn't tell Wyatt that he had disarmed the McLaury-Clanton party.

The Earp party pushed past Behan and slowly walked toward the men. Virgil had been carrying a walking stick in his left hand, likely Doc's, with his right on his pistol. When Behan assured him that he had disarmed the men, Virgil changed hands, placing the walking stick in his right, and slid his pistol around to the left. It was an unspoken gesture that when a man is holding something other than a pistol in his right hand he's not braced for a fight.

The Clantons and McLaurys stood in front of the open lot next to Fly's, while Behan and Billy Allen followed the Earp party from a few paces back. As the distance narrowed, Wes Fuller moved in from the far side of the lot, Behan veered left and found safety near the doorway of Fly's Boarding House. Fuller pulled back to cover, as Billy Claiborne followed suit, and moved out of the group. The Clantons and McLaurys also moved away from the road, and tucked further back into the lot closer to an old house owned by Mr. Harwood.

It was then Virgil realized he'd been lied to. John Behan had not disarmed anyone. Virgil could see Billy Clanton and Frank McLaury with their hands on their six- shooters. To his right, he could also see Tom McLaury reaching for a rifle scabbard that was tied to the saddle. Virgil raised his right hand, showing the walking stick in his gun hand as evidence of his intention to not hurt anyone, then shouted; "Boys, throw

---

[65] John Behan's testimony; Earp-Holliday Hearing November 1881

up your hands, I want your guns." The next thing he heard was the clicking sounds of a cocking hammer and rolling cylinder. Quickly scanning the scene, Virgil saw Billy Clanton and Frank McLaury in motion with their six-shooters rising in their holsters, while Ike Clanton, displayed his normal yellow streak, and threw up his hands to show he wasn't heeled.

"Hold, I don't want that!" Virgil shouted, now with both hands raised to show only a walking stick in his hands. Wyatt had placed his pistol in his overcoat pocket after Behan's assurance of unarming the men. When he saw that they were indeed armed, Wyatt quickly drew his Colt. Through fear or anger, Billy Clanton and Frank McLaury couldn't wait and leveled their sidearms. Virgil said he next heard two shots, almost as one. Wyatt testified that Clanton's first volley was aimed toward him, but missed. This was met with an immediate response from the barrel of Wyatt's Colt. But it wasn't Clanton Wyatt was focused on, it was Frank McLaury. Wyatt considered him to be the most dangerous gun-hand in the group, and aimed to neutralize that threat upfront. Virgil tossed the cane to his left hand and reached for his pistol with his right and "went to shooting, it was all general then and everybody went to fighting," he later recalled.

McLaury was gut shot and mortally wounded, but continued to fire as he stumbled. One round randomly fired from his pistol tore deep into Virgil Earp's right calf muscle. Morgan took a round from Tom McLaury across his back that skirted his left shoulder blade and chipped the edge of one vertebra before coming out at his right shoulder. The bullet stayed in his shirt. Morgan shouted; "I am hit!" then lost his balance, probably stumbling on the muddy pile of dirt from an open waterline trench, but came back to his feet. "Get behind me and stay quiet." Wyatt replied, as he returned fire.

Billy Clanton had been shot twice by this time, one in the chest and one in the wrist. He pulled himself away and fell against the side wall of the Harwood's house next door. Clanton rested his pistol on his knee and continued to fire with his left hand until the cylinder was dry.

After a slight pause following the first four shots, Ike Clanton stepped out franticly waving his hands to show he wasn't armed. The instigator of the entire debacle was now running for his life. When he reached Wyatt, he grabbed his arm, but Wyatt pushed him away and shouted: "The fight has commenced, get to fighting or get away." Ike ran through Fly's house, the lot next door, and a saloon to end up on Toughnut Street, two blocks away.

Doc Holliday had focused his attention on Tom McLaury who was partially concealed behind his rowdy horse. Doc saw him lean across the saddle in a posture of reaching for his scabbard. Doc fired both barrels of his shotgun, hitting McLaury under his right armpit. Some used the angle of entry as proof that McLaury had his hands in the air. Perhaps, but that portion of his body would have been equally exposed had he been reaching across to access the contents of a rifle scabbard. Tom McLaury staggered out into Fremont, and fell near Third Street with twelve shotgun pellets in his side. Doc dropped the shotgun, and pulled his pistol.

While John Behan stood helplessly near Fly's front door, Frank McLaury tried unsuccessfully to use his horse as a shield to get away. Holding fast to the reins, Frank made it to the street, and fired toward Morgan, causing the horse to break loose, leaving him fully exposed. As the first man to feel the wrath of Wyatt's Colt, Frank was weak and in pain, but came back to his feet as Doc Holliday approached. It took all that was left, but Frank stood and raised his pistol then said: "I've got you now."

"Blaze away," Doc replied. "You're a daisy if you have." Both men fired, Doc's bullet tearing its way into Frank's chest, while Frank's only grazed Doc's hip. Morgan Earp, who was back on his feet, took aim at Frank, and shot him in the side of the head. Doc looked to the gash in his pistol pocket; "I'm shot right through," he shouted. Frank McLaury was dying in the street, but somehow still moving. Doc shouted, as he moved toward McLaury; "That son of a bitch shot me, and I mean to kill him." Doc didn't fire again, for he already had. It was thirty seconds of pure hell that cost the lives of three men, but it was far from over.

CHAPTER EIGHT

THE AFTERMATH

The chaos that immediately followed kept everyone on edge. People began to gather on Fremont Street, and into the small lot, while those left standing waited for the unexpected. Stumbling across piles of dirt, and a muddy ditch for the new water line, the Earp party gathered themselves. Wyatt was still holding his revolver, and expecting the worst. Virgil was shot in the leg, Morgan in the back, and Doc with a slight graze from a bullet that was meant to do much more. Wyatt was the only man unscathed. The whereabouts of Wes Fuller, and Billy Claiborne were not known at the moment, but having been there at the start of the fracas, they could easily be ready for retribution, and perhaps amongst the crowd. One would think that Ringo and Curly Bill had also come to mind.

The last shot had been fired, but a squirming Billy Clanton was struggling to reload. C.S. Fly and Bob Hatch walked to Harwood's house, where Billy sat. "Give me some cartridges," he asked. Fly didn't speak, he just reached down and took the pistol, then walked away. Wyatt tended to Virgil and Morgan, while Doc checked his side to assess the damage, but luckily found it had been only a close call.

Several individuals who were standing in close proximity admitted to having come in near contact with stray bullets. One man, an investor from back east, said he was merely walking down the street when a bullet passed through his pant leg. According to Clara Brown, he left town the next morning and never returned. Billy Claiborne was grazed by a bullet as he fled the scene early in the fight. As folks began to gather, three short blast from the Vizina Mine whistle was heard. It was the signal to rally the Safety Committee should there be a second wave of violence, but all was quiet.

John Behan emerged from the safety of Fly's Studio as Wyatt was assisting Virgil, and attempted to assert his authority; "I have to arrest you, Wyatt." Behan barked. "I won't be arrested," Wyatt replied. Neither man backed down. Wyatt stood in confidence, while Behan pondered his next move. Sylvester Comstock, Tombstone's Democrat Party leader stepped in to ease the situation, convincing Behan to hold off for the time being. "There is no hurry in arresting this man," Comstock began. "He done just right in killing them, and the people will uphold them."

"You bet we did right. We had to do it, and you threw us off, Johnny. You told us they were disarmed." Wyatt said. Behan had no reply. All the while, the McLaury brothers, and Billy Clanton were carried into a house on the corner of Third and Fremont Street where they were examined by Coroner Henry M. Matthews. Frank McLaury was dead, Tom was dying quietly, while Billy Clanton was anything but quiet. He proclaimed that he had been murdered, and began to howl, as he told people to go away and let him die. Dr. William Miller soon arrived and injected him with morphine, which quieted him considerably.

Doc Holliday left quietly for his room at Fly's Boarding House. For a man with such a reputation, this had been a traumatic experience for Doc. As Kate later recounted;

After the fight, Doc came in, and sat on the side of the bed and cried and said; "Oh this is just awful – awful."

"Are you hurt?" He said "No, I'm not." He pulled up his shirt. There was just a pale red streak about two inches long across his hip where a bullet had grazed him. Then he went out to see what had become of the two Earps that were wounded. They were afraid to leave them for fear that the cow rustlers would take them in the night.[66]

As the sun began to set, Ike Clanton had been arrested on Toughnut Street, with rumors around town of a possible lynching. Phin Clanton had made it to town, and asked to be placed under sheriff's guard after seeing his brother Billy. He was placed in the cell with Ike, as ten extra men guarded the jail to prevent further trouble.

The Earp family had gathered at Virgil's house across the street from Wyatt's. Virgil and Morgan had been tended to and now had a better grasp on the extent of their wounds. For all other questions, there were no answers. Present at Virgil's house were James Earp, Wyatt Earp, the Earp wives, Sherm McMasters, and Winfield Williams. John Behan paid a visit, but received a less than welcome reception.

ARIZONA WEEKLY CITIZEN; OCTOBER 30, 1881

Tombstone, October 26; A fatal shooting affray occurred on Fremont Street, near Third, about three o'clock this afternoon. It appears that a number of cowboys have been in town for a few days past and have been

---

[66] Doc Holliday; The Life and Legend. Gary Roberts pg. 200

drinking heavily and making themselves generally obnoxious. This morning V. W. Earp, City Marshal, arrested one of them, Ike Clanton, and Ike was fined twenty-five dollars in the Justice's court, and disarmed. He left the court swearing vengeance. The Earp brothers shadowed them. Sheriff Behan also met four of them coming out of the O. K. corral and tried to pacify them. Just after he left them, the Earp brothers and "Doc" Holliday came along and hostilities at once commenced. It is not known who fired the first shot. About twenty-five shots were fired in quick succession. When the smoke of battle cleared away it was found that Tom and Frank McLowry were killed and Bill Clanton mortally wounded, and is now dying. Ike Clanton was slightly wounded and is now in jail. All these were cow-boys. Morgan Earp is badly wounded in the back and V. W. Earp has a flesh wound in the calf of the leg. Holliday has a slight scratch in the leg. The streets were immediately thronged with excited citizens, many of them armed with rifles and pistols. The Sheriff summoned a posse, who are now under arms. No further trouble is apprehended. [67]

The cowboys were struggling to maintain control of the beef market, and continue life as drifters, while Tombstone was growing in population and sophistication. This wasn't the case in Charleston, or Galeyville, but 1881 brought many new opportunities to the area known as Goose Flats only two years removed. Tombstone was a young town, filled with young people, who had dreams of riches and a good life. The rarity of a fresh apple a year earlier was replaced by markets of fresh fruit. Ice cream parlors, which were the favorites of Wyatt Earp and George Parsons, sprang up around town. French restaurants, oyster houses, and wine and spirits shops were tantalizing the desires of the up and coming.

History buffs and movie goers are all too familiar with the modern-day reenactments of the old west. Well, in 1881 Tombstone, they had a fancy for old time reenactments as well. Colorful Colonial costumes were popular, as tea parties, minuets, and seventeenth century gatherings became the fancy of many. Schieffelin Hall hosted Shakespearian readings, plays performed by professional traveling acting troupes, as well as the Tombstone Theater Company, who entertained with their version of popular stage acts. The Russ House, owned by Nellie Cashman, had cold beer, and specialized in the more discerning menu selections. Meals were a bit pricier though, with the least expensive starting around fifty cents.

Such refinement brought with it a clash of cultures. The freewheeling cowboy was becoming more out of place in town, as the heavy hand of the local law overshadowed the capitulation of a cooperative sheriff. The

---

[67] Arizona Weekly Citizen; October 30, 1881 pg. 1

formation of the Citizen Safety Committee, a so-called secret society of vigilantes, which was never much of a secret, also flared the anger of Frank McLaury, Ringo, and the Clantons. When Frank confronted Virgil Earp after the October 8th arrest of Stillwell and Spence, he also brought up the Citizen Committee, asking Virgil if their purpose was to hang him and the 'boys'. Virgil said he was not a part of it, and reminded Frank of the times that 'the boys' had been protected by the law. Siting their protection of Curly Bill after the killing of Marshal Fred White, and Michael O'Rouke (Johnny Behind the Deuce) after he killed Henry Schneider in Charleston, Virgil asked if he still thought they belonged to the Committee. Frank said he did because Johnny Behan had told him so. For Virgil Earp, that statement spoke volumes.

Their runs through Guadalupe to Sonora had become too dangerous, which placed American ranchers at greater risk of losing their stock to rustlers. Along with the vigilance committee in town, ranchers were beginning to talk about bounties placed on the heads of those known as the cow-boy leaders.

John Gosper, acting governor of the Territory of Arizona visited Tombstone in early September to gather a first-hand assessment of the situation. He saw nothing encouraging, including the relationship between John Behan and the Earps. In a letter to Secretary of State, James G. Blaine on September 20, 1881, Gosper wrote the following:

At Galeyville, San Simon and other points isolated from large places, the cow-boy element at times very full predominates, and the officers of the law are at times either unable or unwilling to control this class of outlaw, sometimes being governed by fear, and at other times reward. At Tombstone, the county seat of Cochise County, I conferred with the sheriff of said county upon the subject of breaking up these bands of out-laws, and I am sorry to say he gave me but little hope of being able, in his department, to cope with the power of the cowboys. He represented to me that the Deputy U.S. Marshal, resident of Tombstone, and the city Marshal for the same, and those who aided him (the Deputy Marshal) seemed unwilling to heartily co-operate with him (the Sheriff) in capturing and bringing to justice these out-laws.

In conversation with Deputy U.S. Marshal, Mr. Earp, I found precisely the same spirit of complaint exist against Mr. Behan (the Sheriff) and his deputies.

And back of this unfortunate fact, rivalry between the civil authorities, or an unwillingness to work together in full accord in keeping the peace – I found the two daily newspapers published in the city taking sides with the Deputy Marshal and the Sheriff respectively; each paper backing its civil clique and condemning each other. And still back of all this, the unfortunate fact that many of the very best law-abiding peace-loving citizens have no confidence in the willingness of the civil officers to pursue and bring to justice that element of outlawry so largely disturbing the sense of security, and so often committing highway robbery and smaller thefts. The opinion in Tombstone and elsewhere in this part of the Territory is quite prevalent that the civil officers are quite largely in league with the leaders of this disturbing and dangerous element.

In light of the few facts above given connected with the greatly unsettled state of affairs (and I have only touched the border) one of two results is sure to follow in our time. The cow-boys will come in control and "run" this part of our Territory with terror and destruction, and probably cause serious complications with sister Republic Mexico, with which we are now in fullest peace; or the law-abiding citizens of this county will be compelled to organize vigilant committees to protect their persons and property. I am secretly informed that a movement of that kind is now on foot in the county.

The greatest difficulty now in the way, perhaps of enforcing the law and bringing to justice these reckless spirits is the inability or indisposition of the civil officers of this particular county to do their duty.
Something must be done, and that right early, or very grave results will follow. It is an open disgrace to the very name of American liberty and the peace and security of her citizens, that such a state of affairs should exist as is cursing portions of this frontier country.[68]

In an open letter to Acting Governor John J. Gosper printed in the December 11, 1881 Arizona Weekly Citizen (page 4), the writer who signed the piece as "Clipper" verified Gosper's letter of September 20, 1881 as he wrote the following;

Dear Sir; In reply to your inquiry concerning the cowboys who are reported and have been, and still are raiding along the line of Sonora and Arizona I will say: The gang who are known as "cowboys" are engaging in stock raising in the valleys of San Simon and Cloverdale, in the southeastern portion of Arizona, and from good authority I learn that the cattle, horses, and sheep now controlled by said cowboys have been stolen from the citizens of Sonora, Arizona, and New Mexico. They are reported to have about three hundred head of cattle at or near Granite Gap, in New Mexico, and close to the line of Arizona. It is a well-known fact that they are in the habit of making raids along the border. Until recently it has

---

[68] Acting Governor John Gosper's letter to Sec. of State, James G. Blaine. September 20, 1881

been the custom to steal horses and cattle and drive them into Sonora for sale, and on the return trip to steal stock in Sonora and drive them into Arizona and New Mexico for sale; consequently, quite a traffic was kept up. This practice has abated somewhat lately, on the account of the killing of four cowboys at Fronteras in, I think last June. The circumstances as near as can be ascertained, are these; Last spring George Turner and [M.] McAllister, two well-known cowboys, obtained the contract at Fort Bowie for furnishing beef for the command. They and two assistants went to Sonora to either buy or steal beef cattle. They succeeded in driving a large herd as far as Fronteras, where they were attacked by Mexican citizens. They (the cowboys) were all killed, and one Mexican citizen was killed. Upon the bodies of Turner and McAllister was found the money which it is supposed they ostensibly took to purchase the cattle, which amount compared with what they were known to have started from here with proved that the cattle they were driving had not been paid for. This affair has earned bad blood between the cow-boys and the citizens of Sonora; each party taking revenge upon the other whenever opportunity occurs; consequently, it is unsafe for any person to travel across the border.

As previously noted, M. McAllister is actually Alfred McAllister, a Galeyville butcher, and good friend of George Turner.

By the spring of 1881, the cowboy faction had become a well-organized group of outlaws. Prior to that time, they were a loosely associated band of ruffians, staying to the hills and highways, and rarely seen in Tombstone. Curly Bill Brocius had been proclaimed as the leader, and it seems to be with just cause. His roots trace to the Lincoln County War, as well as running with Texas bandits such as Robert Martin. There were others from Texas, some from New Mexico and Lincoln County, and those such as Johnny Ringo and Joe Hill from Mason County, Texas and the Hoo Doo War. They were fast becoming a serious, calculating, and deadly precursor to the gangs which would follow in Chicago, and New York during the 1920's.

Other documented examples, not folklore or movie drama, include reports such as that of September 4, 1881;

I will also state another case: "Billy the Kid", a stripling belonging to the profession, was arrested for stealing horses. Upon his examination the court ruled that the affidavit upon which he was arrested charged him with the crime of theft, but should have been larceny. Also, the person from whom the horses had been stolen voluntarily stated to the court that he did not want the boy prosecuted as he agreed to return the horses. The same person told me afterward that if he had prosecuted the boy the other cowboys would steal every head of stock he had, which he, being a poor man, could not afford to stand. The cowboys frequently visit our town and often salute us with an indiscriminate discharge of firearms, and after indulging in a few drinks at the saloons, practice shooting at the lamps, bottles, glasses, etc., sometimes going to the lengths of shooting the cigar out of one's mouth. This, of course, produces a nervous feeling.

The situation at this writing is not materially changed from the above. The cowboys, as a class, are not over brave, though there are among them who have gone through so much difficulty that they have become desperate and take desperate chances.

Please note the "Billy the Kid" referred to here is Billy Claiborne, not Henry McCarty who was ostensibly killed in Lincoln, New Mexico on July 14, 1881.

In the same article, the writer reports the theft of a herd of Mexican sheep, which seemed to match the time frame surrounding the August incident in Guadalupe Canyon between Old Man Clanton's crew and a band of Mexican smugglers. In it he states that an outlaw named John R. was in town offering all the mutton the town could consume at a rate of $1.00 per head.

Perhaps the most chilling example of the extent of control levied by the cowboys can be found in the Arizona Star, September 10, 1881;

Permit me to give you a brief history of a trial before a border Justice of the Piece known as G.W. Ellingwood. David Estes was one of two men who robbed a game of about four hundred dollars in cash at the mid-night hour in the town of Galeyville as follows; Estes entered the front door of the saloon in which the game was being played armed with a Winchester and a six shooter; his "pal" passing in at the rear of the house, armed in a similar manner. They ordered the players to throw up their hands and surrender all their cash. This accomplished, Estes proceeded to the corral of Babcock & Co. and extracted and confiscated a valuable horse, making the total clean up about five hundred dollars. Estes was subsequently arrested by Deputy Sheriff Goodman and tried before said Ellingwood and discharged. His honor ruled in the examination of the witnesses that they could not testify to the taking of the money (ordered by the bandits to be left on the table) unless they of their own knowledge knew to whom a particular parcel of money belonged. This could not be proven as all the occupants of the room were commanded to absquatulate instantly, leaving Estes and his pard to take the divide. Thus, you see a single pair in Galeyville wins five hundred dollars. Under the ruling of this astute and honorable judge, no evidence was admitted necessary to conviction.

Sheriff Goodman asked to be sworn to testify that the prisoner offered him five hundred dollars to cast loose his shackles and let him at liberty. The testimony was ruled out by the Court as being irrelevant and not material to the issue. While the trial was in progress, the Judge stated to Quartz Johnson that the prisoner could not be convicted, and subsequently that he (the Judge) would now stand well with the cowboys.

The reality of such situations is the fear a judge would have for his life, and the life of his loved ones. After any trial, the judge would leave the court venue either by carriage or on horseback. Either way, he was in the open and exposed to instant retaliation. Currying favor with the cowboys was better for one's health. By the way, Dave Estes's "pal" in that holdup was Johnny Ringo.

On Sunday March 26, 1882, after the killing of Morgan Earp, the Arizona Daily Star printed a lengthy article on page one, entitled "The Venditti". Written by a San Francisco to Tombstone reporter, the article's purpose was to chronicle the shootout of October 26, 1881 (although he called it November 26th,) and the events which led to the tragic event. The tie between the Benson Stage robbery, the shootout of October 26, 1881, and the attack on the Earp family was as clear then as it is now.

Under the subheading '*The Benson Stage Robbery*' the writer includes the following;

"The trouble between the Earps and the Clanton and McLowry boys grew out of the robbery of the Benson stage. On March 15th 1881, the stage with Wells, Fargo & Co.'s express left Tombstone for Benson with a large treasure, 'Bud' Philpot driving and Bob Paul as Wells, Fargo & Co.'s messenger. The coach left at 6:00pm and at 7:30pm, while only 200 yards out from the first station, the order to halt was given. Simultaneously with it two shots were fired, one of which killed the driver and the other perforated the cushion upon which Paul was setting. The driver fell off, carrying the lines with him, and the horses ran away. Paul emptied his gun, returning shot for shot, but without effect. The horses kept running, and the robbers kept shooting, and in all fired some twenty shots at the retreating stage with its load of ten passengers. They succeeded in killing one man who was on top. Paul managed to stop the team, gathered up the lines and drove rapidly to Benson, where he telegraphed the news to Tombstone. Immediately all was excitement. Agent Williams of Wells, Fargo & Co. and the Earp brothers were rushing around, preparing to hunt the robbers. At 8:30 that same evening Doc Holliday rode up to a saloon in Charleston, ten miles from the scene of the attempted robbery and inquired of Billy Clanton. On being told that he was not there, started

in the direction of Tombstone, which was nine miles distant, and about 10:00 o'clock rode up to a saloon on a back street in Tombstone and called for a big drink of whiskey, which he drank at a gulp, without dismounting. His horse at the time was covered with foam. This all happened before the news of the murder reached Tombstone. At midnight the agent and the Earp brothers, with Holliday, left town to meet Paul. It was too dark to follow a trail when they arrived on the ground, so they camped until morning. They found three masks made of hay rope and about twenty large-size rifle cartridges. They then took the trail and followed it for about three weeks without catching anyone but a supposed accomplice, and he was assisted by some unknown person to escape from the custody of the sheriff while consulting with his lawyer."

'SOME SHADY TRANSACTIONS'

The news of Holliday's ride becoming known, coupled with the facts that he was seen mounted and armed in the early part of the afternoon, ostensibly to go to Mexico, caused many surmises, and not a few made the remark that "the robbers were hunting themselves." Before the return of the agent's posse it became known that Billy Leonard, Jim Crane and Harry Head were interested in the murder, and it was their trail that Paul was following. Wells Fargo & Co. offered a large reward for them, but it was of no use. So, matters rested for some time, until, as Ike Clanton swears, Wyatt Earp called him aside and told him that he would guarantee him all the Wells Fargo & Co's. reward and one thousand dollars more on top of it, if he would induce Leonard and Head to come to some ranch in the neighborhood of Tombstone so that he (Wyatt) could surprise and kill them. He gave as his reasons that they had failed to realize anything out of the attempted robbery and that Leonard and Head might "squeal" sometime. Crane had been killed by the Mexicans with Old Man Clanton, so there was nothing to fear from him. To satisfy Clanton that he meant business, Earp had Wells Fargo's agent telegraph to San Francisco asking whether the reward would be paid dead. The answer came back yes. But while negotiations were pending Leonard and Head were both killed in New Mexico for stealing cattle.[69]

~

On November 8, 1881 the Tombstone Nugget reported that John Ringo of New Mexico was in town to address a legal matter. The matter was in regard to the August poker game in Galeyville in which Ringo and

---

[69] Arizona Daily Star; March 26, 1882

David Estes robbed the participants of $400.00 and a horse. Prior to dealing with personal matters, Ringo became fixated on the Earp-Holliday hearing. He wasn't around for the confrontation, or the role that Ike had played in the run-up, but Ike had Ringo's ear, and he believed every word. As in Mason County, Ringo was willing to stand with his friends. He'd seen retribution by the local law, and if he believed Ike, his thoughts must have gone back to John Clarke, and the death of Tim Williamson.

Ringo attended parts of the hearing with hopes of a murder trial, but left for San Simon before it was over. On November 25th, Joe Hill registered at the Grand Hotel where Ringo had taken a room. George Olney, Joe Hill's brother, and W.H. Miller also checked in. No one is sure of their purpose in town. Curly Bill would probably have been with them, except for the fact that he was in jail in Lordsburg, New Mexico at the time. Neither of them had been around in October, and why Ringo had ridden such a distance to bring them back is unknown. What is known is Judge Wells Spicer declared on November 30, 1881 that no case could be made against the Earps or Doc Holliday and set them free.

CHAPTER NINE

THE COURT OF PUBLIC OPINION

The validity if the Earp Holliday Hearings have always been questioned. Judge Spicer's partiality to the Earps, and his open dislike for the cow-boy faction was widely known. Many believed his conflicts of interest should have disqualified him from hearing the case. Never the less, he did, and the Earps were cleared, but the conflict was far from over.

Ike Clanton had been granted a golden opportunity during the hearing to discredit the Earps. In his testimony he accused them of involvement, along with Wells Fargo agent Marshal Williams, of stage robbery and murder. He had no proof, but Clanton was passionate and convincing enough to plant doubt in the minds of many. During the month of December, Ringo and a hoard of cow-boys convened on Tombstone, boosting Ike Clanton's claims and spreading whatever discourse they could regarding the Earp family.

Wyatt was perplexed and truly didn't understand why they were being perceived in such a light. In his mind they had done what needed to be done, but it was now coming at a heavy price. Virgil was more politically astute, where Wyatt was quite naïve, he realized their time there in law enforcement, as well as any status in town was seriously damaged. For Doc Holliday, he had no status to lose, and inadvertently earned a degree of respect along with a reputation of being fearless.

Ringo fueled the fire with cow-boys creating havoc at every turn, but he had other business in town as well. On November 23, 1881, Ringo surrendered to Deputy Sheriff Dave Neagle. He was in court twice the following week, once on December 1, 1881 where he was given a court date of January 18, 1882 for the August poker game robbery in Galeyville. He was back in court the following day to address the charge of stealing a horse during the same incident. That matter was set for January 23, 1882.

What had started only a month earlier as overwhelming support for the Earps was now beginning to turn. Members of Ringo's crew were seen more in town with the tide against John Clum and the "Law and Order" faction building by the day. Clum, who was no greenhorn, became frightened of the cow-boys after talk of lynching the Earps, and wired Gov. John J. Gosper for weapons.

It was not a good time for Mayor Clum. December 18th would mark the first anniversary of his wife's death. Mary died of the fever only a few days after giving birth to their eleven-pound daughter, Elizabeth. Mary "Mollie" Clum was 27. Elizabeth "Bessie" wasn't healthy from birth, and died early in the summer of 1881.

Clum had nothing left in Tombstone. As the rhetoric increased, he decided that Washington D.C. might be a better place for him than Tombstone for the time being. In the midst of threats and turmoil, Mayor Clum had decided to not run for re-election, choosing instead to board the Kinnear Stage on December 14, bound for Benson.

About four miles out of town, near Malcolm's Water Station, John Clum was taken by surprise. Two rigs had just pulled out of Malcolm's, the stage driven by Jimmy Harrington, and a bullion wagon driven by "Whistling Dick" Richards. With the stage in the lead, the team quickly picked up speed, and were moving along at a lively gait when the order to "Halt" was given from the side of the road. An immediate barrage of gunfire hailed the stage from both sides of the road. The off leader (the front horse on the right side of the team) was hit in the neck, causing the remainder of the team to become unmanageable. The horses ran for about a half mile before the wounded horse fell from the loss of blood. "Whistling Dick" caught a bullet in the leg causing a very painful flesh wound, but he held fast to the team and kept the bullion wagon on the road.

John & Mary Clum

Mayor Clum, assisted by four other passengers, left the stage and cut the down horse from the team. The passengers hurriedly boarded the stage, and off they went. With Clum not in the stage, the passengers assumed that he had taken a seat top-side, but Clum was gone. It wasn't until the stage pulled into Contention City that they realized he was missing. With a telegram back to Tombstone reporting the attack, and the missing mayor, Sheriff John Behan and C.D. Reppy, who was filling in at the Epitaph for Clum, set out around 3:00 am to search for the assailants and the mayor. Behan arrived in Contention around 4:00 am, where he learned the location of the attack, and the particulars of the incident. Behan and Reppy backtracked toward Tombstone until they reached the location of the attack. There was no sign of Clum.

Around 4:00 am a second posse left Tombstone bound for Malcolm's Station where they talked to two teamsters who had witnessed the attack from a close enough vantage point to see the flash from the firearms. They reportedly saw the stage horses' break out in a run for about half a mile before they stopped and cut the wounded horse loose. By the time they got there, the stage was on its way and the horse had wandered off a few hundred yards before it fell for the last time. Leaving a trail of blood, the horse was already coyote meat when they arrived.

With no sign of Clum, or a trail, the posse proceeded to Contention where they heard he was at the Grand Central Mill. Assuming that he was a target of assassination, Clum moved away from the stage in the excitement, and hid himself in the hills until the area was quiet. Finally, he took the ore road, and walked back to Contention where he used the telephone at the mill to call back to Tombstone. After a short rest, Mayor Clum acquired a horse and continued on to Benson, arriving there at approximately 8:00 am.

Judge Wells Spicer

After daybreak the posse searched the scene of attack and found no rifle cartridges on the ground, although passengers had reported fifteen to twenty shots fired in rapid order. Up the gulch, about a hundred yards from Malcolm's, the posse found evidence of a number of horses having been tied in the thick brush. Others at Malcolm's said they had heard the sounds of a number of horses leaving the area in a rush at about that time. The identity of the assailants was never found.[70]

The incident served to increase the tension in Tombstone. In the wake of Judge Spicer's decision in the Earp-Holliday hearing, Earp supporters John Clum, Wyatt's attorney Tom Fitch, and Marshal Williams had received threatening letters, by in large, demanding they leave town or else. Judge Spicer, like John Clum, had decided to not run for re-election. Both men, who had been highly respected, realized they could not win another term. The initial support enjoyed by the Earps had been replaced by doubt, drummed up by people like John Ringo, and Milt Joyce. Folks in town who once supported the outcome of the October shootout, were now second guessing its justification.

Judge Spicer received the following letter:

Tombstone, A.T., Dec. 13, 1881
Sir, if you take my advice you will take your departure for a more genial climate, as I don't think this one healthy for you much longer. As you are liable to get a hole through your coat at any moment. If such sons of Bitches as you are allowed to dispense Justice in this Territory, the Sooner you depart from us the better for yourself and the community at large. You may make light of this but it is only a matter of time you will get it sooner or later. So, with those few gentle hints I Will Conclude for the first and last time.
A Miner

Spicer replied in the December 18th Tombstone Epitaph as follows:

I must regret that the writer of the above did not sign his true name, or at least inform me what mine he works in, for I would really be pleased to cultivate his acquaintance, as I think he would be an amiable companion - when sober...
As I cannot have the pleasure of a personal interview with the amiable 'Miner,' will you allow me the privilege of replying to his charming epistle, and say to him that I have concluded not to go, nor would I ever notice his disinterested advice on the subject were it not for the fact that similar threats have been made by others, and that the threats would be carried into execution if they only dared to do it.
Since the daring attempt to murder Mayor Clum and to wantonly kill a stage load of passengers to accomplish it, these little emanations of

---

[70] Wells Fargo & Co. Stagecoach and Train Robberies 1870-1884. James B. Hume; Pg. 260

bravado do not draw forth admiration as would the beauty of summer clouds with silver linings. They are too somber and surrounded with a deathly black shade of recent transactions- they are bad omens of the future when viewed in the light of the death glare of the past. This style of threat has been made not only against myself, but at the same time against Mr. Clum and others. The attempt has been made to assassinate Mr. Clum - who will come next?

One and all will ask, from whence do these threats emanate? And each will have his own opinion; I have mine. And now I will try to do justice to the Clanton brothers by saying that they and men outside the city, living on ranches and engaged in raising cattle or other lawful pursuit, as heartily condemn the proceedings as any man in our midst, and that they as honestly denounce all such affairs as any man can. That the real evil exists within the limits of our city.

It is needless to try to turn these matters into ridicule or make them a subject of jest for funny squibs. It is a matter of serious importance to the community.

I am well aware that all this hostility to me is on account of my decision in the Earp case, and for that decision I have been reviled and slandered beyond measure, and that every vile epithet that a foul mouth could utter has been spoken of me, principal among which has been that of corruption and bribery.

It is but just to myself that I should here assert that neither directly or indirectly was I ever approached in the interest of the defendants, them or for them. Not so the prosecution - in the interest of that side even my friends have been interviewed with the hope of influencing me with money, and hence all this talk by them and those who echo their slanders about corruption. And here too, I wish to publicly proclaim everyone who says that I was in any in manner improperly influenced is a base and willful liar.

There is a rabble in our city who would like to be thugs if they had courage; would be proud to be called cowboys if people would give them that distinction; but as they can be neither, they do the best they can to show how vile they are, and slander, abuse and threaten everybody they dare to. Of all such I say, that whenever they are denouncing me they are lying from a low, wicked and villainous heart; and that when they threaten me they do so because they are low-bred, arrant cowards, and know that "fight is not my racket" - if it was they would not dare to do it

In conclusion, I will say that I will be here just where they can find me should they want me.

Wells Spicer [71]

On December 15, 1881, Milt Joyce approached Virgil Earp in the Oriental Saloon with remarks regarding John Clum's stage incident the previous evening. Joyce said that "he had been expecting something of this sort ever since they (the Earps and Holliday) had been liberated from jail." Virgil's response was to slap him across the face. Joyce left, but said on the way out; "Your favorite method is to shoot a man in the back, but if you murder me you will be compelled to shoot me in the front."[72]

The following day when Joyce entered the Oriental, Virgil Earp was there at a gambling table. With a revolver in hand he approached Virgil, but was stopped by John Behan who walked Joyce out of the saloon and arrested him for carrying a firearm. Although they had been friends, the incident turned Milt Joyce against Sheriff Behan from there forth.

On Saturday December 17, 1881 George Parsons lamented in his diary of the attempted murder of John Clum. Parsons later spoke of the existence of a "hit list" which included the Earp Brothers, Doc Holliday, Judge Wells Spicer, Tom Fitch, and Marshal Williams. He cited the known letters to several in the group, as well as talk around town to justify his theory.

Although the rhetoric was high, retaliation by the cow-boys was of concern for the entire town. The sight of twenty or so cow-boys haranguing a saloon at any time of night, as well as a barrage of street fights was now a reality. Each effort was well planned, and executed to intimidate those who still stood with the Earp faction.

In the midst of it all, Tombstone was still a growing town. On December 26, 1881 the Bird Cage Theater opened its doors. It would become a central part of Tombstone's entertainment and gambling activity. The basement was  host to the longest running poker game in history running twenty-four

---

[71] Arizona Archives Online
[72] Doc Holliday; The Life and Legend. Gary Roberts pg. 227

hours a day – seven days a week for eight years, five months and three days. Men such as Bat Masterson, Diamond Jim Brady, George Hearst, Doc Holliday, and Adolphus Busch laid their cards on those tables. On the stage, the Bird Cage hosted acting troupes, singers, and comedians from around the country.

Within days, Deputy Breakenridge was walking near the building's side wall to avoid the rain when he suddenly felt a pistol press against his chest. Frank Stillwell stood there in a panic telling Breckenridge that someone was out to kill him.

"I asked him what he was trying to do, and he said that a certain party had boasted that he was going to get him that night, and that he would not do it if he saw him first. I told him that it was too late for him to kill anyone that night, that he was in enough trouble already, and to put up his gun and go home. He did as I told him and went down the side street, and I turned back wondering whom he was after, but about the middle of the block I met Doc Holliday, who roomed a short distance up the street, on his way home. It flashed through my mind that I had inadvertently saved Holliday's life that night." [73]

As the tension in Tombstone was building to yet another tragedy, Crawley Dake picked up John Clum's request for guns and forwarded it to President Chester A. Arthur. Where Clum had asked for guns, Dake asked for an exception to the Posse Comitatus Act and a force of troops to be sent to the border. With such a request having to be heard by Congress, Dake would not receive a timely reply as he'd hoped.

Three days following a less than joyous Christmas for the Earps, Virgil was gunned down. On December 28, 1881 at near midnight, Virgil Earp left the Oriental Saloon for the evening, while Wyatt stayed behind to keep an eye on the gambling tables. As he approached the corner of Fifth Street, on his way to the Cosmopolitan Hotel, a barrage of shotgun fire rang out with Virgil taking the force of the blasts in his left side. His arm was shattered, with shots in his side and leg. One having entered above the groin, and exited near the spine. Several stray shots broke windows in the Eagle Brewery, missing one patron by inches before plowing into the wall. Witnesses spotted three men running through the back of the building then over to Toughnut Street. [74]

Miraculously Virgil remained conscious and on his feet, then made his way back to the Oriental. Wyatt hurriedly took him back to the hotel and summonsed Dr. Goodfellow and Dr. Matthews. On December 28, 1881,

---

[73] Helldorado; William Breakenridge. Pg. 155-156
[74] Arizona Weekly Citizen January 1, 1882

George Parsons, who lived on the second floor of the Eagle Brewery, just above the location where the shots were fired, remarked in his diary;

Tonight about 11:30 Doc G (Goodfellow) had just left and I thought couldn't have crossed the street – when four shots were fired in quick succession from very heavily charged guns, making a terrible noise and I thought were fired under my window under which I quickly dropped, keeping the dobe wall between me and the outside till the fusillade was over. I immediately thought Doc had been shot and fired in return, remembering a late episode and knowing how pronounced he was on the Earp – cowboy question. He had crossed though and passed Virgil Earp who was crossing to the west side of 5th and was fired upon when in range of my window by men, two or three concealed in the timbers of the new two-story adobe going up for the Huachuca Water Co. He did not fall, but re-crossed to the Oriental and was taken from there to the Cosmopolitan, being hit with buck shot and badly wounded in left arm, with flesh wound above left thigh. Cries of "There they go, head them off," were heard, but the cowardly apathetic guardians of the peace were not inclined to risk themselves and the other brave men, all more or less armed did nothing. [It was generally conceded that the attempted assassination of Virgil Earp was carried out by Ike Clanton, Frank Stillwell, Hank Swelling, and John Ringo] Doc had a close shave. Van and I went to hospital for Doc and got various things. Hotel was guarded, so much so that I had hard trouble to get to Earp's room. He was easy. Told him I was sorry for him. "It's Hell, isn't it!" said he. His wife was troubled, "Never mind, I've got one arm left to hug you with," he said. [75]

On December 29th, Parsons provided an update on Virgil Earp's status, and amended the possible names of the shooters;

"Crowds this morning looking at shots and bullet marks on the walls... Longitudinal fracture, so elbow joint had to be taken out today and we've got that and some of the shattered bone in room. Patient doing well. It is surmised that Ike Clanton, Curly Bill, and [William] McLaury did the shooting. Bad state of affairs here. Something will have to be done."

---

[75] A Tenderfoot in Tombstone; George Parsons. Pg.198

CHAPTER TEN

THE WAR OF WORDS

Tombstone was in a state of terror, as danger in the streets intensified. With a "Who's Who" list of suspects for the shooting, it is fair to surmise that the cow-boy leadership was in town, and taking full advantage of the situation. Emboldened by the very incident intended to bring them to their knees, Ringo and Curly Bill now had the upper hand. With upwards of fifty cow-boys coming in from San Simon and Charleston, the Earps were out gunned, and they knew it.

To protect the family, the Earp brothers and their wives had consolidated their living quarters to the Cosmopolitan Hotel. They still had business to tend to, such as the gambling concessions, mining and land deals, and water rights. All but the gambling tables could be managed in the light of day, with none of the Earp brothers venturing out on their own. Their income from the tables was managed at night, leaving them exposed when not in the presence of others. Virgil had survived the attack, but was given only a twenty per-cent chance of pulling through. The protection of the family at large was foremost in Wyatt's mind. Anticipating the worst, Wyatt turned to Crawly Dake for an appointment as Deputy U.S. Marshal to replace Virgil. On the afternoon of the 29th, Wyatt wired Dake;

Virgil was shot by concealed assassins last night. His wounds are fatal. Telegraph me appointment with power to appoint deputies. Local authorities are doing nothing. The lives of other citizens are threatened.

Dake's positive response was immediate. Wyatt Earp was now a Deputy U.S. Marshal with all the authority that comes with the appointment, yet he stayed quiet for better than a week. Wyatt stayed close to Virgil while selecting deputies, and narrowing down suspects. With all the prior conjecture, two solid suspects became obvious to the Earps. Virgil had seen Frank Stillwell enter the vacant building as he was leaving the Oriental Saloon. After the incident, Ike Clanton's hat was found near the rear of the building, where the men had been seen in their escape. Ike may as well have left a calling card.

The cowboys had made their headquarters on the second floor of the Grand Hotel across the street from the Cosmopolitan. It was a strategic move on their part that provided a bird's eye view of Allen Street as well as the Earp's movements to and from their hotel. Wyatt all the while, was busy selling assets including his stake at the Oriental Saloon to stock pile all the cash he could to support the family on the short run.

As they waited for the funds from Crawley Dake, Wyatt secured his posse. Morgan Earp, Doc Holliday, "Turkey Creek" Jack Johnson, "Texas Jack" Vermillion, Sherm McMasters, and Dan Tipton, along with a few lesser known names who were good with a gun. It was a tough cadre of men who wouldn't run, and who weren't afraid to shoot. If Wyatt was to make a dent in the cow-boy faction, and apprehend those who had attempted to murder Virgil, he needed men as tough and as hardy in a saddle as they were.

The second floor of the Cosmopolitan Hotel had become a fortress. Armed supporters stood guard to limit access and protect the family. Drs. Goodfellow and Matthews had done all they could to remove buckshot and bone, now it was up to Virgil to begin the healing process. George Parsons had become a regular visitor, running medical supplies and other necessities from the hospital to the hotel, but even he had a difficult time getting past those committed to protecting the Earp family. At the very least, Wyatt expected the plight of his brother would garner enough sympathy and good wishes from their waning friends and prior supporters to restore their reputation in town just a little. Unfortunately, as the Earps hoped for a little sunshine, the clouds only continued to gather.

The election cycle was in full swing, but without the usual hard line partisan divide. The formation of the People's Independent Party seemed to make the election more of a referendum on the Earps and their associates. In a rare move, the pro Democrat Nugget endorsed Republican candidate John Carr for mayor while the *Epitaph* supported Lewis Blinn, a pro-Earp Democrat. The *Nugget* endorsed Deputy Sheriff Dave Neagle for sheriff. The *Epitaph* in turn supported long time Earp friend, Democrat Jim Flynn. It was an election season where party politics took a back seat to one's impression of the Earp family, none of whom had their name on a ballot anywhere.

Editorials and newspaper pundits who supported Carr and Neagle made every effort to tie their opponents to the Earps. Feeding off their tarnished reputation, newspapers like the *Tombstone Nugget* and the *Prescott Democrat* re-litigated the October shootout to impugn the character of any candidate ever associated with the Earps. As a man without political savvy, Wyatt was stunned and honestly did not understand how it had gotten to that point.

Politics and the truth have never seemed to mix very well. It was no different in those days than it is today. Erroneous articles and editorials tying Wyatt, Doc, and Wells Fargo agent Marshal Williams to every stage robbery since they arrived were commonplace. For some, simply reminding the good people of Wyatt Earp's close friendship with the likes of Doc Holiday was enough to tarnish one's reputation. It was a time when Wyatt Earp expected his name to stand on its own and garner the county's support as their new sheriff. Instead, his name had been muddied and soiled to such a degree that it was used instead to denigrate anyone with whom he had associated.

On Election Day, the *Tombstone Nugget* again reiterated the close alliances between the Earps, Doc Holliday, and candidates Jim Flynn and Lewis Blinn. The encouragement for every miner and businessman to vote was a call to save their city from the Earps and their murderous ways. In the end, John Carr won the mayoral race 830-298 over Lewis Blinn. Dave Neagle beat Jim Flynn by a margin of 590-434. The Independent People's Party also prevailed by securing three of the four city council seats.

BUSINESS AS USUAL

Three days following the elections, it seemed that things hadn't changed. On January 6, 1882, just before 9:00 am, the W.W. Hubbard & Company stage to Bisbee was attacked about six miles from Charleston. Shotgun guard Charles Bartholomew put up a fight, but wasn't able to stop the robbers from making off with the strong box containing $6,500.00. The driver was said to have recognized one of the men, but threatened with his life if he ever talked. He said nothing at the time, but a subsequent report in the Las Angeles Times identified the man as Johnny Ringo.[76]

On the cold evening of January 7th, the Sandy Bob stage driven by Jack Sheldon from Benson to Tombstone was hit just south of Contention. On board that stage was Wells Fargo detective Jim Hume. The take there was small, but Hume was relieved of his two-prize pistols, which for him was more of a humiliation than the monetary loss. For Wyatt Earp, this put him back in the hunt.

When Hume arrived at the Wells Fargo office in Tombstone, Fred Dodge met him at the door. According to Dodge, Hume hardly said hello, but immediately said; "get me Wyatt Earp." Wells Fargo was aware of the rumors and accusations directed at the Earps during the hearing, but they never believed a word. In the early days of Tombstone, Wyatt and Morgan

---

[76] Inventing Wyatt Earp; Allen Barra. Pg.240

Earp had both worked as shotgun riders for Wells Fargo. They would later boast that no stage run by their company was ever robbed with an Earp on watch. For Tombstone, new concerns over rumors that Wells Fargo was pulling out left business owners in fear that they would be isolated without the stage line. The expectations of voters who'd ushered in new leadership, and "showed the Earps a thing or two" just days ago, didn't seem to work out as they'd hoped.

Wells Fargo had the upper hand in Tombstone, and felt Wyatt Earp was their best hope in solving the robberies. With that, the Earp family had new reason to believe they had a place in southern Arizona after all. On January 4th, just three days before Hume arrived in town a well-known mining tycoon from California payed a visit to Tombstone. George Hurst visited town, and spent time at the poker tables of the Bird Cage Theater. Amidst rumors that he might be a kidnapping target, Hurst asked for Wyatt Earp to serve as his body guard while there. It was a short assignment for Earp, but he and Hurst hit it off, and their connection continued. In the early twentieth century, it would be Hurst's son, William Randolph Hurst who would help preserve the legend that was Wyatt Earp.

Even in the dark, Hume had paid close attention to the robber's height, build, and, voice inflections. His description to Wyatt and Fred Dodge was said to be enough that the only thing he missed were their names. Dodge said he knew who they were, and could be found at J.B. Ayres, Saloon, the usual headquarters of the cow-boys in Charleston. Hume wanted to leave immediately, but Dodge advised him that he would only serve to get himself killed. Hume agreed. While Fred Dodge and Wyatt Earp were making preparations to ride out, Hume slipped away without their knowledge.

Wyatt Earp, Morgan Earp, Charlie Smith, and Fred Dodge rode out of Tombstone in the dark of night and made camp on the west side of the Huachuca Mountains around 2:00 am. Making camp until first light, the posse made their way to the homes of those suspected in the robbery, rousting their families out of bed, but neither of the men had returned. It was around 2:00 pm when the posse arrived at J.B. Ayres' Saloon only to find Jim Hume standing in the doorway, as he invited them in for a drink. They left without the men they'd come for, but Hume returned the next day. By then he had concluded that even with the information he had, he had not seen their faces, and had a lack of evidence to arrest the men.[77]

The two stage robberies in as many days proved that neither the bloody gunfight in October, nor the elections of January 3rd had changed a thing. Wyatt Earp's focus was back on being a lawman, but his loss of influence

---

[77] Wyatt Earp Explorers; Jim Rose. www.wyattearpexplorers.com

and informants from the shadier side of town left him with neither an arrest nor a suspect for either robbery.

THE GUNFIGHT THAT NEVER WAS

An overnight snowfall had dusted the streets of Tombstone as the sun rose on Tuesday January 17th. It was cold and windy, with the remaining snow slowly melting away by mid-morning. The Earp family was still holed up at the Cosmopolitan Hotel, and watching the cow-boy's moves around town. Ringo, and an ever changing number of cow-boys, still maintained a headquarters at the Grand Hotel, waiting for their next nefarious opportunity. In yet another confrontation, the townsfolk witnessed one of the greatest "what-ifs" in gunfight history.

Johnny Ringo, who was awaiting a court date the next morning, ran into Wyatt Earp and Doc Holliday on Allen Street in front of the Occidental Saloon around mid-afternoon. Some accounts claim that Ringo calmly walked up to Wyatt and invited him to step out in the street and draw. Others said Ringo walked up to Wyatt and told him what he thought of him. Those who were in support of Ringo said Earp cowardly walked away, while others saw Wyatt as the cooler head who considered it as neither the time nor the place.

Doc Holliday, on the other hand, played it quite differently, and wasted no time in stepping out to challenge Ringo. The story has been told in so many ways that it's hard to know what is true. In one of the least dramatic, and probably most accurate versions, Doc challenged Ringo, and the two began to square off. Wyatt got to Doc and turned him, while Jim Flynn grabbed Ringo from behind. Newly elected police chief Dave Neagle intervened, arresting Wyatt, Doc, and Ringo. The charge for each was carrying a firearm, for which Wyatt was dismissed as a U.S. Marshal. Doc and Ringo were fined $32.00 each.

George Parsons, who surely can be quoted with confidence, wrote in his diary for January 17, 1882;

Snow yesterday. Light fall. Much blood in the air this afternoon. Ringo and Doc Holliday came nearly having it with pistols. Ben Maynard and Rickabaugh later tried to kick each other's lungs out. Bad time expected with the cowboy leader [John Ringo] and DH [Doc Holliday]. I passed both not knowing blood was up. One with hand in breast pocket and the other probably ready. Earp just beyond.

Crowded street and looking like another battle. Police vigilant for once and both disarmed. [78]

The episode between Ben Maynard and Lou Rickabaough stemmed from a confrontation Maynard had with one of the members of Wyatt Earp's posse. Maynard was so angry that he got in Wyatt's face over it. Rickabaugh, a staunch supporter and friend of Wyatt's, took exception to Maynard's actions causing the two men to come to blows. In the days that followed, arguments between those who saw the incident from their own loyalties caused the tension in Tombstone to grow. Some wanted more pressure placed on the cow-boys, while Behan tried to quiet the conversation by claiming the entire episode had been overblown.

On February 4, 1882, *The San Diego Union* ran a column submitted by Clara Brown;

"While there is much to encourage the settlers on this new country, there is also an element of lawlessness, an insecurity of life and property, an open disregard of the proper authorities, which has greatly retarded the advancement of this place. It has occasioned much annoyance and loss among men who have invested their little all in Arizona's resources, not to speak of the lives that have fallen a sacrifice to a set of unprincipled beings who are above working for an honest living. Worse and worse the evil has grown until now the state of affairs in this camp is far worse than in the early days of its settlement."

The next day, January 18, 1882, Ringo appeared in court to stand for the Galeyville saloon robbery. When none of the witnesses showed up, Judge William Stillwell rescheduled the trial for February 1st. On Tuesday January 24th, Ringo appeared in court once again for the charge of stealing the horse with much the same result. Judge Stillwell, a bit fed up, revoked Ringo's initial bond, and had him jailed until the new higher bond was paid. John Dunbar, Al Woods, and Thomas Moses said they would stand for the bond. Believing the bond to have been posted, Breakenridge released Ringo, but in fact it had not been accepted, making Ringo a fugitive the moment he left town.

---

[78] A Tenderfoot in Tombstone; George Parsons. Pgs.201-202

CHARLESTON

Wyatt Earp and his posse left town on Monday the 23rd with warrants for Ike Clanton, Phin Clanton, and Pony Deal. With $3,000.00 in hand, the instruction for use from Marshal Crawley Dake was for the purpose of apprehending stage robbers, and other federal matters. For Wyatt, it was a two-for-one. He wanted these men for their involvement in Virgil's shooting as well as stage robbery. Those who saw the men as they rode out speculated as to their true purpose. Each man was heavily armed, which raised questions from most of the town regarding their true intentions. The cow-boys wondered the same and strengthened their numbers around Charleston. Later in the day, word reached town that the Earp posse had been seen riding very close to a party of fifteen to twenty cowboys, ready for revenge. Tombstone once again waited in anticipation of the worst, but the two factions never crossed.

With Wyatt and Morgan out of town, James Earp initiated the paper work for a warrant to track down Ringo, and return him to custody. James feared a clash between Wyatt and Ringo, and those concerns were justified. Word of a posse in pursuit of outlaws was commonplace, and raised little concern from townsfolk. But, once they realized that Johnny Ringo was free, and riding toward the Earp party, they began to worry.

For Ringo and his experience in Mason County, Texas this was much the same. He seemed to be doing it all over again, protecting his friends, and pushing back against crooked lawmen with an agenda. The reality of which was not so clear cut as in Texas, but perception being reality, to Ringo it was no different. The Earp posse had left Tombstone with Ringo still incarcerated, and hadn't figured him in the equation. That would surely make a difference. In the early hours of Wednesday January 25th, a posse of twenty-one men, led by John Henry Jackson left Tombstone in pursuit of the Earp posse and Ringo. George Parsons wrote;

"Was routed out of bed night before last to help get a horse for posse which left about four am for Charleston to re-arrest Ringo. Jack headed them and they had quite an experience, but no shooting."

According to Billy Breakenridge in his book, *Helldorado,* when the posse reached the bridge into Charleston, they were surrounded by cow-boys, then disarmed and detained in a saloon. Ringo, who was present, rode back to Tombstone to clear up matters, and the posse was released. Others reported the event a bit differently with Jackson running into Ringo quite by chance. After reaching Charleston in the morning hours, Jackson and his men stowed their firearms and entered the Occidental Hotel for breakfast. Much to their surprise, they ran headlong into Ike Clanton and Johnny Ringo. Ringo, apparently unaware that he had left Tombstone ahead of the bail approval, agreed to go back, but he would not be arrested. The posse was detained to give Ringo some distance between them, but released without issue. Holding to his word, Ringo rode into Tombstone and turned himself in. Jackson's posse arrived around 4:00 pm to find their bird already in the cage.

Townsfolk still harbored misgivings with regard to the Earp posse. Those who saw the October shootout as murder, considered the pretense of a law and order posse to be more of the same. To help soothe matters, Jim Carr, the new mayor, issued a statement in support of the Earp posse, and asked that the townsfolk remain calm and let him do his job.

> *"I am informed by His Honor, William H. Stillwell, Judge of the district Court of the First Judicial District, Cochise County, that Wyatt S. Earp, who left the city yesterday with a posse, was entrusted with warrants for the arrest of divers persons charged with criminal offences. I request the public within this city to abstain from any interference with the execution of said warrants."* [79]

Confusion was the norm of the day. With the Earp posse focusing their efforts on Charleston in search of the two Clantons and Pony Deal, John Jackson's posse was back in Tombstone. After a bit of humiliation, the Jackson posse was instrumental in locating Johnny Ringo and initiating his return. At the same time, Charles Bartholomew, driver of the Hubbard & Co. stage which had been robbed, on January 6th, headed up a third posse to find and support the Earp posse. With little rest, the determined John Jackson saddled up and went along.

Wyatt and his men had set up camp approximately three miles outside of Tombstone. William Herring, one of Wyatt's attorneys, had agreed to deliver grain and information to the posse, and did so late on Monday night. Jackson's posse brought word that Ringo was on the loose, and awaiting them on the

Charleston Bridge

---

[79] Tombstone A.T A History of Early Mining Milling and Mayhem; William Shillingberg pg. 298

west side of the Charleston Bridge. Jackson went on from there to his ill-fated encounter with Ike Clanton and Ringo, but returned with Charles Bartholomew the following night.

Once joined by the Bartholomew posse, Wyatt had the force of men he needed to initiate a door by door search which required them to control all movements, both in and out of town. He was now on offense, with no intention of backing down. With his newly found authority and vehemence for apprehending Virgil's assailants, Wyatt and his men terrorized the Charlestown citizenry. They stopped everything and everybody who might have offered the cow-boys shelter, with one of the first being Ben Maynard. Maynard said he was greeted near the bridge with; "Stop you son-of-a-bitch horse thief!" With his animosity toward Wyatt, this didn't set well, but the number of gun barrels focused in his direction was enough to encourage his mouth to stay shut.

Used as a shield, Maynard was forced to knock on the doors of those who might have harbored either of the three suspects. He had every reason to comply, and stayed calm. Being stuck in the middle, he would have been in the first line of fire should things go wrong. Wyatt advised that if a shot was fired from any of the buildings, he wouldn't last as long as "A Snowball in Hell."[80] After canvasing the entire village, it became obvious that neither the Clantons nor Pony Deal were around, but they didn't let up.

From Friday the 27th through Sunday the 29th, Wyatt's posse covered the area from Tombstone to Charleston, and the Huachuca Mountains, which were cold and snow covered. Although they were yet to encounter Wyatt and his posse, the Clantons knew they were there. On January 30, 1882, suspecting their ultimate demise if captured, Pony Deal and the Clantons rode up to the Bartholomew posse and surrendered. In a strange twist, on that same day, Dave Neagle rode into Wyatt's camp with a warrant for Sherm McMasters on a charge of stealing two horses back in September – the same day he slipped away from Virgil and headed for Contention.

Deal and the Clantons were escorted back to Tombstone, and turned over to Sheriff Behan at about 2:30 am. Expecting to be held for the January 7th stage robbery, all parties were surprised to find a much different charge – the attempted murder of U.S. Marshal Virgil Earp. Prosecutor William Herring stated that due to the extreme nature of the charges, he asked Judge William Stillwell for a $5,000.00 bond each. The judge settled instead for a lower bond of $1,500.00 each, which was satisfied that day.

---

[80] Wyatt Earp Explorers. Jim Rose

IKE CLANTON IN COURT FEB. 3, 1882

On Monday January 30, 1882 George Parsons met up with Wyatt Earp just outside of Charleston.

> The preliminary examination of Isaac Clanton, charged with the attempted murder of Virgil Earp, was held last night before Judge Stilwell, who was sitting as an examining magistrate.
>
> Drs. Goodfellow and Mathews, the attending physicians, were called and testified as to the nature of the wounds received by Earp.
>
> Sherman McMasters testified that he was in Charleston about the 1st of January, and that during a conversation Ike Clanton said he "would have to go up and do the job over again"
>
> Messrs. McKelvey, Handy, Russell, Calwell, Ayers, Clark and Frost were then called, and each testified that Clanton was in Charleston on the night of the attempt d murder. These witnesses were subjected to a rigid examination, and an alibi having been established, the accused was discharged.

Arizona Daily Star: February 4, 1882

"Got off this A.M. about 9:30 leading my horse and riding Sam. Packed my horse at Charleston with grub. Met the Earp posse on the outskirts of Charleston returning to town, their parties having surrendered at Tombstone. Came in and delivered up. Charleston looks almost like a deserted village and as though having undergone a siege. Cold in the mountains. Snow and ice." [81]

---

[81] A Tenderfoot in Tombstone; George Parsons pg. 204

THE EARPS RESIGN

With all their exposure and hard work, life was not improving for the Earps. Their true intensions in the backcountry had become suspect at best. Enough so that those for whom they held warrants, chose to turn themselves in rather than risk arrest by the Earp posse. Virgil had been shot in October, and lost his City Police Chief position. In December, he was shot again, and lost his ability to perform the duties of a Deputy U.S. Marshal. In a matter of poor timing, former city policeman, T.J. Cornelison was released from jail after seven months behind bars. Cornelison had been charged with theft after going through a lady's trunk behind her back. Virgil Earp made the arrest. It was a charge, which Cornelison claimed, Virgil told him he could make go away for a bribe of $100.00. According to Cornelison, he refused to pay, choosing jail instead.

BEHAN IN THE HOT SEAT

Not to be left out, Sheriff John Behan was charged with perjury on the same day Pony Deal and the Clantons turned themselves in. The charge was brought against Behan by Tombstone merchant, Sylvester Comstock for twice submitting the same $365.00 bill to the county for payment. When Judge Stillwell was selected for the case, Behan's attorney, James Southard, objected, and shocked the court by asking for a change of venue. Stillwell was insulted, and denied the request, stating that any judge who would not hear a case based on its merit was no more than a prostitute.

It was obvious that Behan was guilty, and it wasn't the first time, which forced Southard to change the argument. It was customary to submit all receipts for reimbursement under oath as a surety that the request was valid. Southard argued that Richard Rule, clerk of the board of supervisors, did not have the authority to administer an oath, therefore no perjury could exist. Judge Stillwell concluded that by technicality Southard was correct and dismissed the charge.

The disharmony spawned by Behan's arrest simply threw another log on the fire. The *Epitaph* editorialized the evidence of a dishonest sheriff, while the *Nugget* railed against a trumped-up charge designed to craft further discourse in town.

On February 1, 1882 a meeting of the Tombstone Republican Club was held in the courtroom of Judge A.O. Wallace. In that meeting was United States Marshal Crawley Dake. The stated purpose of the gathering was; "to take steps toward harmonizing the Republican Party in view of present complications." More plainly said, they wanted Marshal Dake to appoint new deputy marshals. The desired outcome as stated by city council clerk B.C. Quigley was to appoint "men who were not allied with either faction of the parties who are now distracting our community." Quigley's sentiment was reinforced

Crawley P. Dake

by a number of speakers expressing the same concern. As a result, a five-man council headed by Mayor Jim Carr was appointed to recommend proper replacements for the Marshal's consideration. It was a direct and unapologetic repudiation of the Earps.[82]

The Earps were done, and they knew it. The only option they had was to proactively resign simply to avoid the inevitable dismissal. On February 2, 1882 Wyatt presented Marshal Dake with a letter written by Earp attorney Tom Fitch, and signed by Wyatt and Virgil Earp.

"While we have a deep sense of obligation to many of the citizens for their hearty cooperation in aiding us to suppress lawlessness, and their faith in our honesty of purpose, we realize that there had arisen so much harsh criticism in relation to our operations, and such a persistent effort having been made to misrepresent and misinterpret our acts, we are led to the conclusion that it is our duty to place our resignations as deputy United States marshals in your hands, which we now do, thanking you for the continued courtesy and confidence in our integrity, and shall remain subject to your orders in the performance of any duties which may be assigned to us, only until our successors are appointed."[83]

A slightly different version was printed in the Tombstone Epitaph on February 2, 1882; Major C.P. Dake, United States Marshal, Grand Hotel, Tombstone-

---

[82] Tombstone A.T.; A History of Early Mining, Milling and Mayhem. Pg. 302
[83] Ibid.

Dear Sir:

In exercising our official functions as deputy United States marshals in this territory, we have endeavored always unflinchingly to perform the duties entrusted to us. These duties have been exacting and perilous in their character, having to be performed in a community where turbulence and violence could almost any moment be organized to thwart and resist the enforcement of the process of the court issued to bring criminals to justice. And while we have a deep sense of obligation to many of the citizens for their hearty cooperation in aiding us to suppress lawlessness, and their faith in our honesty of purpose, we realize that, notwithstanding our best efforts and judgement in everything which we have been required to perform, there has arisen so much harsh criticism in relation to our operations, and such a persistent effort having been made to misrepresent and misinterpret our acts, we are led to the conclusion that, in order to convince the public that it is our sincere purpose to promote the public welfare, independent of any personal emolument or advantages to ourselves, it is our duty to place our resignations as deputy United States marshals in your hands, which we now do, thanking you for your continued courtesy and confidence in our integrity, and shall remain subject to your orders in the performance of any duties which may be assigned to us, only until our successors are appointed.

Very respectfully yours,

Virgil W. Earp.
Wyatt S. Earp.[84]

Marshal Dake accepted the Republican Club's recommendation of John Jackson as a Cochise County deputy marshal, and appointed him as the "regular" deputy. He did not, however, accept the Earp's resignations nor rescind their appointments. In an effort to calm the waters, Wyatt sent a message to Ike Clanton, expressing a desire to end their feud. Clanton without hesitation rejected Wyatt's overture. To the contrary, Ike Clanton had retained attorneys Ben Goodrich and J.S. Robinson. In Contention City on February 9th, they filed a complaint before Justice of the Peace J.B. Smith against the three Earp Brothers, and Doc Holliday for the murder of Billy Clanton, and Tom and Frank McLaury. In return, Judge Smith issued an order; "To any Sheriff, Constable, Marshal, or Policeman in the

[84] Tombstone Epitaph February 2, 1882

Territory of Arizona, Greetings." The order commanded those addressed to "arrest the above-named Wyatt Earp, Morgan Earp, Virgil Earp, and J.H. Holliday and bring them forthwith before me at my office on Main Street in the Village of Contention, in the County of Cochise, Territory of Arizona."[85]

On February 11th, William Herring filed a writ of habeas corpus with Judge J.H. Drum. Drum quickly recused himself as he had served as Doc Holliday's attorney during the initial Spicer hearing. The writ, and the case was passed back to Justice of the Peace J.B. Smith who denied the habeas request. February 14th was a dark and rainy day in Tombstone, but failed to hinder yet another flurry of activity. To avoid an arrest, Wyatt informed Sheriff Behan that they would go to Contention to answer the charge. Having been cleared of the shootings back in November, the Earps considered Ike's purpose for filing another charge in Contention to be nothing more than a set up for an ambush. To avoid trouble, twelve armed men rode with the Earps, Doc Holliday, and their attorney, William Herring, to Contention. Before they left Tombstone, John Behan asked Wyatt to give up his pistol, but Wyatt refused. Behan didn't press the matter any further.

On February 15th George Parsons wrote;

Weather rainy and very disagreeable Bad time on street today. Policeman just prevented Ben Maynard and [Dan] Tipton from shooting one another. Yesterday Earps were taken to Contention to be tried for the killing of Clanton. Quite a posse went out. Many of Earp's friends accompanied armed to the teeth. They came back late in the day, the good people below beseeching them to leave and try case here. A bad time is expected again in town at any time. Earps on one side of the street with their friends and Ike Clanton and Ringo on the other side with theirs – watching each other. Hope no innocents will be killed.[86]

In court at Charleston William Herring made a motion that the case be transferred to Tombstone, which Judge Smith happily granted. On February 15th, the defendants, along with William Herring stood before Judge Smith, where attorney Herring asked to see "the complaint and depositions upon which said warrant had been alleged and issued."[87] Judge

---

[85] And To Die in the West; The Story of the O.K. Corral Gunfight; Paula Mitchell Marks. Pg. 334
[86] A Tenderfoot in Tombstone; George Parsons Pg. 206
[87] And Die in the West; The Story of the O.K. Corral Gunfight. Paula Mitchell Marks. Pg.335

Smith admitted to not having it with him, and attempted to continue the case once again. Herring immediately went to Judge Lucas with another writ of habeas corpus, which he granted. The case was dismissed on the grounds that it had already been heard and decided by Judge Wells Spicer on November 30, 1881.[88] Although he was cleared, Wyatt was placed under additional financial stress with the cost of representation by William Herring. Wyatt was cleared, but forced to take a loan for $365.00. Attorney James Howard loaned Wyatt the money, in today's dollars' worth approximately $9,250.00, using his Fremont home as security. Wyatt was never able to repay the loan. In 1884 Howard foreclosed on the property.

IN the police court yesterday before Judge Wallace, Ben Maynard and D. G. Tipton were each fined $30 and costs for carrying deadly weapons.

ROBERT ECCLESTON, ESQ., returned from his visit East last evening looking hale and hearty. His many friends were pleased to welcome his return.

A WARRANT was issued by Judge Spicer yesterday for the arrest of Ben Maynard, charged with an assault with attempt to kill, being sworn out on complaint of B. R. Tipton.

Tombstone Weekly Epitaph Feb. 20, 1882

Change was inevitable. Lou Rickabaugh had had enough, and left Tombstone for San Francisco on February 3rd. A few days later, Wells Fargo agent, Marshal Williams left town heading for Brooklyn, New York. Rumors swirled concerning Williams' business practices, but an audit of the Wells Fargo books found no worthy improprieties.

February 18, 1882, Wyatt Earp and his posse were back on the trail in search of Pony Deal for the January 6th stage robbery. At least that was what they said. Pony Deal was rumored to be in jail in Cisco, Texas at the time, but the Earp posse didn't return to Tombstone until February 24th. When word reached Marshal Dake that Wyatt was still leading a posse as

---

[88] The Truth About Wyatt Earp; Richard Irwin. Pgs. 391-392

a U.S. Marshal, Dake became concerned. He assumed, for Wyatt's sake, that he was out serving old warrants, but advised the locals that John Jackson was now his deputy in the area.

CHAPTER ELEVEN

SHOT IN THE DARK

March seemed to martial in a long overdue respite for the folks in Tombstone. The weather was becoming more agreeable, with the muddy streets becoming more passable. The cowboys weren't dominating every corner, and even the Apache had left the area after a bloodless run through Sulphur Springs Valley, where they stole approximately 200 horses from Henry Hooker.

On March 10th, Clara Brown wrote;

> *"There being a lull in cow-boy criminality, which we hope is something more than temporary, and the Indians apparently having left the Dragoons, Tombstone people have been obliged to look to other causes for excitement.[89] "*

March 15th, Virgil Earp ventured out of the Cosmopolitan Hotel for the first time since the shooting. It was an unusual quiet, which made Wyatt Earp very uneasy. He too was aware of the absence of known cowboys roaming the streets, and making themselves a nuisance. But what he saw, which eluded the attention of others, were the unfamiliar faces showing up in town. On March 17th, the weather had turned once again to a cold wind and rain. Wyatt was vigilant, and watching for strangers. Late in the day, he witnessed a small gathering of men he'd never seen. It was a bad sign, and the one he'd expected.

The next day, Wyatt met Briggs Goodrich on the street and pulled him aside. Goodrich was the older brother to Ben Goodrich who had represented most of the cow-boys at one time or another, Briggs knew them all as well.

---

[89] Printed in the San Diego Union March 13, 1882

"I think they were after us last night." Wyatt began. "Do you know anything about it?"

"No." Goodrich replied.

"Do you think we are in any danger?" Wyatt asked.

"You're liable to get it in the neck anytime." Goodrich replied.

Wyatt led Goodrich a bit by saying that he hadn't seen any of the crowd in town lately. Goodrich's reply confirmed Wyatt's take on the situation; "I think I see some strangers here that I think are after you." Goodrich replied. Before Wyatt spoke, Goodrich added; "By the way, John Ringo wanted me to tell you that if any fight came between you all, that he wanted you to understand that he would have nothing to do with it; that he was going to look out for himself, and anybody else could do the same.[90]

Later in the day, Goodrich met up with Ringo on Allen Street where they saw two heavily armed men pass by. Goodrich assumed they may be friends of the Earps carrying extra firearms to the Cosmopolitan for increased protection. Ringo disagreed. He was sure they were not connected to the Earps.[91]

The conversation between Goodrich and Ringo would suggest his lack of personal involvement in the current conflict. As on other occasions, Ringo wished to make it clear that he was looking out for himself, and should trouble arise, to leave him out of it. In such regard, Ringo was rarely, if ever, at the center of prior conflicts, he seemed to come in after the fact. His role, as he proved time and again, was in support of others. Ringo seemed to constantly be at odds with the law, but by his own actions, not as an instigator, as were others.

Wyatt's Worst Fear

March 18, 1882 - The rain didn't let up, and neither did Morgan Earp. He was thirty years old, just a month shy of his thirty first birthday, but Morgan was still very much a kid at heart. He was a prankster, and risk taker, which is perhaps the reason that Doc Holliday favored his company. Wyatt had told Morgan of his concerns, but in spite of the inclement weather, and warnings from his brother, Morgan was insistent upon attending the latest play at Schieffelin Hall.

---

[90] Goodrich provided this information while under oath during the Morgan Earp coroner's inquest #68 on March 22, 1882

[91] Tombstone A.T. A History in Milling, Mining and Mayhem. Wm.Shillingberg. Pg. 307

It was opening night of a new comedy named *Stolen Kisses*. It was against his better judgement, but Wyatt, along with Dan Tipton, and Doc Holliday, conceded to Morgan's request and went along. In the lobby of Schieffelin Hall, Briggs Goodrich saw the Earps, and told them what he and Ringo had seen. "You fellows will catch it tonight if you don't look out." He warned.

After the play, Wyatt insisted they get off the street, and return to the hotel. Doc Holliday went home, but Morgan talked Wyatt into stopping off at Campbell & Hatch's Saloon for a game of billiards on the way. Wyatt relented. Dan Tipton went along. Together they walked the two hundred forty-two steps from the front door of Schieffelin Hall, crossing Fremont, then down Fourth Street, turning left onto Allen

Dan Tipton

Street before entering the billiard hall on the left. For three men walking in conversation, the time frame would be approximately three and one-half minutes.[92] The shooters had total cover to wait on the Allen side of Fremont, watch for the Earp party to leave the hall, then slip in behind Campbell & Hatch before they arrived. Sherm McMasters was there when they walked in at approximately 11:00 pm. Morgan and Bob Hatch chose a table in the back, near the door. Wyatt and McMasters sat near the wall, across from the door, while Tipton pulled up a chair closer to the table.

---

[92] Based on a man six feet tall walking at a normal stride. The author made the walk to verify the time and distance involved.

At the beginning of their second game, two rifle shots rang out. The door glass shattered, as one bullet hit the wall just above Wyatt's head, and the other tore its way through Morgan Earp's body. The bullet entered his back on the left side near the spine, ripping through his left kidney, and his liver before exiting the right side near the gallbladder. George Berry, who was standing near the stove at the front of the saloon, caught the spent round in his right thigh. When Morgan fell, Wyatt, McMasters, and Tipton pulled him away from the door, as Bob Hatch

Louisa Earp

ran into the back yard through the card room, but they were gone. Sherm McMasters and Pat Holland, who was in the card room, searched the area behind the building, but the rain and mud had covered any tracks.

Within moments, Dr. William Miller was at the scene, with Drs. Goodfellow and Matthews close behind. Morgan was in great pain as they moved him to a sofa in the card room. His insides were torn up, and he knew he was going to die. Even with three doctors looking on, there was nothing to be done. Once they laid him down, Morgan looked to Bob Hatch; "Hatch, I've played my last game of pool."

With family and friends gathered 'round, Morgan languished for some forty minutes. Virgil, along with Allie, walked the distance from the Cosmopolitan Hotel to be with him. Wyatt, James, and Bessie stood close by. Warren was not in town that evening, but was back to help his brothers transport Morgan's body the next day. Morgan had convinced Louisa to head back to Colton for a while for her own safety. She was in California visiting family at the time of the shooting. Doc was there with Dan Tipton, and Sherm McMasters, waiting for the inevitable, as well as instructions from Wyatt.

George Parsons wrote on March 19th – It was Wyatt Earps thirty fourth birthday, by the way.

Another assassination last night about eleven o'clock. I heard the shots, two in number, but hearing so many after dark was not particularly startling, though I remarked to Redfern about it. Poor Morgan Earp, was shot through by an unknown party. Probably two or three in number in Campbell and Hatch's, while playing pool with Hatch. The shots, two, came from the ground window leading into the alley running to Fremont Street – on east side of Otis' & Co's store. Geo Berry received the spent ball in his thigh, sustaining a flesh wound. The second shot was fired apparently at Wyatt Earp. Murderers got away, of course, but it was and is quite evident who committed the deed. The man is Stillwell in all probability. For two cowardly, sneaking attempts at murder, this and the shots at Virgil E, when I came nearly getting dose, rank at the head. Morgan lived about 40 minutes after being shot and died without a murmur. Bad times ahead now.[93]

On Sunday, Andrew Ritter was tasked with transporting Morgan's body from Tombstone to the Contention railhead. Around 12:30 pm, the hearse, accompanied by family and armed protectors proceeded down Allen Street in route for Contention. It was, for the entire town, a sad sight to watch as the small precession rolled down the street toward the stage road. Once at the train station, Morgan's remains were loaded onto the train, with James Earp riding along to see his brother home. Wyatt, Warren and the rest of the Earp posse returned to Tombstone to ride the same route again the next day.

Allie Earp

Virgil and Allie packed what they could take with them, and prepared for the trip back to Colton California the next day. On March 20th, they boarded the train in Contention. Wyatt's intention was to escort them as far as Benson, expecting a safe transfer in Tucson. From there it should have been an uneventful ride to the safety of Colton California. Wyatt got word in Benson that Ike Clanton and Frank Stillwell were in Tucson, with cow-boys watching every train with hopes of killing Virgil. Wyatt's decision to go on to Tucson was twofold. Virgil's protection was paramount, but Frank Stillwell was there, which would save him a lot of time.

---

[93] A Tenderfoot in Tombstone; George Parsons. Pg.212

When they arrived in Tucson, Doc left the train first to check the platform, and stow his shotguns at the station. Deputy U.S. Marshal J.W. Evans met Wyatt and his posse as they exited the train along with Virgil & Allie Earp in route for the Potter Hotel for dinner. As they walked back to the train, Wyatt spotted two men lying flat on one of the cars close to the engine, he recognized one of them as Frank Stillwell, and suspected the other to be Ike Clanton. They spotted Wyatt looking their way and ran, but Wyatt followed, catching up with Stillwell, while the one he suspected to be Clanton had slipped away in the dark.

In the darkness, Stillwell stood shaking before Wyatt Earp with a shotgun pointed at his belly. Stillwell couldn't move. Wyatt later recalled; "What a coward he was. He couldn't shoot when I came near him. He stood there helpless and trembling for his life. As I rushed upon him. He put out his hands and clutched at my shotgun. I let go both barrels, and he stumbled down dead and mangled at my feet."[94] Although he was armed, John Behan's ex-deputy was too afraid to pull his pistol.

George Parsons, March 20, 1882;

A little cool again. Morg Earp's body sent to Colton yesterday, and today Virgil Earp and his wife left for that place. A body guard, well-armed, accompanied Virg Earp, and tonight came news of Frank Stillwell's body being found riddled with bullets and buckshot. A quick vengeance, and a bad character sent to Hell, where he will be the chief attraction until a few more accompany him.[95]

George Hand, butcher, saloon owner, and diarist, was in Tucson, and viewed the body the next morning. He wrote;

George Hand

Frank Stillwell was shot all over, the worst shot up man I ever saw. He was found a few hundred yards from the hotel on the railroad tracks. It is supposed to be the work of Doc Holliday and the Earps,

---

[94] The Life and Times of Doc Holliday; Gary Roberts. Pg.246
[95] A Tenderfoot in Tombstone. George Parsons. Pg. 212

but they were not found. Holliday and the Earps knew that Stillwell shot Morg Earp and they were bound to get him.[96]

Dr. Dexter Lyford examined Stillwell's body the next morning at Smith's Funeral Parlor. His report included wounds coming from a heavily charged buckshot blast at close range which shredded the liver and abdomen. Another shotgun blast that shattered the left leg. A single shot from a rifle or revolver had passed through the body from armpit to armpit, passing through the upper portion of both lungs, the gunpowder burning his coat. There was also a rifle wound in the upper left arm, and another in the right thigh.[97]

BEHAN'S ALLIANCE

To say that John Behan and Wyatt Earp were adversaries would be a gross understatement. By the time Behan arrived in Tombstone in 1880, his resume in law enforcement was more extensive than Wyatt's, but Behan was first and foremost a politician. Wyatt, by contrast was dedicated to the "law and order" ambitions held by many of the town's newcomers, but he had no political instincts. Behan held an upper hand on Wyatt in many ways, but he never had the grit to be an effective lawman. Behan was a Democrat in an area settled by Texans and Southerners bringing with them a strong Democratic leaning. The Earps, coming from the mid-west, were northern supporters, with Virgil and James having fought for the Union Army. They were staunch Republicans attempting to effect change in an area of dominate Democrat philosophies.

PACIFIC COAST NEWS.

The Arizona Trouble—The Earps and Their Opponents.

TOMBSTONE, March 23d.—The Coroner's jury find that Morgan S. Earp came to his death at the hands of Frank Stillwell, who was killed next day at Tucson. Pete Spence, one Freis and two half-breed Indians. Pete Spence's wife exposed the plot. A Sheriff's posse, consisting of twenty men, mostly cowboys, left this morning for Dragoon mountains, where the Earps are supposed to be at present. The Sheriff made a weak attempt to arrest them at the Cosmopolitan Hotel before they left, but Wyatt Earp told him he didn't want to see him; that he had seen him once too often, and thereupon the Earp party mounted their horses and rode away. There is a very uneasy feeling among the cowboy element, as the Earps are rendered desperate by the attempted assassination of Virgil Earp and the cold-blooded murder of Morgan Earp.

---

[96] Next Stop: Tombstone. George hand's Contention City Diary, 1882. Neil Carmony. Pg. 10
[97] Tombstone A.T. A History of Milling, Mining, and Mayhem. William Shillingberg. Pg.313

Alliances for the Earps were not difficult with the influx of businessmen and investors wishing to protect their stake in an unsettled land, but the numbers were in Behan's favor. He too had a plethora of supporters who liked the quick and easy money brought to town through the auspices of 'ranchers' who were nothing more than rustlers and highwaymen selling cheap stolen cattle. When the two clashed, the Earps always seemed to win the legal arguments, but never got a conviction, or locked away any cow-boy from their efforts in a Tombstone court.

After the shooting of Virgil Earp in December '81, Ike Clanton's hat was found near the scene. It was enough for an arrest and indictment, but with a few dubious alibis swearing on the Holy Bible that he was somewhere else at the time, the judge had no choice but to dismiss the charge. It was bad enough for Judge William Stillwell to pull Wyatt aside and offer a bit of sober advice. "You will never clean up this crowd this way. Next time you'd better leave your prisoners out in the brush where alibis don't count." It was time for Wyatt to do just that.

On Tuesday night, March 21st, the Earp party quietly returned to Tombstone and the Cosmopolitan Hotel. They had left Tucson on foot, and quickly walked to the Papago railroad station then flagged down a freight train back to Contention, where they picked up their horses from the livery then back to Tombstone. It was to be a short stay, only to gather ammo, and supplies for a long stay in the backcountry. Charles Meyer, Pima County justice of the peace, had wired Tombstone to let the sheriff know that Wyatt was wanted for the murder of Stillwell, and to arrest him if he returned.

Make no mistake, Behan was afraid of Wyatt Earp. His failure to arrest the Earp party came as no surprise, and was followed by the usual litany of excuses. He first said they had all pulled their weapons on him, which was disputed by every bystander on the street. What Behan had tried to pass off as brandishing their firearms was said to be rifles pointed up in a usual fashion. Others, including Wyatt, said he never attempted an arrest, only to approach the party with; "I want to see you." He had no warrant, and made no gesture to execute an arrest, to which Wyatt replied; "If you're not careful, Johnny, you might see me once too often." As Behan watched, Wyatt Earp and his men saddled up, and rode unmolested toward the Dragoons.

George Parsons March 21, 1882;

Exciting times again this evening. The Earp party returned this afternoon and Behan tried to arrest them tonight from a telegram. They refused arrest, and retired from town, first though waiting for

Behan and Neagle to do what they threatened. Bad muss this. Sheriff is awake now that one of his friends is killed. Couldn't do anything before. Things are very rotten in that office.[98]

---

[98] A Tenderfoot in Tombstone; George Parsons Pg. 213

CHAPTER TWELVE

THE RECKONING

"Oh, make no mistake, it's not revenge he's after... It's a reckoning."

I know, it's a movie line, yet a most accurate description for a man whose purpose was to exact justice. It was about making it right, not just getting even. In a world that had turned upside down, Wyatt Earp was doing his best to make sense of it all. Although he still wore a badge, he was now a fugitive. In turn Johnny Ringo was riding lead behind Sheriff Behan, deputized, and wearing a badge.

Behan left Tombstone with a posse of six men who rode directly to Contention to meet up with Pima County Sheriff Bob Paul. Paul carried the original warrants for the men suspected in the killing of Stillwell, but his primary motivation was more likely to keep an eye on those who would be chasing down his friend. Behan asked Bob Paul to join him, but Paul refused by saying he would never ride with such a gang.

Behan was in a predicament of his own making. The honest men of Tombstone would have nothing to do with his posse, and truth be known, most were invigorated by Wyatt Earp's endeavor. Behan went to Charleston where he would find men who weren't afraid, or even relished the idea of facing down the Earp party. Behan knew that without a band of rustlers, and outlaws to call a posse, that he had no chance. Of the twenty-five men he deputized, half were cow-boys including Hank Swilling, and Phin Clanton, with Ringo riding close to the front. Behan's posse wasn't well received by Tombstone residents. The town's impression of their sheriff as less than a brave man was solidified with a low expectation that he would be successful.

Always the insider, George Parsons penned the following on Thursday March 23rd;

...Paul is here, but will not take a hand. He is a true, brave man himself and will not join the murderous posse here. If the truth were

known he would be glad to see the Earp party get away with all these murderous outfits...[99]

His expectation of the men he'd chosen, was seriously overrated. In reality, it was more likely that most of the men in whom he'd placed his trust wouldn't stand and fight. Ike Clanton ran from every fight he ever started. Hank Swilling was a back-shooter, who knew Wyatt Earp was after him. He knew the fate that awaited him from Frank Stillwell's demise. Other than John Ringo, the rest were good at ambushing a man, but not so much at standing face to face. Ringo had proven his grit in Texas, and probably the only one in the bunch that would actually stand for a fight.[100]

George Parsons, March 22, 1882:

"Excitement again this morning. Sheriff went out with a posse supposedly to arrest the Earp party, but they will never do it. The cowboy element is backing him strongly, John Ringo being one of the party. There is a prospect of a bad time and there are about three men who deserve to get it in the back of the neck. Terrible thing, this, for our town, but the sooner it is all over the better.[101]"

MORGAN EARP INQUEST
ARIZONA DAILY STAR MARCH 24, 1882

[On March 21st,] Marietta D. Spence, being sworn, testified as follows; Resides in town, and am wife of Peter Spence. Statement –

On last Saturday night, the 18th of March, was in my home on Fremont Street; for two days my husband was not home, but in Charleston, but came home about 12 o'clock p.m. Saturday. He came with two parties, one man named Freis, a German, I don't know the name of the other man, but he lives in the home of Manuel Acusto. Each one had a rifle. Immediately after arriving, he sent a man to take care of the horses, and take them to the home of Manuel Acusto. They then entered the front room and began to converse with Frank Stillwell. When they finished, Frank Stillwell went out, and Spence went to bed. This is all that happened that night. Spence remained in bed until 9 o'clock a.m. Sunday. Freis slept there. The other man went to his house; I never heard his name. Stillwell came to the house on

---

[99] A Tenderfoot in Tombstone; George Parsons. Pg. 213
[100] John Ringo; The Gunfighter Who Never Was. Jack Barrows. Pg. 40
[101] A Tenderfoot in Tombstone. George Parsons. Pg. 213

Friday and stayed all day; went out Friday night, but returned in a short time to sleep. Saturday he was out all day and up to 12 o'clock at night when Spence came in. There was an Indian with Stillwell called Charley. He was armed with a pistol and carbine. He left Saturday morning with Stillwell and came back with him at 12 o'clock at night, and left about two hours after Stillwell did. Both Charley and Stillwell were armed with pistols and carbines when they returned to the house Saturday night. The conversation between Spence and Stillwell and the others was carried out in a low tone. They seemed to be talking some secret. When they came in I got out of bed to receive them and noticed they were excited. Why I didn't know ... On Saturday morning Spence told me to get breakfast about 6 o'clock, which I did, after we had a quarrel, during which he struck me and my mother, and during which he threatened to shoot me, when my mother told him he would have to shoot her too. His expression was that if I said a word about something I knew about he would kill me; that he was going to Sonora and would leave my dead body behind him. Spence didn't tell me, but I knew he had killed Morgan Earp ...

Marietta's testimony concerning the time line of Pete Spence's whereabouts was a bit contradictory, but she was convinced they had killed Morgan Earp. The other men involved were Florentino Cruz, and Hank Swilling. The man she called Fries was a German by the name of Frederick Bode.

On Wednesday March 22, 1882, the Earp posse broke camp at the Dragoons, and headed toward the South Pass. They had a short, but concise roster of men involved in the death of Morgan Earp. Marietta had given up the names at the inquest the day before, but they were already known by the Earp party. It was around noon on March 22nd when the Earp party consisting of Wyatt & Warren Earp, Doc Holliday, Sherm McMasters, "Turkey Creek" Jack Johnson, "Texas Jack" Vermillion, Charlie Smith, and Dan Tipton, broke over the hill approaching Pete Spence's wood cutting operation. Little did he know, but Florentino Cruz would be the first name scratched from the list.

Pete Spence wasn't there, but five men including Sam Williams, Ramos Acosta, Florentino Cruz, another half-breed, and Theodore Jude were at the camp, which was little more than a rendezvous point for rustlers. Sam Williams rode off on horseback just before noon to search for mules that had strayed from the camp. Moments before the Earp party arrived, Cruz had left on foot for the same reason. Jude was the first man to encounter Wyatt when he rode up and asked if Spence was there. Jude said no. Spence was actually sitting in jail in Tombstone awaiting trial for the killing of Morgan Earp. Wyatt continued to ask questions about the whereabouts of Hank Swilling, and if Jude was a friend of Spence, and Frank Stillwell. To which he replied that he was. The Earp party soon turned about and headed back to the road.

Cruz saw the posse when they reached the road, and realized he was in trouble. When Wyatt saw him, he left the road in chase, followed by the rest of his men. Jude and Acosta ran toward the hill after the posse left, and got there in time to see Cruz running with shots being fired in his direction. Acosta said he didn't see Cruz fall, but did see the men dismount, then spread out and follow after him. After the report of more gunfire, Jude saw the posse casually walking back to their horses, then ride off in an easterly direction on the road.

It was the next morning when Jude when back to the top of the hill where he'd seen the posse, and began to look for Cruz. When Jude found his body, it was face down with his right arm under his head a few feet from the tracks left by the Earp party. He left the body in place, then saddled a mule and went to Tombstone to report the killing. Accompanied by the coroner, Jude returned to the scene where the body was removed, and examined by Dr. George Goodfellow.

At the coroner's hearing, Dr. Goodfellow testified that he found four wounds on the body. The first shot entered at the right temple, penetrating the brain; the second produced a slight flesh wound in the right shoulder; the third entered the right side of the body, near the liver, and made its exit to the right side of the spine, about five or six inches to the right. The fourth struck in the left thigh and made its exit about six or eight inches above the point of entry.[102]

There was much commentary amongst the townsfolk, as well as the ecclesiastical bloviating in the *Nugget* railing against the unjustified killing of "Indian Charley". Some said he was harmless, although he was a known horse thief. Wyatt Earp saw him as a lookout, and the man who held the horses for those who'd killed Morgan. It was a harsh sentence, and one for which Wyatt Earp had overstepped the bounds of the law. He had now killed two men in cold blood, and there was no turning back.

There were reportedly two posses' now in search of Wyatt Earp. One led by John Behan and Johnny Ringo, the other Charleston cow-boys, deputized by Behan and turned loose to do whatever.

George Hand was in Contention City and wrote in his diary for March 24th;

---

[102] Tombstone Weekly Epitaph; Marsh 27, 1881. Pg.1

"The cow-boys, twenty or more, have been prowling around all morning. They are well mounted, well-armed, and seem intent on business. They are in search for the Earp party, who took breakfast 2 miles above here this morning, 3 a.m. they again came from the direction of Tombstone, watered their horses here

Curly Bill Stood Here

and started again at the double quick for Kinnear's ranch.[103] "

In need of cash and supplies, the Earp party rode back in the direction of Tombstone and rested while waiting to meet with supporters. The only law in town were deputies Billy Breakenridge, and Dave Neagle. They were there keeping up the routine of law and order while Behan and Ringo roamed around from the Dragoons and points west. There was word from Contention that Curly Bill was riding lead in another posse comprised entirely of Charleston outlaws, who were now chasing down the Earp party. Behan would swear he never commissioned their posse, or deputized Curly Bill or any of his crew. Whether that be true or not, he opened that door the moment he pinned a badge on Ringo and Ike Clanton.

On Thursday evening March 23rd, John Behan, who had returned alone, arrested Dan Tipton and Charlie Smith as they entered town. The charges were resisting an officer of the law, and conspiracy, but they were bogus. George Parsons – *"Tip and Smith arrested this evening while entering town. Much excitement. Behan will get it yet."* Bail was quickly raised with Tipton and Smith back on their mission of raising money. Behan quickly left town to join his posse as they rode the Arizona backcountry and making every effort to avoid the Earp party.

Wyatt needed $1,000.00, and sent word to mining executive E.B. Gage. Gage eagerly agreed, and provided Charlie Smith with the cash. Smith ran into Dave Neagle, who arrested him again, requiring the Citizen Safety Commission to call on Tony Kraker and Whistling Dick Wright to retrieve the funds and make the delivery.

Friday March 24, 1882. This is where history takes a detour. Wyatt told his biographer, John Flood, that he and his men were camped in an

---

[103] Next Stop Tombstone. George Hand's Contention Diary. Neil Carmony. Pg. 9

area known as "Iron Springs". The purpose for meeting there was to rendezvous with Whistling Dick Wright for the delivery of the loan provided by E.B. Gage. The historic controversy which later arose, (proving there is no such thing as settled history), was that his description of that location did not match the topography of Iron Springs. Wyatt spoke of cottonwood trees, there are no cottonwoods at Iron Springs. According to a hand drawn map, and his memory of events, Wyatt Earp speaks of a shelf at the top of the ridge, which dropped off, and a lone hill to the right of the road. This ridge is actually a small plateau which drops off almost straight down, with the hill that rises several hundred feet to the left as you look down. Wyatt was not familiar with a good portion of the Arizona backcountry, making it quite easy for him to confuse names of one for another.

In 2008, Bill Evans studied the topography of both locations, and began a serious discussion of the true location. Jim Rose, who has studied the site extensively, has misgivings concerning the accuracy of the Iron Springs location, giving its distance from the San Pedro, and North Contention. In 2009, the author visited the location along with historian, and author, Bob Boze Bell, owner and editor of *True West Magazine*, historian Steve Shaw, of *Great American Adventures*, Kevin McNiven, one of the greatest horsemen I've ever ridden beside, and a number of expert riders.

When comparing the location of the line shack, the plateau, and the hills, the Cottonwood Springs location makes sense. Wyatt talks about surprising Curly Bill and his crew. On horseback, as you approach the edge of the plateau, it is the final step of the horse before the valley floor comes into view. That would certainly offer a surprise to those below as well as the rider.

Lone Hill, which is referred to in other writings, is not at Cottonwood Springs, and approximately four miles away. Next to the plateau rises a hill called "Rock Shoulder" several hundred feet in height. We rode to its peak, and down the other side, making our own switch-back as we climbed. It wasn't difficult to cross. It is elevated, but not intimidating. A good horseman accustomed to those mountains, might easily refer to it as a "hill". Other evidence that gives the location credibility, are the remnants of a line shack. Wyatt talked of two men coming out of a line shack and firing upon them. In that visit, we found the crude stone foundation of a line shack with evidence of an outhouse approximately twenty feet away.

Much has been written about the events of those first few moments – how Wyatt was surprised, and how Warren, Doc, and the rest turned tail at the sound of gunfire. With a proper understanding of the terrain, it all makes sense. Riding horseback around Rocky Shoulder you will find the area around the foot to be sandy. No large rocks, or rock shelf, for horseshoes to announce "that company's coming." Also, the horses were tired, and could smell water, they were relaxed and knew it was time for a break. Wyatt was riding ahead. When the first shot was fired by Curly Bill, its report echoed off the hill like thunder. Those slow walking, relaxed horses perked their heads, and with the instincts of a prey animal, bolted, one after another around that hill. Wyatt said his horse reared, and became unmanageable.

By the time Doc, McMasters, and the rest got their horses under control and returned to the plateau, the fighting had commenced. On the floor below, stood Curly Bill Brocius, Pony Deal, Johnny Barnes, Frank Patterson, Milt Hicks, Bill Hicks, Bill Johnson, Ed Lyle, and Johnny Lyle. They were by any definition, John Behan's Charleston posse. As the Earp party regrouped, Texas Jack's mount was shot from under him, pinning his leg under the horse. He tried to pull his Winchester from the scabbard, but it was wedged between the horse and the ground.

Wyatt was taken completely off guard. He had loosened his cartridge belt while riding, and felt it slip down to his knees when he dismounted. In the space of a movement, Wyatt dismounted, pulling at his cartridge belt, while holding the reins of an unruly horse, and unlimbered his shotgun. All the while, gunfire is blazing. Within minutes, the saddle horn was shot off Wyatt's saddle, he took a bullet in the heel of his boot, which convinced him that he'd been shot in the leg, not to mention his long coat was riddled with buckshot. All the while...Wyatt Earp never got so much as a scratch.

Once he was square on his feet, Wyatt leveled his shotgun and fired. Curley Bill was cut almost in half with the full force of the buckshot drilling him directly in his chest. Doc said he counted some thirty or forty shots before they made it to safety. In the aftermath, Curley Bill was dead, Johnny Barns had been shot, and would later die of his wounds. On the Earp side, their only loss was Texas Jack's horse. Wyatt tried to remount his horse, but his cartridge belt was still too low to swing his leg over. Pulling at the leather once again, he finally made it in the saddle, then freed Texas Jack's leg from his horse before riding off to safety.

George Parsons, Saturday March 25, 1882;

"A very disagreeable day indeed. Tip and Smith discharged this a.m. Rumors of a battle and four of Earp party killed received this a.m. Discredited. I got strictly private news though later that "Curly Bill" has been killed at last – by the Earp party and none of the latter hurt. Sheriff Behan has turned all the cowboys loose against the Earps and

with this lawless element is trying to do his worst. I am heartily glad at this repulse and hope the killing is not stopped with the cut-throat named. Feeling here is growing against the ring, Sheriff, etc.; and it would not surprise me to know of a neck tie party some fine morning. Things seem to be coming to pass. "Then let it come the time is ripe and rotten ripe for change." [104]

On the same day that Wyatt Earp killed Curly Bill in the uncivilized backcountry, Pete Spence was scheduled to stand trial for his role in the death of Morgan Earp. The proceedings before Justice A.O. Wallace, contained a hostile witness, hearsay, and conjecture. No one saw the shooter, or could identify any of the men who fled the scene. As a result, on April 4, 1882 Pete Spence, and all others named in the complaint were freed. Judge Stillwell was right, they would never be convicted in a court of law.

Wyatt didn't receive the $1,000.00 provided by E.B. Gage. By the time Whistling Dick Wright and Tony Kraker reached the rendezvous point, the Earps were gone. At the springs, they encountered four cow-boys, and quickly told them they were out looking for lost mules. After having a meal with them, not to seem suspicious, they made their way back to Tombstone. Wyatt and his party headed back toward Tombstone and camped in the Dragoons, about six miles north of town. Wyatt's intention was to meet with supporters and recover the $1,000.00, but was apparently unsuccessful on both counts. He was able to pick up Charlie Smith who re-joined the posse bringing the number back to six.

The Earp party headed north through the Dragoons, stopping at Summit Station for dinner before pushing on toward the ranch owned by Jim and Hugh Percy. Behan, Ringo, and their posse had been in the area roaming the hills, in all probability doing everything they could to stay clear of the Earp party, but soon headed back toward Tombstone. When the Earps reached the Percy Ranch, they were met with apologies. Hugh and Jim fed the men and horses, but asked them to move on for fear of cow-boy retaliation if they helped. It was later revealed to be more than just that.

Cochise County Deputy, Frank Hereford, had been hiding in one of Percy's corn cribs for fear of his life the entire time. Frank was not known for his bravery, and probably hired due to his family connections. Frank Hereford was the son of noted Tucson attorney Benjamin Hereford, brother-in-law to Gov. Tritle, and law partner of James Zebriskie, who had connections with both Wyatt Earp and Johnny Ringo.

---

[104] A Tenderfoot in Tombstone. George Parsons. Pg. 214

Wyatt and his men camped on a grassy spot about a mile beyond the Percy Ranch, and rested for a few hours before leaving around 3:00 a.m. on Monday morning March 27th. In route for Wilcox, and the Sierra Bonita Ranch of Henry Hooker, Wyatt somehow got a message to Dan Tipton to tell him where they were heading, and to bring the $1,000.00 to them there. Tipton was able to retrieve the funds, and left Tombstone on the 5:00 a.m. stage the next morning.

By then, Behan was back in Tombstone, but struck out early on Monday morning March 27th. He and Ringo picked up the Earp trail again at Summit Station heading north. Behan had received a message from Deputy Hereford informing him that Wyatt had been to the Percy Ranch, and now in route to the Sierra Bonita in Wilcox. Wyatt was well beyond Behan's reach, giving him and his men time to rest. Hooker graciously welcomed Wyatt and the posse, and offered them food and fresh mounts, although it is likely that they left on their own horses. Dan Tipton arrived with the much needed $1,000.00 later in the day. Lou Cooley, one of Hooker's employees, and former stage driver arrived before they left with an additional $1,000.00 from Wells Fargo & Co. Later that afternoon, Behan and his men were spotted in the area. Hooker wanted Wyatt to stay there and make his

Henry Hooker

stand, but Wyatt chose to move up to Reilly Hill, about three miles from the ranch.

It was Tuesday morning when Behan's posse arrived at the Sierra Bonita, without the welcome extended to Wyatt Earp. He was close enough to be there by Monday evening, but it seemed that Behan was hoping to give the Earp party enough distance to avoid an encounter. Hooker loathed the sight of Behan arriving with a group of outlaws, some of whom had probably stolen cattle from the ranch. They didn't receive the hospitality that a badge would normally receive. When Behan asked Hooker if he knew where the Earp party was, he said he did not, and wouldn't tell them if he did.

Henry Hooker was not a man to hold his tongue. A heated exchange between him and Behan concerning his associates ensued, causing Billy

Whelan, Hooker's foreman to step in. After looking over Behan's party, Hooker replied; "These are a pretty set of fellows you have with you; a set of horse thieves and cut-throats."[105] Behan disavowed their association, and replied they were only there for the purpose of a posse. Hooker wasn't impressed. As would any gentleman, he offered them food, but not lodging. After they ate, the Sheriff's posse left, but not in the direction of the Earp party.

Graham County sheriff, George H. Stevens was also perturbed by the presence of John Behan and his posse running around his county. Behan had not contacted the sheriff, and had no jurisdiction, which suggests he was only racking up miles, and was anything but serious. Stevens knew the Earp party was in his county, and made no effort to restrict their travels, or interfere with their mission. Behan's presence, on the other hand, wasn't so welcome.

Behan roamed around the countryside for two additional days before returning to Tombstone on March 30th. He did not return with any of the men he was ostensibly chasing, but he did accrue a hefty bill for the county. His bill for Pima County alone was $2,593.65 for him and Ringo to ride the countryside in search of nothing. That's $60,588.00 in current value.

As the chase waned, Wyatt Earp and his men kept to the springs and countryside for a few days. They were still in search of cow-boys, but they had scattered with the wind. In Wyatt's August 9, 1896 installment of his three-part column for the *San Francisco Examiner*, Wyatt tells of the cow-boys that escaped to New Mexico. Major Albert Jennings Fountain and the First Battalion of Volunteer Calvary was tasked by Governor Lionel Sheldon to search the water holes for the Arizona cow-boys who had come their way. "The gallant Major Fountain at the head of his rangers, chased and killed the wayward cow-boys Wyatt's posse had chased out of Arizona."[106]

Behan was no longer a threat. He was back in the safety of Tombstone, awaiting his reimbursement checks from Pima and Cochise counties. Ringo was lost with nowhere to turn. His friends had either been killed, or skipped out. The legacy of the "Vendetta Ride" as it was called, was primarily about the plight of the Earp family, but in many ways, it was also about Johnny Ringo. Riding in solitude beside a man who he knew was a coward, Ringo watched his friends die, one by one, with no one held accountable. A paradox of sorts, with a conclusion as inevitable as time itself.

---

[105] The Life and legend of Doc Holliday; Gary Roberts. Pg. 261
[106] Wyatt Earp's Cow-boy Campaign. Chuck Hornung.

The Earp brothers, who'd been inseparable, were now scattered. On his course out of Arizona, Wyatt Earp stopped in Camp Grant and met with Henry Morgan, a notary public who witnessed Wyatt's signature as he transferred property to his sister in California. In what appeared to be a snag, Col. James Biddle approached Wyatt and told him that he would be held there for warrants to be served. Biddle then invited Wyatt and his men to join him for a meal, during which time, Biddle made himself scarce. Wyatt and his coterie soon slipped out, and rode off on fresh horses that had been left at the gate. Wyatt Earp still had friends in the right places. Friends who saw his actions as heroic, and necessary to clean out the undesirable element of the territory. A number of businessmen, lawmen, and politicians, who wished not to make a lot of noise, gave safe harbor, and passage to the Earp party to see them safely out of the territory.

Life in Tombstone was forever changed. O'Brien Moore, a trusted journalist for the Arizona Star, reported the following;

"I am now more than a week in Tombstone, and haven't so far seen a single killing. If I should make this statement in an Eastern newspaper I would immediately be dubbed a liar of a high order of genius. But such is the real state of affairs, without gloss or glamor. There hasn't even been a street fight, a knock down, or a game of fists." .... "The Republicans are in a terrible state of demoralization owing to the Earp imbroglio, a good portion of the party being still firm adherents of the outlaws. These may be called the 'swallow tails'... There is hardly a doubt that the best feelings of the people are in unison with the county government regarding the Earps."[107]

John Clum left Arizona for Washington D.C., and a federal post office appointment. With the sale of the Epitaph, the once strong Republican voice of Tombstone, became yet another outlet for Democrat propaganda. Sam Purdy, the Epitaph's new editor, also controlled the Associated Press reports that left the city, which meant he controlled what the world saw of their town. There were no Earps', no Hollidays', and no Curly Bills', creating what Purdy called; "a most peaceful state as any other section of the country."

There was, however, Johnny Ringo. Ringo was a loner who interacted with society only when necessary, but a man who never ran. As the Earp party disbursed and headed for Colorado, Ringo still facing charges in the case of Morgan Earp, stayed in Tombstone to stand before his accusers. He was thought to be out of the territory for most of April, some speculate

---

[107] Wyatt Earp; The Life Behind the Legend. Casey Tefertiller. Pg. 252

this to be one of three possible timeframes in which he visited his family in San Jose.

His whereabouts are among the hardest to track. In October 1934, Ringo's sisters, Mattie Belle, and Mary Enna, penned a letter to Mrs. Minerva Letton in response to an upcoming family newsletter scheduled to feature their brother. The sisters had misgivings about false information, in particular, that which was included from Walter Noble Burns; "Tombstone; An Iliad of the Southwest". They considered much of his research to be inaccurate, and written from bad sources. In their letter, the sisters' said that Ringo visited them in 1880, and was a stand-up gentleman. This clearly rebuffs later assertions that he was turned away in shame. Their letter was fifty years after the fact, and they could easily have been off by a year or two.

Their recollection is contrary to information provided by Charles Ringo, a distant relative who, without personal knowledge, said Ringo had visited his sisters in San Jose sometime in 1881. When Ringo actually visited his sisters' is lost to time, but he was present for his May 12, 1882 court date. As what seemed to be a pattern for Ringo, the case was continued twice, and finally dismissed on May 18th with all charges dropped, and the return of his $3,000.00 bond. He was once again a free man.

TRAGEDY IN TOMBSTONE

Only one week later, tragedy struck Tombstone once again. On May 25, 1882, a lantern in a water closet located at the rear of the Tivoli Gardens on Allen Street tipped over and became the source of Tombstone's second major fire. In minutes the fire had swept throughout the building, and was out of control. When firemen realized they could not contain the flames, they turned their attention to the north side of Allen Street, but their efforts were in vain. Within an hour, the blaze had spread to the businesses on the north side of the street, consuming the Alhambra Saloon, the Cosmopolitan Hotel, Campbell & Hatch Saloon, and the Occidental Saloon.[108]

Tombstone, May 25, 1882 – *A fire broke out in the rear of the Tivoli Gardens on Allen Street this afternoon at about half past three o'clock and immediately communicated to the surrounding structures. The Grand Hotel and magnificent rooms of the Tombstone Club adjoined were immediately enveloped in flames. The fire spread rapidly and soon the entire block between Toughnut and Allen Streets, and Third and Fourth Street were in flame. The fire department fought the flames like heroes,*

[108] True West Magazine; February 24, 2016

but it was evident that the heart of the city was doomed. The flames spread across Allen Street and destroyed the entire block to Fremont Street and again across Fourth Street, destroying the block bounded by Allen, Fremont, Third, and Fourth. Here the flames were conquered through the combined aid of firemen, police, and deputies under command of Sheriff Behan. The portion of the city destroyed comprised almost the entire business portion. The three principal hotels – The Grand, Cosmopolitan, and Brown's – were reduced to ashes. The Nugget newspaper office was completely destroyed, not a type or pound of stock being rescued from the flames. The fire spread destruction and desolation all around, but the people pluckily expressed their determination to commence to build immediately. The entire city would have succumbed to the flames were it not for the herculean efforts of Sheriff Behan and deputies, Chief of Police Nagle, and our gallant little Fire Department. The Western Union Telegraph Office was among the first to hug the flames, but the manager, C.E. Donnelly, at the risk of his life, saved the records and instruments, and established another office in a distant quarter within an hour. It is impossible at present to estimate the loss, perhaps half a million will cover it, but it certainly will not be less. The Epitaph office suffered a loss of something less than $1,000, through the breaking and wear of furniture and material. The newspaper offered the use of all material not in actual use to the Nugget, but the loss of the latter was too complete to attempt an immediate resurrection. The insurance on the property destroyed will foot up to about $250,000, but the loss will certainly double that. It will not affect the town, as most of the property destroyed was owned by solid business men who will immediately rebuild.[109]

Ringo was apparently not in town at the time of the fire. It was July 2, 1882 when he is documented to be back in Tombstone, clear with the law, and without enemies standing on each corner. Ringo had thoughts of moving to town. Most of his San Simon friends were gone. Some were killed by Wyatt Earp and his men while others moved on to Texas and New Mexico. It could have been a fresh start for a man who was now alone, with no direction and no other place to go. Life, however, or what was left of it, got in his way. Stuck in a mood of morose solitude, Ringo flooded his soul with rye whiskey that followed him to his death only two weeks later.

---

[109] Los Angeles Herald. May 26, 1882

CHAPTER THIRTEEN

THE DEATH OF JOHNNY RINGO

Friday July 14, 1882. It was a day like any other, until a cold dead body changed everything.

It was a hot afternoon. John Yoast, a German freighter for Sorghum Smith, was making a familiar run from Morse's Mill to Tombstone when he reined up near a tree he'd passed many times. Spurred by the barking of a dog, his eyes focused on a place known for respite, only today it offered the aftermath of a violent death. In the July heat, the body had turned black, and begun to swell. There was no doubt the man sitting in the fork of the tree was dead. Yoast shoed the flies as he approached, gaining a better view of the gunshot near the man's right temple that exited the left side of his head. As he focused on the scene, he fanned his hat once more to brave the stench, which overpowered the usual sweet smell of juniper and pine. The flies soon returned, fighting to regain their place in the dried blood and gaping wound in the man's head. There was also a swatch of open flesh within the hairline that stirred their appetite as well. The man had also been scalped. John Yoast was looking upon the remains of a man he had known both in Arizona, and the Texas Hill Country. His name was Johnny Ringo.

Yoast pondered the scene, with only the sound of swarming insects breaking the silence. Time had become irrelevant until the resonances of a creaking buckboard overpowered the serenade of flies. Breaking from the surreal moment, Yoast turned to realize the presence of a second man now at the scene.[110]

Robert Boller, an eighteen-year-old freighter also transporting lumber to Tombstone that day, tied up just after Yoast. What he saw was much the same, as they reported later in the day of a body, leaning back, and facing west between two jack oaks. There was a hole conducive with that of a large caliber bullet in his right temple, with an exit wound to the top left side of the skull.

---

[110] December 29, 1929 interview for the Arizona Historical Society as recorded by Mrs. George Kitt.

The location of the body was some fifty miles northeast of Tombstone in lower Turkey Creek Canyon, approximately twenty yards north of the road leading to Morse's Mill, and a quarter mile west of the home of Mr. B.F. (Coyote) Smith. Ringo's Winchester was buttressed against the tree next to him.

The location was well known by the lumber haulers who routinely made their way on that road. The area consisted of five jack oak trees, growing from one stump, with a flat rock in the center. It was a routine stopping place for the freighters around mid-day. Under the shade of the trees, with the creek close by, they'd found an ideal place to enjoy their lunch and cool down.[111] Perhaps while too drunk to ride, Johnny Ringo had the same idea the day before.

According to the Tombstone Weekly Epitaph, eleven men were at the scene within fifteen minutes of the discovery.[112] Among the gathering was Mr. B.F. (Coyote) Smith, whose wife heard a single shot at approximately 3:00 pm the previous day. This circumstantially sets the time of death, meaning Ringo's remains had been exposed to the heat and elements for a period of twenty-four hours. The condition of the body would be conducive with that time frame. On the afternoon of July 13, 1882, Mrs. Morse and Mrs. Young saw the body as they walked along the road.[113] As a well-known resting spot for passers-by, they assumed the man to be asleep, and thought no more of it, as they continued along their way. For an investigator, it provides a statement from two eyewitnesses, further substantiating the approximate time of death.

Having spent time in the dry, one-hundred-degree heat of an Arizona July, it's quite easy to determine the condition of the remains. In the twenty-four hours since death, by written account, the body had turned black. What accompanied the discoloration was the presence of flies, the formation of maggots, and swelling caused by bacteria in the gut, which decomposes at an accelerated rate in the dry heat. These conditions would have been accompanied by an almost unbearable stench, followed by rigor mortis. Thus, the consensus of the witnesses was to immediately bury the remains at that spot.

The coroner's jury included, John Yoast, Robert Boller, Thomas White, John Blake, John W. Bradfield, B.F. Smith, A.E. Lewis, A.S. Neighbors, James Morgan, Frank McKenny, W.J. Dewelt, J.C. McGray, and Fred Ward.

---

[111] Tombstone; An Iliad of the Southwest; Walter Noble Burns pg.265
[112] Tombstone Weekly Epitaph July 22, 1882
[113] Tombstone Weekly Epitaph July 22, 1882

Turkey or Morse's Mill Creek
July 14, 1882

STATEMENT FOR THE INFORMATION OF THE CORONER AND
SHERIFF OF COCHISE COUNTY, ARIZONA TERRITORY.

There was found by the undersigned John Yoast the body of a man in a clump of oak trees about 20 yards north from the road leading to Morse's mill and about a quarter mile west of the house of B.F. Smith. The undersigned reviewed the body and found it in a sitting position facing west, the head inclined to the right. There was a bullet hole in the right temple the bullet coming out on top of the head on the left side. There is apparently a part of the scalp gone, including a small portion of the forehead and part of the hair, this looks as if cut out by a knife. These are the only marks of violence on the body. Several of the undersigned identify the body as that of John Ringo, well known in Tombstone. He was dressed in light hat, blue shirt, vest, pants, and drawers, on his feet were a pair of hose and undershirt torn up so as to protect his feet. He had evidently traveled but a short distance in this foot gear. His revolver, he grasped in his right hand, his rifle rested against the tree close to him. He had two cartridge belts, the belt for the revolver cartridges being buckled on upside down.

The undernoted property were found with him and on his person: 1 Colt revolver Ca. 45, #222 containing five cartridges; 1 Winchester Model 1876, No. 21896, containing a cartridge in the breech and 10 in the magazine; 1 cartridge belt containing 9 rifle cartridges; 1 cartridge belt containing 2 revolver cartridges; 1 silver watch of American water company, No. 9339 with silver chain attached; 2 dollars and 60 cents ($2.60) in money; 6 pistol cartridges in his pockets; 5 shirt studs; 1 small pocket knife; 1 tobacco pipe; 1 comb; 1 box matches; 1 small piece of tobacco.

There is also a portion of a letter from Messrs. Hereford & Zabriskie, Attorneys at Law, Tucson (to the deceased John Ringo).

The above property is left in the possession of Frederick Ward, teamster between Morse Mill and Tombstone. The body of the deceased was buried close to where it was found. When found deceased had been dead about 24 hours.

Coroner's Jury:
Thomas White
John W. Bradfield
W.W. Smith

John Blake
B.F. ("Coyote") Smith
A.E. (Bull) Lewis

A.S. Neighbors

James Morgan
J.C. McGregor
Fred Ward [114]

Robert Boller
(Second man on the scene. Boller was 18 years old)
W.J. Dowelt
John Yoast (First on the scene, Yoast was age 25)

A more comprehensive inventory of belongings was published in the Tombstone Weekly Epitaph on July 22, 1882 as follows;

"The undernoted property was found with him and on his person; 1 Colt revolver caliber 45, No.222, containing five cartridges; 1 Winchester rifle octagon barrel, caliber 45 model 1876, No. 21,896, containing a cartridge in the breach and ten in the magazine; 1 cartridge belt, containing 9 rifle cartridges, 1 cartridge belt containing 2 revolver cartridges, 1 silver watch of American Watch company, No. 9339, with silver chain attached; two dollars and sixty cents ($2.60) in money; six pistol cartridges in pocket; five shirt studs; 1 small pocket knife; 1 tobacco pipe; 1 comb; 1 box matches; 1 small piece of tobacco. There is also a portion of a letter from Messrs. Herford & Zebriskie, attorneys at law, Tucson, to the deceased, John Ringo. The above property is left in the possession of Fred Ward, teamster between Morse's Mill and Tombstone."

The accuracy of this report should have undergone additional scrutiny. First, it was a citizen report, filed as provided to the Cochise County coroner, Dr. Henry M. Matthews. Ringo was a resident of that county; therefore, the report was filed there. The incident took place in Apache County, now Navajo County, fifty miles from the city of Tombstone. There's no record of any jurisdictional authority responding to the scene. Officially, all we have is a compilation of eye-witness accounts from untrained drovers and freighters, trampling a contaminated crime scene, and reporting on a salacious death from their point of view. Dr. Henry Matthews, by the way, is the same coroner who examined the bodies of Billy Clanton, and the McLaury brothers following the shooting on October 26, 1881.

The inventory of Ringo's possessions, as written by those at the scene, and presented to Dr. Matthews is quite telling. The list of property is described in such fine detail as to include "a *small* piece of tobacco" - "A *portion* of a letter; who it was from and who it was addressed to;" - "A *small* pocket knife." – "5 shirt studs" - Etc. Their description of the

---

[114] Statement of Henry Matthews, Coroner July 14, 1882. Filed in the Cochise Clerk's Office, Bisbee, Arizona.

Winchester rifle includes the model number, caliber, barrel style, serial number, the number of rounds in the magazine, and the fact that there was a round in the breach. For the Colt pistol, the description included similar information including the caliber and serial number, and listed the number of cartridges in the cylinder as five. These men made no mention of a spent round in the chamber, which would preclude any possibility of that weapon having been fired. Sometimes what isn't said speaks the loudest.

Writers and historians have written for years of a spent round resting under the hammer. That information came from Robert Boller's letter to Frank King dated September 20, 1934. In that letter Boller says; "There was an empty shell in the sixshooter and the hammer was on that." In that same letter, Boller said Ringo's "other cartridge belt was full *if I remember correctly.*" Ringo was wearing two belts, one with nine rifle cartridges, and one with two pistol cartridges. Neither would be considered full. He also said; "The Earps learning Ringo was one of Sheriff Behan's posse they hightailed out of Arizona." When considering the known inaccuracies of Mr. Boller's statements fifty-two years after the fact, one must call into question the existence of the spent round in the chamber.

Although some details seem to be carefully worded, other information leaves a lot to interpretation. For example, the official document states that Ringo "was dressed in a light blue hat". The inference is that the hat was on his head. There was no mention of any bullet hole in the hat – and the hat would surely have been blown from his head from the gunshot. According to Robert Boller in his letter to Frank King in 1934, the hat was lying on the ground next to the Winchester. That part of his recollection does make sense.

There are conflicting stories regarding the recovery of Ringo's horse. Burns said it was found a week later with a broken picket rope at Robert's Cienega in Sulphur Springs

of violence visible on the body. Several ot the undersigned identify the body as that of John Ringo, well known in Tombstone. He was dressed in light hat, blue shirt, vest, pants and drawers. On his feet were a pair ot hose and an undershirt torn up so as to protect his feet. He had evidently traveled but a short distance in this foot gear. His revolver he grasped in his right hand, his rifle resting against the tree close to him. He had on two cartridge belts, the belt for revolver cartridges being buckled on upside down. The undernoted property was found with him and on his person; 1 Colt's revolver, calibre 45, No. 222, containing five cartridges; 1 Winchester rifle octagon barrel, calibre 45, model 1876, No. 21,896, containing a cartridge in the breech and ten in the magazine; 1 cartridge belt, containing 9 rifle cartridges; 1 cartridge belt, containing 2 revolver cartridges; 1 silver watch of American Watch company, No. 9339, with silver chain attached; two dollars and sixty cents ($2 60) in money; 6 pistol cartridges in pocket; 5 shirt studs; 1 small pocket knife; 1 tobacco pipe; 1 comb; 1 block matches; 1 small piece tobacco. There is also a portion of a letter from Messrs. Hereford & Zabriskie, attorneys-at-law, Tucson, to the deceased, John Ringo. The above property is left in the possession of Frederick Ward, teamster between Morse's mill and Tombstone.

Valley, approximately six miles away.[115] Ringo's horse was still saddled, and wandering the country side. On the horse was one of Ringo's boots, with his coat tied in a roll to the back of the saddle. In a coat pocket was a letter from Hereford and Zabriskie, a law firm in Tucson. The content of the letter is unknown. In the breast pocket, was a group of photos, presumed to be of Ringo's family.[116] One would wonder how, or why, the horse would be found six miles away. At the scene of the crime, there was sufficient grass and water to hold the animal's attention, and by nature, he would have stayed close by. It also calls the broken picket line into question. Was it broken as suggested, or perhaps cut?

The Tucson Weekly Citizen reported on July 30, 1882 that the 1000lb. Bay was found two miles away by the son of B.F. (Coyote) Smith. This statement is a direct contradiction to the recollection of Smith's daughter, Rosa Ann Smith, who said the horse was found in Sulphur Springs Valley. There is no dispute regarding the personal effects attached to the horse. Ringo's mount is also reported to have been stolen from a Mexican a few weeks earlier.

SO – WHAT HAPPENED IN THE DAYS LEADING UP TO HIS DEATH, AND WHO WAS THE LAST PERSON TO SEE RINGO ALIVE?

On July 2, 1882, Ringo was in Tombstone, reportedly with plans for moving to town. According to The Epitaph editor, Sam Purdy, he spoke with him at length. In that conversation Ringo stated to Purdy that "he was as certain of being killed, as he was of being living then. He said he might run along for a couple of years more, and might not last two days."[117] Ringo was still there for the 4th of July celebration, and spent time with a number of his friends including Billy Claiborne and Frank Leslie. As reported by the Epitaph on July 22nd, Ringo spend his time there in a drunken binge, or as Purdy described it "an extended jamboree". It was July 8th when he saddled up with an extra bottle of whiskey, and headed toward Galeyville. Witnesses confirmed that Claiborne, and Leslie left town shortly thereafter.

Along the South Pass toward the Chiricahua, Billy Breakenridge claims to have run into Ringo on his way to Galeyville;

---

[115] Walter Noble Burns; An Iliad of the Southwest. Pg. 265
[116] Tombstone; An Illiad of the Southwest; Walter Noble Burns pg.265
[117] Tombstone Epitaph July 22, 1882

"I met John Ringo in the south pass of the Dragoon Mountains. It was shortly after noon. Ringo was very drunk, reeling in the saddle, and said he was going to Galeyville. It was in the summer and a very hot day. He offered me a drink out of a bottle half-full of whiskey, and he had another full bottle. I tasted it, and it was too hot to drink. It burned my lips. Knowing that he would have to ride nearly all night before he could reach Galeyville, I tried to get him to go back with me to the Goodrich Ranch and wait until after sundown, but he was stubborn and went on his way."[118]

- From a rider's point of view, Breakenridge is right. The author has run those trails on horseback in the summer. A canteen of cold water, hung over a saddle horn at first light, will be hot by mid-day. It still gets the caked dust out of your mouth, but I swear I could make coffee with it.

Billy Breakenridge

Ringo stopped at Dial's Ranch, in the South Pass of the Dragoons late the next evening, in all probability it was after he saw Breakenridge. He was still drinking. On the 10th, he, Frank Leslie, and Billy Claiborne met up at the Cienega Saloon run by "Widow" Patterson, where they drank and stayed for the night. Ringo arrived in Galeyville the next day, still in a drunken stupor. He stayed there for the day, and didn't let up on the whiskey. Mrs. Patterson said he left on July 11th, still drunk, and taking a bottle of whiskey with him.

Bill Sanders, who owned the property where Ringo was killed, reports that he passed Ringo on the road while he was in route to Bisbee with a load of wood. By his account, Ringo was slumped over in the saddle as he rode. Sanders also passed Billy Claiborne and Frank Leslie, who said they were looking for Ringo. Whether they found him or not, was never known.

There has been an abundance of speculation concerning Ringo's final hours. With no basis in fact, some have claimed Ringo to be crazed, and dying of thirst. No doubt he was dehydrated, alcohol is a diuretic, but he was within sight of water in West Turkey Creek. Some speculate that he stopped to remove his boots, and the horse wandered off from him, perhaps. According to Josephine Earp, Ringo suffered from "whiskey

---

[118] William Breakenridge; Helldorado pg.313

shakes"[119] and would see things when he was drunk. She recalled that he would see snakes in his boots, and pull them off to get away from the snakes. At the end, Ringo suffered from alcoholism. It wasn't an issue until he reached Arizona, but became progressively worse. When he reached his final resting place, he was drunk, and may have thought there was something in his boots, so he removed them. Did the horse walk away from him? Very likely. The only relevance here is in trying to piece together Ringo's final movements before he sat down next to that tree. He was drunk, and apparently confused. He buttressed his rifle against the tree, took off his hat, sat down in a cool spot, and fell asleep. Putting the speculation aside, that's really all that matters.

In retrospect, Ringo's death and discovery by John Yoast validates the strange evidence of karma. John Ringo, a man who played a major role in the Mason County War, ends up scalped and decomposing against an Arizona tree. Looking down, was a familiar Texas face glaring at his cold dead body.

Who Killed Ringo?

THE CASE AGAINST 'BUCKSKIN' FRANK LESLIE

In the aftermath, Billy Claiborne blamed "Buckskin" Frank Leslie for the death of his friend Johnny Ringo. After Ringo's death Claiborne left Tombstone, and took a job working in a mine in Globe. He is said to have told acquaintances there that he planned to go back to Tombstone to kill Leslie for what he'd done. On the evening of November 11, 1882, a drunken Claiborne entered the Oriental Saloon where Leslie was working as a bar tender. He started making trouble, presumably over a political discussion, and refused

William Claiborne

Leslie's demand that he leave. Leslie led him by the collar until they were at the door, and asked him not to go away mad. Claiborne walked outside, but didn't leave. Minutes later, Leslie was told that a man was waiting

---

[119] Jack Barrow; The Gunfighter Who Never Was.

outside to kill him. When Leslie walked out, he saw a rifle barrel sticking out from a fruit stand where Claiborne had hunkered down.

He told Claiborne "Don't shoot, I don't want you to kill me, nor do I want to have to shoot you," but Claiborne, still drunk, raised his rifle and fired the weapon, missing Leslie. Leslie returned fire and hit Claiborne in the chest. "I saw him double up and had my pistol cocked and aimed at him again... I advanced upon him, but did not shoot, when he said, "Don't shoot again, I am killed." Claiborne was taken to a doctor by friends, where he died six hours after being shot. His last words were reportedly, "Frank Leslie killed Johnny Ringo, *I saw him do it"* [120]

There was no evidence at the time that he'd killed Ringo, and if he had, why did Billy Claiborne wait four months to take action? Moreover, Leslie and Ringo had a friendly relationship, so what was his motive? Leslie took credit for killing Ringo while he was in Yuma Territorial Prison. Frank King, who was a guard at the facility revealed later that Leslie had told him and others. He didn't believe his story, and neither did anyone else. Although still considered a possible suspect today, most believed that Leslie made the claim for the notoriety.

So why did he and Claiborne leave Tombstone on the 8th of July in search of Ringo?

There was rumor and speculation around Tombstone that led to talk of a conspiracy between Claiborne and Leslie to murder Ringo. This theory is illogical for several reasons. First, the three men were known to be friendly... Although Ringo and Leslie had an argument just prior to Ringo leaving town. Perhaps significant, or perhaps a routine event amongst drunken friends, that ended with Leslie saying; "we'd better go find him." Not sure, but plausible. Second, if Leslie held such a grudge, he surely wouldn't have told Claiborne, much less solicited his help. Third, there is no record of animosity placing Ringo at odds with Frank Leslie. Surely not enough for him to demonstrate a desire to execute such a deed.

---

[120] Tombstone Epitaph November 18, 1882

THE CASE AGAINST
WYATT EARP & DOC HOLLIDAY

The court of public opinion has produced some less than plausible suspects in the Ringo case, but none as far-fetched as Wyatt Earp. Earp himself pressed the theory in the 1920's, telling a number of writers that he had killed Ringo. With all due respect, many of Mr. Earp's assertions in his elderly years could not be verified, with some quite easily dismissed. Mrs. Earp also put forth her account of how her husband had killed Ringo, although her version didn't match his. This has been a favorite theory for a number of writers. The perfect dramatic ending to a righteous vendetta where the good guy returns to finish off the one that got away.

John Gilchrise, renowned Earp researcher, believed, that based on John Flood's manuscript, it would have been possible for Wyatt to accomplish the mission as detailed. Gilchrise never actually accused him of executing the murder, only that he thought it possible. As with most, he approached the situation as a writer/historian, not from the perspective of an investigator. Unlike writers, cops recreate the crime from every possible angle – touch it – smell it – and let it speak, to determine the truth. Gilchrise didn't know the lay of the land, and often had Earp traveling in the wrong direction. The timing of railroad schedules, his ability to obtain a horse and saddle, not to mention a trail that skirted hostile Indian territory leave his hypothesis as less than credible.

Tales of Doc Holliday's presence have been included, but Doc was known to be in Gunnison, Colorado on July 1st, where he soon departed alone for Pueblo to appear in court over a larceny charge. Doc was indicted by the grand jury on the morning of July 11th, where he was granted bail of $500.00. By July 18th, he was known to be in Leadville, Colorado. He therefore could not have assisted Wyatt on such a post vendetta mission.[121]

Other accounts are remiss in considering the travel routes, both by trail and train of the 1880's and rely on the configuration of rail and road for the twentieth century. It is nearly impossible to determine a reasonable set of circumstances by which Wyatt Earp could have accomplished such a feat.

---

[121] The Life and Legend of Doc Holliday; Gary L. Roberts. Pgs. 317-318

SUICIDE

Did John Ringo die by his own hand? It was the conclusion of those at the scene that he surely had, but by what authority or expertise? The men who viewed the scene were freighters and ranchers. They had no forensic abilities, limited as it was in those days, to reach any informed conclusions. Dr. Matthews, who signed the coroner's report, did so with the information provided, having never viewed the body.

Too many unexplained facts existed to draw such a conclusion.

1. Why was there a missing section of hair that appeared to have been scalped?
2. Why didn't the recoil from the pistol knock it from his hand?
3. "The pistol was caught in his watch chain". Was that on the way up, or the way down?
4. There was no mention of blood on the pistol or on Ringo's hands.

There are a number of circumstantial conclusions that one could draw, given Ringo's melancholy demeanor, but not enough for an untrained eye to distinguish the difference between a homicide from a suicide. Had Ringo been sitting in a drunken state with his head cocked to the left, a bullet fired from several feet away would have that same upward trajectory. It's one of those unsolved mysteries that may never find an answer, but for the expediency of all, suicide seemed to be an acceptable answer for Sheriff Behan and all involved to neatly close the case and move on.

There were several people at the scene who disagreed. Henry Smith and his mother saw the body before the bulk of onlookers arrived, and never believed that Ringo took his own life. Foremost to them was the lack of powder burns. When firing a black powder round at close range, there will be a discharge of burned powder, as well as muzzle fire. It was not uncommon for a man shot at point blank range, to also find his clothes on fire. Dodge City lawman, Ed Masterson, was shot at close range on April 9, 1878 causing his coat to catch fire. In the February 25, 1881 confrontation between Luke Short and Charlie Storms, Short shot Storms in the chest at point blank range, catching his shirt on fire. Smokeless gunpowder wasn't invented until 1886.

There was no mention of blood. At very close range, after an explosive shot, high velocity impact blood spatters travel back toward the gun barrel, as the projectile hits a surface area. This causes internal muzzle staining, also known as 'back spatter', or blowback'. In addition, the larger the projectile, or bullet, the more spatter. Had Ringo shot himself, there would have been blood spatter on, and in the gun barrel, and even on his hand. Another very important consideration involves 'stippling' on the victim, which is caused by burning from gunpowder.[122] Given the detail of the coroner's report, the presence of blood on the pistol or hands would probably have been mentioned.

Although "Coyote" Smith signed the coroner's report, he too believed that someone else had killed Ringo. Some years later, Henry explained the quick and unanimous verdict as one of expediency. "The verdict of suicide was returned as the easiest and quickest way out of the affair. The jurors didn't want to lose time in a long coroner's investigation."[123]

---

[122] Forensics Science Weebly/Bloodstain Pattern Analysis. Author's conversation with Steve Sederwall.
[123] The Cochise Quarterly; Volume 3 No.1 Spring 1973. Pg. 12

CHAPTER FOURTEEN

THE CASE AGAINST JOHN YOAST

There are times when the answer is staring you in the face, from the person you were least likely to suspect.

It was a hot July afternoon. John Yoast, a German freighter for Sorghum Smith, was making a familiar run from Morse's Mill to Tombstone when he reined up at a place he'd passed many times. Spurred by the barking of a dog, his eyes focused on a place known for respite, only today it offered the aftermath of a violent death. In the July heat, the body had turned black, and begun to swell. There was no doubt the man sitting in the fork of the tree was dead. Yoast shoed the flies as he approached, gaining a better view of the gunshot near the man's right temple that exited the left side of his head. As he focused on the scene, he fanned his hat once more to brave the stench, which overpowered the usual sweet smell of juniper and pine. The flies soon returned, fighting to regain their place in the dried blood and gaping wound in the man's head. There was also a swatch of open flesh within the hairline that stirred their appetite as well. The man had also been scalped. John Yoast was looking upon the remains of a man he had known both in Arizona, and Texas Hill Country. His name was Johnny Ringo.

I recently received a telephone call from Steve Sederwall, Cold West Investigation's owner and senior investigator. It was nothing unusual, as a rule we talk a couple times a week about one case or another. This call was different. "I know who killed Johnny Ringo," he began. Always with an open mind when Steve compiles a theory, I simply replied; "I'm listening."

"John Yoast, the man who found him, is the man who killed him." Steve replied.

Without speaking, my first thoughts were, this is the man who told me that he knew where the shell casing to the bullet that killed John Tunstall was located. "You're crazy." I thought.

"It was a lever action Winchester. The first thing any shooter would do in that circumstance is to lever that rifle to reload, which kicks out the shell. I can find it" Needless to say, he was right. He found it, and I've held it in my hand.

He's the man who concluded that Billy the Kid did not shoot J.W. Bell at the bottom of the stairs. His forensic investigation, and the application of luminol found blood at the top of the Lincoln County Courthouse stairs, right where he said it would be.

I never disagreed, and began my investigation. Damn! I think Steve was right.

I started at the scene of the crime, the day Ringo was found. Did a barking dog actually draw Yoast's attention to the dead body next to the tree? He may, perhaps, have been startled that it was still there – black, swollen, and baking under the hot sun, and yet undiscovered. But for the horrific change in Ringo's dead body, the scene was much as he'd left it only 24 hours prior. Yoast now finds himself in a dilemma…he must have thought: "Do I drive on, or call for help? After all, it's been a full day, and no one will ever suspect that I had any involvement, there would be no reason. Confident that he will be hailed as the man who discovered Ringo's body, Yoast fires three shots into the air, the international code for distress, to summon for help. According to reports, eleven men were at the scene in a matter of fifteen minutes. Yoast is now lost in the crowd, with he and Robert Boller heralded for their discovery. Yoast is in the clear.

With a group of medically non-qualified freighters and drovers hovering over Ringo's dead body, there was no way a proper coroner's report could ever be written. No law enforcement officer, doctor, or coroner ever saw the body. No professional conclusions, only that of the locals who signed their report back to Dr. Henry Matthews. Much of the report is non-medical such as an inventory of possessions, position of the body, time of day, and so forth. There were, however, other clues that were overlooked, perhaps because those at the scene didn't know what they were seeing.

FACTS

- Ringo was missing a part of his scalped, cut clean as though with a knife.
- Ringo's right hand gripped his pistol which was drawn and caught in his watch chain.
- His horse was nowhere to be found.
- Yoast made the admission that he'd known Ringo both in Texas and in Arizona.

Four very important pieces of evidence, when coupled with the man who found him.

BACKGROUND

- John Benson Yoast was born in Bastrop, Texas on November 29, 1857 to Frank and Mahala Yoast. He died February 5, 1922 in Las Cruces New, Mexico
- John's mother, Mahala died on January 4, 1870 when John was twelve years of age. His father, Frank, died on May 7, 1882 – two months before the death of Johnny Ringo. John was twenty-four years of age.
- The Yoast's were no strangers to confrontation. On August 14, 1871, one of Frank's sons – who was unnamed in the Austin Weekly Statement, was engaged in a fight when Frank rode up, showing his sidearm, and demanding that everyone back off and allow a fair fight. A matter of deduction, but given the ages of John's brothers, the choices narrow down to either him, at age fourteen, or his brother Amos at age 20. Price was age 10, and Hiram age 5, sort of leaves them out. The Austin Weekly Statement Thursday August 24, 1871 reported the following:

We learn from a gentleman just from Bastrop of the following particulars of a difficulty there on Monday evening after the voting was over. A son of Frank Yoast got into a fight with a Negro, when Mr. Yoast rode up and drawing his pistol demanded a fair fight, threatening to shoot anyone who interfered. Messrs. Green and Burleson did interfere and separate them, when Sheriff Jung and a policeman attempted to arrest Frank Yoast, who was fired at from behind by Mr. Warner, another policeman. Yoast then fired three shots, his six-shooter having only three loads in it, killing Warner, but only striking the clothes of Jung and the other policeman.

Mrs. Halter, a lady subject to hemorrhage of the lungs, came out of a house nearby and became excited from hearing or seeing the difficulty, on returning to her house, fell on the steps and in about half an hour afterwards died from internal bleeding.

A Mr. Procop and a machinist was shot and wounded in the legs and hip accidently by the deceased policeman when firing at Yoast.

Politics as far as we can learn had but nothing to do with the occurrence which was caused by mean whisky and is to be regretted by all.[124]

- The connection between John Yoast and Johnny Ringo originated in the Texas Hill Country during the Mason County War. Yoast's whereabouts can be placed in and around the Loyal Valley of Mason County by his association with Carrie Ann Stone, daughter of the Rev R.G. Stone and his wife Carolyn. Carrie was born in Mason County on August 8, 1864, and resided in Loyal Valley. Yoast and Carrie Stone were married in July 1883.
- Ringo resided in Loyal Valley.
- Yoast said he knew Ringo in Texas – highly unlikely to have been from personal interaction. He could well have known Ringo by reputation, doubtful that Ringo would have known him.
- Yoast was German – Ringo an American, at a time when ethnic animosity ran higher in Mason County than any of the surrounding localities.
- Yoast was a young man in his early twenties, likely as full of piss and vinegar as any young man, with lots of reasons to dislike John Ringo.
- In the press, Ringo was included in each action undertaken by Scott Cooley, as well as those of his own. Cooley, a tough ex-Texas Ranger and Indian scout, scalped John Wohrle, as well as Karl Bader, and carried the scalps with him. An ultimate sign of disrespect which was highly publicized as related to the death of each victim.
- John Yoast's opinion of Johnny Ringo was formed in Texas.
- Yoast said he knew Ringo in Arizona.
- John Yoast lived in the Tombstone area, and worked as a freighter hauling wood from Morse's Mill back to Tombstone on a regular basis. This would be in proximity to the route followed by Ringo as he traveled from Charleston to Galeyville.
- Again, it is doubtful that Ringo interacted with Yoast, but Yoast must have been more than disappointed to find Ringo in the area when he moved to Tombstone.

We have established a connection between the two men. Yoast's normal (perhaps daily) routine was on the road past those trees. If he was there the day before, then he had access and opportunity.

---

[124] The Austin Weekly Statement August 24, 1871

RINGO WAS SCALPED

- Why was a piece of Ringo's hair missing? "Removed as though it was cut by a knife." Doesn't sound like a buzzard plucked it.
- That information was never explained, and rather ignored because it didn't fit. It's there, it has to fit somewhere.
- Why would someone scalp him? If he did in fact commit suicide, as the coroner concluded, then how did a clean-cut section of his hair go missing? Had he been murdered by anyone on the list of public opinion, what would be the motivation of any suspected to scalp Ringo?
- Yoast had memories of fellow German's John Wohrle, and Karl Bader being scalped by Scott Cooley, or perhaps John Ringo back in Texas not so long ago.
- John Yoast had <u>motive</u>.

WHERE WAS RINGO'S HORSE?

- There are conflicting accounts as to the whereabouts of Ringo's horse. According to one report, he was found two miles away, still with Ringo's coat draped across the saddle. Another has the horse six miles away at Sulphur Springs. Rosa Ann Smith, 'Coyote' Smith's daughter stated in her 1939 interview with the *Douglas Daily Dispatch* that the horse was in Sulphur Springs Valley.
- Horses don't tend to wander off, not two miles, not six. The area where his horse would have been grazing after Ringo dismounted is covered in tall grass, with cool shade, and water nearby. A horse's paradise that he would not be inclined to leave. Horses aren't inquisitive enough to roam alone from safety.
- The most curious account is that of the horse being found a week later near Sulphur Springs Valley, six miles from the scene. The horse, again, would not have moved that far on his own for no reason.[125]

---

[125] Rosa Ann Smith, Coyote Smith's daughter, Douglas Daily Dispatch, January 31, 1939.

RINGO'S PISTOL:

-WAS CAUGHT IN HIS WATCH CHAIN

- Every discussion of this possibility that I've ever seen assumes that his pistol caught the watch chain on its way down, after being discharged. In fact, it was quite the opposite.
- Had the pistol been fired, the recoil would have kicked it outward (equal and opposite reaction), not falling straight down into Ringo's lap.
- Having a sidearm hang up in a watch chain while in the process of clearing leather was a common occurrence. It happened to John Westley Harden on August 23, 1877 in a rail car in Pensacola, Florida. That few seconds provided the edge needed by the Texas Rangers to capture Harden. Charley Storms made the same mistake on February 25, 1881 in Tombstone. In a confrontation with Luke Short, Storms drew first, catching the hammer of his Colt in his swinging gold watch chain. Short had all the time in the world and shot Storms twice in the chest. Short was faster, and he would have killed him anyway, but Storm's mistake allowed him more time.

One Spent Round in the Chamber?

- Writers and Historians have written for years that the hammer of Ringo's Colt was resting on a spent round. According to the inventory list at the scene, Ringo's Colt was said to have *five rounds in the cylinder*. The use of that term has a specific meaning for people who know guns, as these men obviously did. It simply means there are five live rounds with the hammer resting on the empty bore.
- If there were five rounds as reported, with no mention of a spent round, this pistol could <u>not</u> have been fired.

CONCLUSION

It seems more than plausible that John Yoast traveled along his normal route on the afternoon of July 13, 1882 and encountered a drunken Johnny Ringo sleeping against the oak where he 'found' him the next day. Recognizing the man as John Ringo, someone he knew as an outlaw, the murderer of German citizens in Texas, who took their scalps, Yoast stopped his wagon, and walked toward Ringo. Perhaps with only a notion of confronting the man when given the opportunity, Yoast very likely had no intention of doing bodily harm to Ringo. In an unexpected moment, he saw a man he didn't like, and planned to tell him so. As he draws near, Ringo is rousted, and sees an approaching man, thereby trying to draw his sidearm against his body while seated, getting it tangled in his watch chain as it came across.

Yoast became afraid, and in the moment clears his pistol and shoots Ringo in the head. In his mind in self-defense. Now he's screwed. Yoast is rattled and not thinking, but decides the horse needs to go. If he was traveling toward Tombstone as indicated, he would have passed through the southern part of Sulphur Springs Valley, and could easily have taken the horse there. John decided to leave the body exactly where it was in hopes that someone will find him. He feels in the clear, and if the body is found later in the day, his name will never be connected with the incident.

To his surprise, it was still there when he rode by the next day. How many people rode past that body, thinking it was a sleeping man? The day of Ringo's death, Mrs. Morse and another lady took a stroll by the area. They later said that they had seen the man leaned against the tree, but

---

Killing at Bastrop.

We learn from a gentleman just from Bastrop the following particulars of the difficulty there on Monday evening after the voting was over. A son of Mr. Frank Yoast got into a fight with a negro, when Mr. Yoast rode up and drawing his pistol demanded a fair fight, threatening to shoot any one who interfered. Messrs. Green and Burleson did interfere and separated them, when Sheriff Jung and a policeman attempted to arrest Frank Yoast, who was fired at from behind by Mr. Waruer another policeman. Yoast then fired three shots, his six shooter having only three loads in it, killing Warner, but only striking the clothes of Jung and the other policeman.

Mrs. Halter, a lady subject to hemorrhage of the lungs, came out of a house near by and becoming excited from hearing or seeing the difficulty, on returning to her house, fell on the steps and in about half an hour afterwards died from internal bleeding.

A Mr. Procop and a machinist were shot and wounded in the legs and hip accidentally by the deceased policeman when firing at Yoast.

Politics as far as we can learn had but nothing to do with the occurrance which was caused by mean whisky, and is to be regretted by all.

thought he was asleep. How many others traveled by from the afternoon of the 13th, until Yoast stopped some twenty-four hours later?

We submit that John Yoast killed John Peters Ringo in the flash of a moment that he wished had never occurred. He was probably a good man, who'd just done a bad thing. As the man who found Ringo twenty-four hours after the murder, he lost himself in the crowd, and was never suspected.

Johnny Ringo came to Arizona in late November 1879 and died there in July 1882. He was a resident of the territory for only two years and eight months, nevertheless, in history, Arizona dominates all other aspects of his life. Far more compelling were the five years he spent in Texas. From his Christmas Day 'pistol-firing' celebration in the Burnet County town square, until his departure in November '79, Ringo never experienced the normalcies of life. He could have lamented the death of his friend Moses Baird, and moved on, but that wasn't in Ringo. He spent whatever life had in store for him on making things right, at least in his mind. Branded as an outlaw, his purpose in Texas was anything but.

Arizona was a different story. Perhaps from the trauma of fighting for his life, or the influence of such a man as Scott Cooley, Ringo came to Arizona a different man than the one who had chosen Texas five years earlier. He left Texas, but the events of The Texas Hill Country never left him. I would submit, that if the evidence before us proves John Yoast to be the man who killed Ringo, it will definitely make him the last victim of the Mason County War.

APPENDICES

DOCUMENTS
PHOTOS
NEWSPAPER ACCOUNTS
SUPPLEMENTAL INFORMATION

THE UNFORESEEN LEGACY OF AN OUTLAW

The census of 1882, taken shortly before Ringo's death, shows the occupants of the Hill home as Joe Hill, John Ringo, Phin Clanton, Ike Clanton, as well as Lula Belle Olney, age 7.

Joe Hill

Every name in an investigation is subject to scrutiny, even with no direct indication of involvement, and even if they are seven years old. The purpose is not to find blame, but to find the truth, both incriminating and exculpatory. There was obviously no culpability found with the child, but Lula Belle's story is quite interesting. Her parents died when she was quite young.

Her father, Texas outlaw, Joseph Olney, alias Joe Hill, had been a rustler and murderer for most of his adult life. By 1882, after the deaths of Curly Bill Brocius and his friend from Texas, John Ringo, Joe decided to settle down. He and his wife Agnes Jane had reunited, and lived in Animas Valley with their five children. Joe had finally straightened out his life, but was unfortunately killed on December 3, 1884 when his horse rolled over him. On October 3, 1887 Agnes Jane passed away, leaving Lula Belle and her siblings as orphans.

Most of Lula's youth was spent at a convent in Tucson where she attended school. Lula graduated in 1895. From there she taught school, and soon met a young man by the name of John J. Rath. She and John married in 1896. In December 1897, John began construction of their new home, in Cochise, Arizona. It was late February 1898 when he and Lula Belle moved in. A small community approximately 57 miles north-northeast of Tombstone, Cochise was settled primarily as a water stop for the Southern Pacific Railroad. Life for Lula Belle was far different from the days of her childhood.

Lula Olney Rath

John J. Rath was an industrious young man with a vision. He homesteaded 120 acres in Cochise, and was granted a deed to the property on October 13, 1899. John became known as the Town Father of Cochise.

In November 1899, the Cochise Royal Hotel, also known as the Hotel Rath, opened for business. It was an adobe structure thirty feet by sixty feet, and was advertised as having large, well furnished rooms, with courteous service. The irony of it was that when the Raths' opened the hotel, Lula

John J. Rath

needed to bring on some help. The woman she hired just happened to be Mary Katherine Cummings. There is some speculation that Lula Belle may not have known the history of Mrs. Cummings, and perhaps Mrs. Cummings did not know Mrs. Rath. Mrs. Cummings was better known, just a few years earlier, as Big Nose Kate, the lady friend of Doc Holliday. Doc and Lula's father, Joe were very much on opposite sides during their time in Tombstone. The story would have been nice had it stopped there, but history always provides an unexpected twist.

Unfortunately, on September 17, 1905 John and several of his friends were heading out on a hunting trip when tragedy struck. Just outside of town, the buckboard in which John and his friends were riding, hit a bump, causing a jolt. John lost his grip on his shotgun, causing it to slip. As he quickly moved to retrieve the firearm, the hammer caught and fired, discharging the round that entered the side of his neck, killing him instantly. John and Lula had three girls. Edith, born in 1899, Lillian in 1902, and Agnes, named for her mother, born in 1905.

Joe Hill may have been gone, but Lula and her brothers remained close. Lula and John were married at her brother, William's house in 1896. John Rath is buried in the Olney family plot at the Desert Resort Cemetery. It was William who took Lula and the girls in for a while after John's death, and George who bought the girl's share of John's estate at probate to keep it in the family. He immediately returned ownership to Lula. Lula returned to Cochise in 1907 to assume the position of postmaster, and reopened the boarding house.[126]

Too often we look at events through the prism of history, but fail to remember that life still remains for those left behind. The sun still rises, and families carry on. For Lula and her family, the ways of an outlaw father became a memory as they lived the joys and tragedies of their own lives. All too often, we forget how they were real people with dreams and desires of their own. They lived as we do, hoping for the best with each rising sun.

Letter from Robert Boller to Frank King

As they say, there are times when you have to take things "with a grain of salt". Robert Boller's letter to Frank King exemplifies this old idiom better than most. While working through the obvious nonsense, such as Boller's description of the utter fear Ringo had instilled in the Earps, there are a few nuggets of helpful information. It's a matter of separating the wheat from the chaff.

Fifty-two years after the death of Ringo, Robert Boller, a member of the coroner's jury, wrote the following letter.

September 20, 1934
Mr. Frank M. King
Los Angeles, California

My dear Mr. King:

In your letter of Sept. 17, you asked me if I noticed powder marks on Ringo's head. I am going into detail quite a bit.

I was driving team for McGregor—seven yoke of cattle. Smith's outfit was just ahead with five teams, seven yoke to the team. If they beat us to the mill, we would be delayed a day in getting our load. They would get the

---

[126] The Early History of the Town of Cochise; Brad Smith

mining timbers which was the choice of loads. Just before we reached the camp grounds, John Yoas stopped his team and called to the teamsters he had found a dead man. They had driven by and didn't notice him. He, Yoas, hesitated to go near the corpse until I got there. The first word he said after looking closely at the corpse was "My God, it's John Ringo!" The body had turned black and was smelling. Yoas said, "Some more dirty work of the Earps." I said, "John, you are crazy to think the Earps would dare follow Ringo. Hasn't he made them take water in their dumps in Tombstone, when Fred Ward and Bull Lewis went into the saloon and lead Ringo out telling him the Earps would shoot him in the back. You have heard Lewis and Ward both tell how he cowed Doc Holliday and three of the Earps singlehanded, then run them out of the territory." The Earps learning Ringo was one of Sheriff Behan's posse they hightailed out of Arizona.

Three trees had grown around a boulder about eighteen inches across and to this day looks like they're planted there to make a chair. Leaning against the tree on his right was his Winchester rifle. His hat, a light colored Stetson about three inch rim, lay beside the rifle. He sat on the rock. He had taken his boots off. He had drawers, tore them up and wrapped them around his feet. He had on two belts, one was upside down. That was his rifle cartridge belt, only seven cartridges in it. The other belt was full, if I remember rightly, Colt's 45. He wore no coat. He had on a vest. He wore a very heavy silver link watch chain attached to a very heavy silver watch. The hook on the chain was hooked into his vest on his right side. The vest was unbuttoned. In his right hand he held his 45 Colt's. The sight on the barrel had caught on his watch chain and held his hand from dropping into his lap. He had held the sixshooter against his head about an inch above his right ear and pulled the trigger. That is the way we all agreed that it happened except John Yoast, and he too was convinced when I showed him where the bullet had entered the tree on his left side. Blood and brains oozing from the wound and matted his hair. There was an empty shell in the sixshooter and the hammer was on that.

I called it suicide fifty-two years ago. I am still calling it suicide. I guess I am the last of that coroner's jury.

With my best wishes, I am,

Sincerely yours,

Robt. M. Boller

The Wild Goose Chase

Research is not always a perfect science. To our surprise, we found a second John "Yost" living in Cochise County. The spelling was different, without the "a", which is more conducive with most of the eastern members of the "Yost" family. John lived in Cochise County for about six years, but passed away on December 3, 1909 at the age of 31. His body was taken back to his home town of Pleasant Dale, West Virginia, and buried there. He would have been four years old at the time of Ringo's death. There was no way he could have known him "both in Texas and Arizona."

We found numerous references to Bert Yoast in the Arizona press. Two articles spelled the last name as "Yoast", with several using the "Yost" spelling. Most interesting, was a social blurb from February 1907 that really caught our attention. Did John Yoast have a brother in town? The family genealogy said no.

> Bert Yoast was in the city last evening from the Sulphur Spring Valley to meet his brother, John Yoast, who who will spend a few weeks out in the valley with Bert.

Tombstone Weekly Epitaph; February 17, 1907

This advertisement for Kenny's Wild West Show was in the Arizona Daily Orb in Bisbee on Saturday July 22, 1911. Bert, who still lived in Sulphur Springs Valley was riding in the Wild West Show.

Kenney's Wild West Show

Immediately After Ball Game
22 Outlaw Horses--6 Riders--Cowboy Band

During the Wild West Show, Joe Kline, from Alpine, Texas, will ride Big Snake, the S. V. Gray, Sandy Bob and Sheeney.

Bert Yost, the famous Arizona rough rider, will ride the S. O. Black, the S. O. Sorrel, the S. O. Pinto and the Mexican Outlaw.

Luther Graham, of New Mexico, formerly with Buffalo Bill and Pawnee Bill, will ride the Lazy S Sorrel, Wild Bill, the Bouquillas Roan and Silvertail.

Jim Kenney will ride the notorious Pinto, (under a guarantee to hit it with his quirt every time it strikes the ground) the S. O. Bay, Squabble O. Bay and the Pete Johnson outlaw.

Willie Hileman, of Bisbee, will ride the Baby Sorrel.

George Smith, of Lowell, will ride Waumpas.

Kid Kenney will show the people that he can ride the gray outlaw that threw him on the Fourth.

Jim Kenney challenges all comers to a mile relay race with four changes.

Admission to both ball game and Wild West Show 50 cents. Music by Cowboy Band.

--- TICKETS ON SALE---

BREWERY GULCH, Shattuck Inc., Hileman's Cigar Stand, Hartelano Pax. MAIN STREET, K. B. Wallace Cigar Stand, Antlers Pax. Exchange Inc., Mass Cigar Stand, Hix box Drug Co., Indian Busbee, Chisholm's Cigar Stand. LOWELL, Legal Tender, Waite House, Arizol.

Grand Free Street Parade at 10 a. m. in Naco Road and Tombstone Canyon

Bert "Yoast" turned out to be the brother of John Yost from West Virginia. Initially, we began with the possibility of Bert being the brother of John Yoast from Texas. Had he been, and lived in close proximity of Sulphur Springs at the time of Ringo's death, then we had a possible connection with the horse. Our research eliminated that possibility.

Bert was a well-known rodeo rider in the time frame around 1910, and worked horses for James Kinney at his ranch in Sulphur Springs Valley. Bert headlined Kinney's Wild West Show as the "Arizona Rough Rider." Sometimes research can be interesting, but turn out to be irrelevant. We must always remember, these were real people with real families. Respect for the truth, and for those involved is as important today as when they were alive.

EPITAPH, THE STATEMENT OF WYATT EARP, NOV. 17, 1881
FIFTEENTH DAY
THE STATEMENT OF WYATT EARP

Q. What is your name and age?

A. Wyatt S. Earp; age 32 last March.

Q Where were you born?

A. Monmouth, Warren County, Illinois.

Q. Where do you reside and how long have you resided there?

A. Tombstone; since Dec. 1st, 1879.

Q. What is your business or profession?

A. Saloon keeper; have also been employed as a deputy sheriff, and also as a detective.

Q. Give any explanation you may think proper of the circumstances appearing in the testimony against you, and state any facts which you think will tend to your exculpation.

A. The difficulty between deceased and myself originated first when I followed Tom McLowry and Frank McLowry, with Virgil and Morgan Earp and Captain Hearst and four soldiers to look for six government mules which were stolen. A man named Estes told us at Charleston, that we would find the mules at McLowry's ranch, that the McLowrys were branding "D. S." over "U. S." We tracked the mules to McLowry's ranch, where we also found the brand. Afterwards some of those mules were found with the same brand. After we arrived at McLowry's ranch there was a man named Frank Patterson who made some kind of a compromise with Captain Hearst. Captain Hearst came to us boys and told us he had made this compromise and by so doing he would get the mules back. We insisted on following them up. Hearst prevailed upon us to go back to Tombstone, and so we came back. Hearst told us two or three weeks afterwards that they would not give up the mules to him after we left, saying they only wanted to get us away: that they could stand the soldiers off. Captain Hearst cautioned me and Virgil and Morgan to look out for those men; that they had made some hard threats against the lives. About one month after that, after those mules had been taken, I met Frank and Tom McLowry in Charleston. They tried to pick a fuss out of me, and told me that if I ever followed them up again as close as I did before that they would kill me.

Shortly after the time Budd Philpot was killed by those men who tried to rob the Benson stage, as a detective I helped trace the matter up, and I was satisfied that three men, named Billy Leonard, Harry Head and Jim Crane were in that robbery. I know that Leonard, Head and Crane were friends and associates of the Clantons and McLowrys and often stopped at their ranches. It was generally understood among officers, and those who have information about criminals, that Ike Clanton was a sort of chief among the cowboys; that the Clantons and McLowrys were cattle thieves, and generally in the secrets of the stage robbers; and that the Clanton and McLowrys ranches were the meeting place, and place of shelter for the gang.

I had an ambition to be sheriff of this county next election, and I thought it would be a great help to me with the people and the business men if I could capture the men who killed Philpot. There were rewards offered of about $1,200 each for the robbers. Altogether there was about $3,600 offered for their capture. I thought that this amount might tempt Ike Clanton and Frank McLowry to give away Leonard, Head and Crane; so, I went to Ike Clanton and Frank McLowry, when they came in town. I had an interview with them in the back yard of the Oriental saloon. I told them what I wanted. I told them I wanted the glory of capturing Leonard, Head and Crane; if I could do so, it would help me make the race for sheriff next election. I told them if they would put on the track of Leonard, Head and Crane--- tell me where those men were hid---I would give them all the reward, and would never let anybody know where I got the information. Ike Clanton said that he would be glad to have Leonard captured, that Leonard claimed a ranch that he claimed, and if he could get him out of the way he would have no opposition about the ranch. Ike Clanton said that Leonard, Head and Crane would make a fight, that they would never be taken alive, and that I must first find out if the reward would be paid for the capture of the robbers dead or alive. I then went to Marshall Williams, the agent of Wells, Fargo & Co., in this town, and at my request he telegraphed to the agent of Wells, Fargo & Co., at San Francisco to find out if the reward would be paid for the robbers dead or alive. He received in June, 1881 a telegram which he gave me, promising that the reward should be paid dead or alive. I showed this telegram soon after I got it to Ike Clanton in front of the Alhambra and afterwards told (approx. 26 lines in the copy of the Epitaph had been covered by a white rectangle. This section will be replaced by the report for the Nugget.) ***Frank McLowry of its contents. It was then agreed between us that they should have all the $3.600 reward outside of necessary expenses for horses in going after them and Joe Hill should go to where Leonard, Head, and Crane were hid, over near Eureka, in New Mexico, and lure them in near Frank and Tom McLowry's ranch near Soldier Holes, 30 miles from here, and I would be on hand with a posse and capture them. I asked Joe Hill, Ike Clanton and Frank McLowry what tale they would make to them to get them over here. They said they had agreed upon a plan to tell them that there would be a pay master going from Tombstone to Bisbee shortly to pay off the miners, and that they wanted them to come in and take them; Ike Clanton then sent Joe Hill to bring them in; before starting Joe Hill took on his watch and chain and between two and three hundred dollars in money, and gave it to Virgil Earp to keep for him until he got back. He was gone about ten days and returned with the word that he had got there a day too late; that Leonard and Harry Head had been killed the day before he got there by horse thieves. I learned afterward that the thieves had been killed subsequently by members of the Clanton and McLowry gang.

After that Ike Clanton and Frank McLowry said I had given them away to Marshal Williams and Doc Holliday, and when they came in town they shunned us, and Morgan and Virgil Earp and Doc Holliday and myself began to hear of their threats against us. I am a friend of Doc Holliday, because when I was city marshal of Dodge City, Kansas, he came to my rescue and saved my life, when I was surrounded by desperadoes. A month or so ago Morgan and I assisted to arrest Stillwell and Spence on the charge of robbing the Bisbee stage. The McLowrys and Clantons have always been friendly with Spence and Stillwell, and they laid the whole blame of their arrest on us, though the fact is, we only went as a sheriff's posse. After we got in town with Spence and Stillwell, Ike Clanton and Frank McLowry came in. Frank McLowry took Morgan into the middle of the street, where John Ringgold, Ike Clanton and the Hicks boys were standing, and commenced to abuse Morgan Earp for going after Spence and Stillwell. Frank McLowry said he would never speak to Spence again for being arrested by us. He said to Morgan, "If ever you come after me you will never take me." Morgan replied that if he ever had occasion to go after him he would arrest him. Frank McLowry then said to him, "I have threatened you boys' lives, and a few days ago I had taken it back, but since this arrest it now goes." Morgan made no reply, and walked off.

Before this and after this, Marshal Williams and Farmer Daly, and Ed. Burns and three or four others, told us at different times of threats made to kill us, by Ike Clanton, Frank McLowry: Tom McLowry, Joe Hill and John Ringgold. 1 knew that all these men were desperate and dangerous, cattle thieves, robbers and murderers. I knew of the Clantons and McLowrys stealing six government mules. I heard of Ringgold shooting a man down in cold blood near Camp Thomas. I was satisfied that Frank and Tom McLowry killed and robbed Mexican in the Skeleton Canyon two or three months ago, and I naturally keep my eyes open, and I did not intend that any of the gang should get the drop on me if I could help it.

Three or four weeks ago Ike Clanton met me at the Alhambra, and told me that I had told Holliday about this transaction, concerning the capture of Head and Leonard. I told him I never told Holliday anything. I told him when Holliday came up from Tucson I would prove it. Ike Clanton said that Holliday had told him so; when Holliday came I asked him and he said no; I told him that Ike Clanton had said so.

On the 25th of October Holliday met Ike Clanton in the Alhambra saloon and asked him about it. Clanton denied it, and they quarreled for three or four minutes. Holliday told Ike Clanton he was a d-d liar, if he said so. I was sitting eating lunch at the time. They got up and walked out on the street. I got through and walked out, and they were still talking about it. I then went to Holliday, who was pretty tight, and took him away. Then I came back alone and met Ike Clanton. He called me outside and said his gun was on the other side of the street at the hotel. I told him to leave it there. He said he would make a fight with Holliday any time he wanted to. I told him Holliday did not want to fight, but only to satisfy him this talk had not been made. I then went away and went to the Oriental, and in a few minutes, Ike Clanton came over with his six shooter on. He said he was not fixed right; that in the morning he would have man for man that this fighting talk had been going on for a long time, and it was about time to fetch it to a close. I told him that I wouldn't fight no one if I could get away from it. He walked off and left me, saying, "I will be ready for all of you in the morning." He followed me into the Oriental, having his six shooter in plain sight. He said, "You musn't think 1 won't be after you all in the morning." Myself and Holliday walked away and went to our rooms.

I got up next day, October 26, about noon. Before I got up, Ned Bolye came to me and told me that he met Ike Clanton on Allen street, near the telegraph office that morning; that Ike was armed; that he said "As soon as those d-d Earps make their appearance on the street to day the battle will open," That Ike said, "We are here to make a fight, we are looking for the sons of b--s." Jones came to me after I got up and went to the saloon, and said, "What does all this mean?" I asked what he meant. He says, "Ike Clanton is hunting you Earp boys with a Winchester rifle and a six shooter. "I said, I will go down and find him and see what he wants." I went out, and on the corner of Fourth and Allen streets I met Virgil Earp, the marshal. He told me how he had heard that Ike Clanton was hunting us. I went up Allen Street, and Virgil went down Fifth Street and then Fremont Street. Virgil found Ike Clanton on Fourth Street in an alley. He walked up to him and said, "I hear you are hunting for some of us." Ike Clanton then threw his Winchester rifle around towards Virgil. Virgil grabbed it and hit Clanton with his six shooter and knocked him down. Clanton had his rifle, and his six shooter was exposed in his pants. By that time I came up, and Virgil and Morgan took his rifle and six shooter away and took them to the Grand Hotel after the examination, and took Ike Clanton before Justice Wallace. Before the investigation Morgan Earp had Ike Clanton in charge, as Virgil Earp was out. A short time after I went into Wallace's court and sat down on a bench.

Ike Clanton looked over to me and says, "I will get even with all of you for this. If I had a six shooter I would make a fight with all of you." Morgan then said to him, "If you want to make a fight right bad, I will give you this one." At the same time offering Ike Clanton his (Ike's) own six shooter. Ike Clanton started to get up to take it, when Campbell, the deputy sheriff, pushed him back on his seat, saying he wouldn't allow any fuse. I never had Ike Clanton's arms at any time as he has stated.

I would like to describe the position we occupied in the courtroom at that time. Ike Clanton sat down on a bench, with his face fronting to the north wall of the building. I myself sat down on a bench that was against the north wall right in front of Ike. Morgan Earp stood up against the north wall with his back against the north wall, two or three feet to my right. Morgan Earp had Ike Clanton's Winchester in his left hand and his six shooter in his right hand, one end of the rifle was on the floor. Virgil Earp was not in the court room any of the time, and Virgil Earp came there after I walked out.

I was tired of being threatened by Ike Clanton and his gang. I believed from what they had said to others and to me, and from their movements, that they intended to assassinate me the first chance they had, and I thought if I had to fight for my life against them, I had better make them face me in an open fight. So, I said to Ike Clanton, who was then sitting about eight feet away from me, "you d--d dirty cur thief, you have been threatening our lives, and I know it. I think I should be justified shooting you down any place I should meet you, but if you are anxious to make a fight, I will go anywhere on earth to make a fight with you, even over to the San Simon among your own crowd." He replied, "all right, I will see you after I get through here. I only want four feet of ground to fight on." I walked out and just then outside the court room, near the justice's office, I met Tom McLowry. He came up to me and said to me, "If you want to make a fight I will make a fight with you anywhere." I supposed at the time he had heard what had first transpired between Ike Clanton and me. I knew of his having threatened me and I felt just as I did about Ike Clanton, that if the fight had to come, I had better have it come when I had an even show to defend myself, so I said to him all right "make a fight right here," and at the same time I slapped him in the face with my left hand, and drew my pistol with my right. He had a pistol in plain sight on his right hip, but made no move to draw it. I said to him, "Jerk your gun use it." He made no reply and I hit him on the head with my six shooter and walked away down to Hafford's corner. I went into Hafford's and got a cigar, and came out and stood by the door. Pretty soon after I saw Tom McLowry, Frank McLowry and William Clanton. They passed me and went down Fourth Street to the gunsmith shop. I followed down to see what they were going to do. When I got there Frank McLowry's horse was standing on the sidewalk with his head in the door of the gun shop. I took the horse by the bit, as I was deputy city marshal, and commenced to back him off the sidewalk. Frank and Tom McLowry and Billy Clanton came to the door, Billy Clanton had his hand on his six shooter. Frank McLowry took hold of the horse's bridle. I said "you will have to get this horse off the sidewalk." He backed him off on the street Ike Clanton came up about that time and they all walked into the gunsmith's shop. I saw them in the shop changing cartridges into their belts. They came out of the shop and walked along Fourth Street to the corner of Allen street. I followed them as far as the corner of Fourth and Allen streets, and then they went down Allen Street and over to Dunbar's corral. Virgil Earp was then city marshal; Morgan Earp was a special policeman for six weeks, wore a badge and drew pay. I had been sworn in Virgil's place to act for him while Virgil was gone to Tucson on Stillwell and Spence, on the charge of robbing the Bisbee stage trial. Virgil had been back several days, but I was still acting. I know it was Virgil's duty to disarm those men. He suspected he would have trouble in doing so; and I followed up to give assistance if necessary, especially as they had been threatening us, as I have already stated. About ten minutes afterwards, and while Virgil, Morgan, Doc Holliday and myself were standing in the center of Fourth and Allen streets several persons said, "there is going to be trouble with those fellows," and one man named Coleman said to Virgil Earp, "they mean trouble. They have just gone from Dunbar's corral into the O. K. corral, all armed. I think you had better go and disarm them." Virgil turned around to Doc Holliday, Morgan Earp and myself and told us to come and assist him in disarming them. Morgan Earp said to me, "they have horses; had we not better get some horses ourselves, so that if they make a running fight we can catch them?" I said, "No, if they try to make a running fight we can kill their horses, and then capture them." We four then started through Fourth to Fremont Street. When we turned the corner of Fourth and Fremont streets we could see them standing near or about the vacant space between Fly's photograph gallery and the next building west. I first saw Frank McLowry, Torn McLowry, Billy Clanton and Sheriff Behan standing there. We went down the left-hand side of Fremont Street. When I got within about 150 feet of them I saw Ike Clanton, Billy Claiborne and another party. We had walked a few steps further when I saw Behan leave the party and come towards us, every few steps he would look back as if he apprehended danger. I heard Behan say to Virgil Earp, "For God's sake don't go down there or you will get murdered." Virgil replied, "I am going to disarm them"-- he, Virgil Earp, being in the lead. When I and Morgan came up to Behan, he said "I have disarmed them." When he said this I took my pistol, which I had in my hand, under my coat, and put it in my overcoat pocket.

Behan then passed up the street, and we walked on down. We came up on them close-Frank McLowry, Tom McLowry and Billy Clanton standing all in a row against the east side of the building on the opposite side of the vacant space west of Fly's photography gallery.

Ike Clanton and Billy Claiborne and a man I did not know were standing in the vacant space about halfway between the photograph gallery and the next building west. I saw that Billy Clanton and Frank McLowry and Tom McLowry had their hands by their sides and Frank McLowry's and Billy Clanton's six shooters were in plain sight. Virgil said, "Throw up your hands. I have come to disarm you." Billy Clanton and Frank McLowry had their hands on their six shooters. Virgil said, "Hold, I don't mean that; I have come to disarm you." They-----Billy Clanton and Frank McLowry---commenced to draw their pistols, at the same time Tom McLowry threw his hand to his right hip and jumped behind a horse.

I had my pistol in my overcoat pocket where I had put it when Behan told us he had disarmed the other party. When I saw Billy and Frank draw their pistols, I drew my pistol. Billy Clanton leveled his pistol at me but I did not aim at him. I knew that Frank McLowry had the reputation of being a good shot and a dangerous man, and I aimed at Frank McLowrv. The two first shots which were fired were fired by Billy Clanton and myself he; shot at me, and I shot at Frank McLowry. I do not know which shot was first; we fired almost together. The fight then became general. After about four shots were fired Ike Clanton ran up and grabbed my arm. I could see no weapon in his hand and thought at the time he had none, and so I said to him, "The fight has now commenced, go to fighting or get away."

At the same time, I pushed him off with my left hand. He started and ran down the side of the building and disappeared between the lodging house and the photograph gallery.

My first shot struck Frank McLowry in the belly. He staggered off on the sidewalk but first fired one shot at me. When we told them to throw up their hands, Claiborne held up his left hand, and then broke and ran. I never saw him afterwards until later in the afternoon, after the fight. I never drew my pistol or made a motion to shoot until after Billy Clanton and Frank McLowry drew their pistols.

If Tom McLowry was unarmed I did not know it. I believe he was armed and that he fired two shots at our party before Holliday, who had the shotgun, fired at and killed him. If he was unarmed there was nothing to the circumstances or in what had been communicated to me, or in his acts or threats, that would have led me even to suspect his being unarmed. I never fired at Ike Clanton, even after the shooting commenced, because I thought he was unarmed and I believed then, and believe now, from the acts I have stated, and the threats I have related, and other threats communicated to me by different persons, as having been made by Tom McLowry, Frank McLowry and Isaac Clanton, that these men, last named, had formed a conspiracy to murder my brothers Morgan and Virgil, and Doc Holliday and myself.

I believe I would have been legally and morally justified in shooting any of them on sight, but I did not do so or attempt to do so; I sought no advantage. When I went as deputy marshal to help disarm them and arrest them, I went as a part of my duty and under the direction of my brother, the marshal. I did not intend to fight unless it became necessary in self-defense, and in the performance of official duty. When Billy Clanton and Frank McLowry drew their pistols, I knew it was a fight for life, and I drew and fired in defense of my own life and the lives of my brothers and Doc Holliday.

I have been in Tombstone since December 1, 1879. I came here from Dodge City Kansas, where, against the protest of business men and officials, I resigned the office of City Marshal, which I held from 1876. I came to Dodge City from Wichita, Kansas. I was on the police force in Wichita, from 1874 until I went to Dodge City.

The testimony of Isaac Clanton that I had anything to do with any stage robbery, or any criminal enterprise, is a tissue of lies from beginning to end. Sheriff Behan made me an offer in his office on Allen Street, and in the back room of the cigar store, that if I would withdraw and not try to get appointed sheriff of Cochise County, that we would hire a clerk and divide the profits. I done so; and he never said another word to me afterward in regard to it. The reasons given by him here for not complying with his contract are false.

I give here as a part of this statement, a document sent me from Dodge City, since my arrest, and marked Exhibit "A", and another document sent me from Wichita, since this arrest, which I wish attached to this statement, and marked Exhibit "B".

Myself and Doc Holliday happened to go to Charleston the night that Behan happened to go down to subpoena Ike Clanton. We went there for the purpose of getting a horse that had been stolen from us a few days after I came to Tombstone. I had heard several times that the Clantons had him. When I got there that night I was told by a friend of mine that the man that carried the dispatch from Charleston to Ike Clanton's ranch had my horse. At this time, I did not know where Ike Clanton's ranch was. A short time afterward I was in the Huachucas, locating some water rights. I had started home to Tombstone, and had got within twelve or fifteen miles of Charleston, when I met a man named McMasters. He told me if I would hurry up I would find my horse in Charleston. I drove to Charleston, and saw my horse going through the streets toward the corral. I put up for the night at another corral. I went to Barnett's office, to get out papers to recover the horse. He was not at home, having gone to Sonora to see some coal fields that had been discovered.

I telegraphed to Tombstone, to James Earp, and papers were made out and sent to Charleston that night. While I was in town waiting for the papers, Billy Clanton found out I was there. He went and tried to take the horse out of the corral. I told him that he could not take him out, that it was my horse. After the papers came he gave the horse up without the papers being served, and asked me "if I had any more horses to lose." I told him I would keep them in the stable after this, and not give him a chance to steal them.

In one of the conversations I had with Ike Clanton about giving away Leonard, Head and Crane, I told him one reason why I wanted to catch them was to prove to the citizens of Tombstone that Doc Holliday had nothing to do with it, as there were some false statements circulated to that effect. In following the trail of Leonard, Head and Crane, we struck it at the scene of the attempted robbery, and never lost the trail or hardly a footprint from the time that we started from Drew's ranch, on the San Pedro, until we got to Helm's ranch, in the Dragoons.

After following about eight miles down the San Pedro river and capturing one of the men, named King that was supposed to be in with them, we then crossed the Catalina mountains within fifteen miles of Tucson, following their trail around the front of the mountain after they had crossed over to Tres Alamos, on the San Pedro river. We then started out from Helm's ranch and got on their trail. They had stolen fifteen or twenty head of stock so as to cover their trail. Wyatt Earp, Morgan Earp, R.H. Paul, Breckenridge, Johnny Behan and one or two others still followed the trail up into New Mexico. Their trail never led south from Helm's ranch, as Ike Clanton has stated.

We used every effort we could to capture these men. I was out ten days. Virgil Earp and Morgan Earp were out sixteen days, and we done all we could to capture these men, and I safely say if it had not been for myself and Morgan Earp, they would not have got King, as he started to run when we rode up to his hiding place, and was making for a big patch of brush on the river, and would have got in it if it had not been for us.

DEFENSE EXHIBIT "A"

To All Whom It May Concern, Greetings:

We, the undersigned citizens of Dodge City, Ford County, Kansas, and vicinity do by these present certify that we are personally acquainted with Wyatt Earp, late of this city; that he came here in the year 1876; that during the years of 1877, 1878, and 1879 he was Marshal of our city; that he left our place in the fall of 1879; that during his whole stay here he occupied a place of high social position and was regarded and looked upon as a high-minded, honorable citizen; that as Marshal of our city he was ever vigilant in the discharge of his duties, and while kind and courteous to all, he was brave, unflinching, and on all occasions proved himself the right man in the right place.

Hearing that he is now under arrest, charged with complicity in the killing of those men termed "Cow Boys." From our knowledge of him we do not believe that he would wantonly take the life of his fellow man, and that if he was implicated, he only took life in the discharge of his sacred trust to the people; and earnestly appeal to the citizens of Tombstone, Arizona, to use all means to secure him a fair and impartial trial, fully confident that when tried he will be fully vindicated and exonerated of any crime.

R.M. Wright	Representative, Ford County
Lloyd Shinn	Probate Judge, Ford County, Kansas
M.W. Sutton	County Attorney, Ford County
George F. Hinkle	Sheriff, Ford County, Kansas
J.W. Liellow	Ford County Commissioner
F.C. Zimmerman	Ford County, Treasurer and Tax Collector
G.W. Potter	Clerk of Ford County
Thomas S. Jones	Police Judge and Attorney at Law
A.B. Weber	Mayor, Dodge City, Kansas
C.M. Beeson	City Council, Dodge City, Kansas
Geo. Emerson	City Council, Dodge City, Kansas
A.H. Boyd	City Council, Dodge City, Kansas
J.H. Philips	Deputy County Treasurer, Ford County
R.G. Cook	U.S. Commissioner
Wright, Beverly & Co.	Dodge City Merchants
Herman F. Fringey	Postmaster, Dodge City, Kansas
O.W. Wright	Pastor, Presbyterian Church
March and Son	Merchants
W.W. Robins	Groceries

H.P. Weiss	Shoemaker
Fred T. M. Wenir	Notary Public and Insurance Agent
R.C. Burns	Attorney
H.M. Bell	Deputy United States Marshal
T.L. McCarty	M.D.
D.E. Frost	Ex-Police Judge
Beeson and Harris	Liquor Dealers

(an additional 35 citizens signed the paper).

THE TOMBSTONE EPITAPH, A FATAL GARMENT, JULY 25, 1880

About 7 o'clock last evening the pistol was used with fatal effect on Allen Street, resulting in the death of T.J. Waters from gunshot wounds from a weapon in the hand of E.L. Bradshaw. The causes which led to this unfortunate tragedy are brief. Waters was what is considered a sporting man, and has been in Tombstone several months. He was about forty years of age, powerful build, stood over six feet in height and weighed about 190 pounds. When sober he was a clever sort of man but quite the opposite when under the influence of liquor. Yesterday he won considerable money and had been drinking a great deal, hence was in a mood to be easily irritated. Bradshaw was an intimate friend of Waters but a very different character, being a man of medium size, over fifty years of age and very reserved and peaceable in his disposition. We understand that these two men had prospected together and when Waters first came to Tombstone he lived in Bradshaw's cabin. Yesterday morning Waters purchased a blue and black plaid shirt, little dreaming that the fated garment would hurl his soul into eternity before the sun had set. It so happened that several good-natured remarks were made about the new shirt during the day until Waters had taken sufficient liquor to make the joking obnoxious to him, and he began to show an ugly resentment and was very abusive, concluding with, "Now, if anyone don't like what I've said let him get up, G-d d-n him. I'm chief. I'm boss. I'll knock the first s--- of a b--- down that says anything about my shirt again." This happened in the back room at Corrigan's saloon and as Waters stepped into the front room Bradshaw happened in, and seeing what his friend was wearing made some pleasant remark about it, whereupon Waters, without a word, struck Bradshaw a powerful blow over the left eye which sent him senseless to the floor. Waters then walked over to Vogan & Flynn's, to see, as he said, "if any s--- of a b--- there didn't like this shirt." He had just entered the street when Ed Ferris made some remark about the new shirt, which Waters promptly resented in his pugilistic style. After some more rowing Waters went back to Corrigan's saloon. As soon as Bradshaw recovered from the knockdown he went into the back room, washed off the blood, went down to his cabin, put a bandage on his eye and his pistol in his pocket. He then came up to Allen Street and took his seat in front of Vogan & Flynn's saloon. Seeing Waters in Corrigan's door, Bradshaw crossed towards the Eagle Brewery, and walking down the sidewalk until within a few feet of Waters, said: "Why did you do that?" Waters said something whereupon Bradshaw drew his pistol and fired four shots, all taking effect, one under the left arm probably pierced the heart, two entered above the center of the back between the shoulders and one in the top of the head ranged downward toward the neck, any one of which would probably have resulted fatally. Waters fell at the second shot and soon expired. Bradshaw was promptly arrested and examination will be had in the morning before Justice Gray.

THE TOMBSTONE EPITAPH, THE DEADLY BULLET, MARCH 20, 1882
THE ASSASSIN AT LAST SUCCESSFUL IN HIS DEVILISH MISSION.
MORGAN EARP SHOT DOWN AND KILLED WHILE PLAYING BILLIARDS

At 10:00 Saturday night while engaged in playing a game of billiards in Campbell & Hatch's Billiard parlor, on Allen between Fourth and Fifth, Morgan Earp was shot through the body by an unknown assassin. At the time the shot was fired he was playing a game with Bob Hatch, one of the proprietors of the house and was standing with his back to the glass door in the rear of the room that opens out upon the alley that leads straight through the block along the west side of A.D. Otis & Co.'s store to Fremont Street. This door is the ordinary glass door with four panes in the top in place of panels. The two lower panes are painted, the upper ones being clear. Anyone standing outside can look over the painted glass and see anything going on in the room just as well as though standing in the open door. At the time the shot was fired the deceased must have been standing within ten feet of the door, and the assassin standing near enough to see his position, took aim for about the middle of his person, shooting through the upper portion of the whitened glass. The bullet entered the right side of the abdomen, passing through the spinal column, completely shattering it, emerging on the left side, passing the length of the room and lodging in the thigh of Geo. A.B. Berry, who was standing by the stove, inflicting a painful flesh wound. Instantly after the first shot a second was fired through the top of the upper glass which passed across the room and lodged in the wall near the ceiling over the head of Wyatt Earp, who was sitting as a spectator of the game. Morgan fell instantly upon the first fire and lived only about one hour. His brother Wyatt, Tipton, and McMasters rushed to the side of the wounded man and tenderly picked him up and moved him some ten feet away near the door of the card room, where Drs. Matthews, Goodfellow and Millar, who were called, examined him and, after a brief consultation, pronounced the wound mortal. He was then moved into the card room and placed on the lounge where in a few brief moments he breathed his last, surrounded by his brothers, Wyatt, Virgil, James and Warren with the wives of Virgil and James and a few of his most intimate friends. Notwithstanding the intensity of his mortal agony, not a word of complaint escaped his lips, and all that were heard, except those whispered into the ear of his brother and known only to him were, "Don't, I can't stand it. This is the last game of pool I'll ever play." The first part of the sentence being wrung from him by an attempt to place him upon his feet.

The funeral cortege started away from the Cosmopolitan hotel about 12:30 yesterday with the fire bell tolling its solemn peals of "Earth to earth, dust to dust."

Guadalupe Canyon in relation to the Arizona - New Mexico – Mexico Border

To understand the movements of the cow-boy ring, you have to understand the tactics behind the geography of their headquarters and placement of cattle. Utilizing the border of Arizona and New Mexico, Ringo and his bunch could maintain a jurisdictional advantage. With one foot across the line, that could move cattle in a moment's notice if any serious involvement by the law came to the door.

The Gird Block

Much of Tombstone's commerce, civic, and legal activity took place here. In the center building, was the office where the November '81 hearing for Wyatt Earp and Doc Holliday was held. The Tombstone miming company was also in that building, were the first telephone was installed in December 1880.

Schieffelin Hall in the distance has been restored, and promotes a number of shows and events annually in the old tradition. The buildings in the foreground are sadly gone. By the time an effort to restore the town was underway, these buildings were too far gone. That space is now a parking lot.

W. John Parks, taken several months before he left Texas for the West in 1879.

Mrs. John Parks, in 1885

Sheriff Jim Parks and wife. Taken during his first term as sheriff of Graham County

John Parks, chief deputy for his brother Jim for six years, when the latter was sheriff of Graham County

TESTIMONY OF MR. R.F. COLEMAN; EARP-HOLLIDAY HEARING; CASE #48 NOVEMBER 1881

TERRITORY OF ARIZONA)
) SS
COUNTY OF COCHISE   )

R.F. Coleman being duly sworn deposes and says that his name is R.F. Coleman and that he resides in the City of Tombstone, Cochise Co., A.T. and that his business that of a mining man.

I saw the trouble that occurred on Oct. 26, 81.

Statement:

I saw the arrest of Ike Clanton before the shooting commenced.

I saw the City Marshal go up to Ike Clanton from behind and partially towards his side Marshal Earp spoke to him but I did not hear what he said. The Marshal made a grab and took a rifle out of Clanton's Hand. There then seemed to be a bit of a scuffle by both of them when Clanton fell. I did not see the Marshal strike him but I saw Clanton fall and they took his revolver from him and took him into the Police Court.

Earp had a revolver in his hand but whether he took it from Clanton or not I could not say. After the trial was over Marshal Earp offered Ike Clanton his rifle some words passed between them. I could not hear what it was. He did not take his rifle, some words passed between them Ike Clanton said all I want is ~~four~~ 4 ft. of ground. They then passed out of Court. Ike Clanton went across to Smith's old store. That is the last I saw of him 'til I saw him with his brother Billy on Allen Street going down towards Dunbar's Corral. I was standing at the front of the OK Corral on Allen Street, in Dunbar's Corral I saw the 2 Clantons and 2 McLowery boys in one of the stalls in deep conversation. I saw Mr. J. Dolling speaking to Ike Clanton. After they had got through with the talk amongst themselves they then came out of the coral and came over towards the OK Corral, I mean the 2 Clantons and 2 McLowery.

Billy Clanton was on horseback Frank McLowery was leading his horse when they came up to where I was standing. Billy Clanton remarked to me it was very cold. He asked me then where the West End Corral was. I told him it was down on Fremont Street. Frank McLowery had passed on before this talk between me and Billy Clanton. Ike Clanton fetched up the rear. As soon as they left me, I walked up Allen Street. There I met Sheriff Behan I told him that he should go and disarm those men. I thought they meant mischief – he asked me where they had gone [and] I told him. – I walked up a few steps farther and met Marshal Earp – I then walked back and passed through the OK Corral towards Fremont Street taking Billy Allen with me. I passed down Fremont Street till I got about to the front door of Fly's Gallery I saw Johnny Behan the Sheriff just leaving there – I heard one of the Clanton party say you need not be afraid Johnny – Johnny was about 12 ft. from them walking up the street – You need not be afraid Johnny we are not going to have any trouble or something to that effect.

I saw standing there Billy Clanton Frank McLowery Tom McLowery Ike Clanton Wm. Clanton – Billy Allen was standing right at the north east angle of the little building below Fly's – his horse at his side his back to the building and facing up the street. Frank McLowery stood next to him – Ike Clanton Tom McLowery and Wm. McLowery were standing 3 or 4 ft. from them – That is the position in which I saw them when I saw Johnny Behan leaving them – I turned around and went up Fremont Street – I got as far as Bauer's Meat Market – nearly opposite me at the time was Wyatt Earp Virgil Earp Morgan Earp Doc Holliday walking down the center of Fremont Street.

Johnny Behan walked up towards them [and said] "Hold boys, I don't want you to go any farther." I don't think they made any reply to his remark at all but passed on down the street till they came opposite to the Clanton party- the Earp party advanced towards the Clantons – I heard "sons-of-bitches" mentioned by which party I could not say. I was about 30 feet away – "throw up your arms, give up your arms" was said by the Earps – I think it was Wyatt – I then thought I was a little close. I turned around and as I turned, or, in the act of turning, two shots were fired – when the firing became general after the first two shots were fired Ike Clanton ran up and ran through Fly's Gallery – One shot fired at him came pretty near to me and struck a wagon standing in front of [the] Barber-shop – there was a second shot fired in that direction – Tom McLowery, after the two shots were fired, ran down Fremont Street and fell. Billy Clanton stood in the same position as when I first saw him, firing two or three shots while in a crouching position – I saw one of the shots hit Morgan Earp – he stumbled or fell – jumped up again commenced firing – about that time Frank McLowery ran out in the road towards Doc Holliday- some words passed between them as Frank McLowery advanced toward him kind of running.

Frank McLowery said "I have got you now", firing a shot at the same time which struck Doc Holliday on his hip or his scabbard – I hollered to Doc Holliday saying you have got it now – He remarked "I am shot right through." Frank McLowery then passed on across the street and fell with his head toward the north. Billy Clanton, after I think he must have been struck, went down in a crouching position. Taking his pistol across his knee, he fired two shots, one of which struck Marshal Earp. Wyatt and Morgan were still firing at Billy Clanton and he raised himself up and fell down still holding his pistol in his hand – then the shooting was over.

Just after the last shot was fired, Mr. Fly came running out of his Gallery with a rifle in his hand. I called Mr. Fly to take Billy Clanton's revolver out of his hand – at this time Billy Clanton was lying on his back trying to fire again with his head raised up a little – that is when I called to Mr. Fly to take the revolver from him.

After the shooting I saw Sheriff Behan and Wyatt Earp talking. I went up to the crowd – Johnny Behan said "I will have to arrest you" – Wyatt Earp said to Johnny Behan "I won't be arrested, you deceived me Johnny. You told me that they were not armed" and he repeated again "I will not be arrested but I am here to answer what I have done I am not going to leave town."

Someone spoke up and said there was no good in arguing the question now. I was not in a position to see whether they threw up their hands or not - I was near enough but I was just in the act of turning – I could not have seen whether they had their hands up or not except Billy Clanton – Billy Clanton had his hand on his pistol which was in the scabbard. His right hand was on his left hip as if in the act of drawing. This was after the first two shots were fired – I could not swear how many of the Clanton party were armed – I do not believe Ike Clanton was armed. When I spoke to the Marshal and told him that he ought to disarm those parties he said that he did not intend to disarm them – I do not know who jumped between me and Ike Clanton when he fell – I don't think there was anybody with the marshal when he arrested Ike Clanton – I think that the report I gave the Epitaph was pretty near correct as published.

I do not know who fired the shot at Ike Clanton as he was running off – Frank McLowery was approaching Holliday quartering just after Holliday said he was shot through – I can't say that I saw a shotgun in the hands of either party – I saw a Winchester rifle, I think. I don't remember seeing a shotgun or rifle during the trouble. I don't know who fired the first two shots but I had the impression it was from the road and the Earp party were in the road but I don't feel justified in swearing that the shots were fired from the road – I think that Billy Clanton was not hit at the 1st 2 shots – I do not think that Billy Clanton was hit before he commenced firing – I did not see Tom McLowery with a pistol – I could not have seen him for he was standing in a lot – my impression as that Tom McLowery started to run after the first 2 shots – my mind is a little confused about that part of it. At the time that the 1st 2 shots were fired I think that the two parties were 10 or 12 ft apart – It was my impression that Tom McLowery was running to get out of the shooting.

/s/R. F. Coleman

TESTIMONY OF MR. C.H. LIGHT; EARP-HOLLIDAY HEARING; CASE #48 NOVEMBER 1881

TERRITORY OF ARIZONA	)	
	) SS	
COUNTY OF COCHISE	)	

C. H. Light being duly sworn deposes and says that his name is C. H. Light and that he resides in Tombstone, Cochise County, A.T. and that his business is mining.

I was in Tombstone on the afternoon Oct. 26, '81 - I was a witness of a portion of the shooting affray which took place here between Doc Holliday and the Earp boys and the Clanton and McLowery boys - I only know Ike Clanton - I know the Earps and Holliday – have known Holliday since the shooting [and] have no personal acquaintance with him - I have since saw Doc Holliday and I know he was one of the party

Statement:

On the afternoon of the shooting I was in the barber shop getting shaved this was before the shooting - The barber told me that there was likely to be trouble between the Earps and the cowboys. He said the Earps had just passed down the street with their guns. I passed from there down to my house on the corner of Fremont Street and Third and I was in there when the shooting commenced - I heard two shots as quick as you could count 1,2. I jumped to the side window on Third St. looking up Fremont St. I saw several men in the act of shooting. At that instant, I saw a man reel and fall on the Corner of Fremont and 3rd Sts. on the south side right directly on the corner of the house. I do not know who that man was.

I looked up the street again. I saw three men standing at an angle about 10 or 15 ft apart about the center of the street facing Fly's photograph gallery. A man with a horse stood between them- between the men in the street and a vacant lot below Fly's Gallery and the house below - I then saw another man standing leaning against a building joining the vacant lot. There appeared to be two men firing at the man standing beside the horse. That man appeared to be struck from the motions that he made. Then he fired one shot at the lower man, at the northwesterly man, which I afterwards understood was Holliday. That shot appeared to take effect which was fired by the man with the horse for the other man turned partially around. I then looked at the man against the house expecting every moment to see some of them fall and he was in the act of sliding down on the ground, apparently wounded.

At that instant, the horse vanished. I do not know where he went to. This lower man was firing, apparently up the street. He fired one or two shots. I then saw the man who slid down the side of the house, lying down with his head and shoulders lying against the house, place his pistol on his leg and fire two shots - he tried to fire a 3rd shot but he was apparently too weak, the shot went into the air. At this time there was a tall man with grey clothes and broad hat standing about the middle of the street [who] fired two shots apparently in the direction of the man who had been leaning against the house.

Then, there appeared to be one party in the middle of the street firing down the street. This man who laid on the ground near the corner of the house never fired but 3 shots. He appeared to be disabled. Then there was a few more shots fired by parties on the north side of the street. The parties on the north side of the street has passed from my view and I was not able to see them my view was obscured.

The next thing I observe was two men standing beside the man that slid down on the south side of street near the corner of the building. A tall man dressed in black appeared on the scene with a rifle in his hand and said "take that pistol away from that man", meaning the man who was wounded or he would kill him. At this time the shooting was all over and I do not think the whole of it occupied over 10 or 15 seconds.

The tall man dressed in black was not a participant in the affray. There seemed to be six parties firing - four in the middle of the street and one on the south side of the street and the one with the horse. Afterward I recognized the man with the grey clothes as to be Doc Holliday. I think there was about 25 or 30 shots fired all together. I did not see any of the parties have a shotgun.

The fight occurred about 130 or 140 feet away from where I was. I think from the report that the first two were pistol shots. I think that there was one report from a shotgun. I saw the man who fell at the corner of the street lying there all the time of the fight. I did not see him shoot. He seemed to me to be the first man shot. There was not time enough for a man to draw a pistol to fire a shot between the first two shots - they must have been from two pistols. The man who fired the second shot must have been prepared to fire when the 1st shot was fired. These two shots I heard were fired before I went to the window but it did not take me but a second to get there.

/s/ C . H. Light

TESTIMONY OF MR. W.C. CLAYBORN[127]; EARP-HOLLIDAY HEARING; CASE #48 NOVEMBER 1881

TERRITORY OF ARIZONA)
) SS
COUNTY OF COCHISE   )

W. C. Clayborn being duly sworn deposes and says that his name is W. C. Clayborn and that he resides at Hereford, Cochise County A.T. His business is a driver in the employ of a New York M Co.

A. I was present on the afternoon of Oct. 26th, '81 when the shooting commenced between certain parties.
A. I am acquainted with the parties engaged in that affair.
A. There was Frank and Tom McLowery and Ike and Billy Clanton on one side and the Earp boys and Doc Holliday, Morgan Earp and two other brothers I do not know their names on the other side.
A. I was present at the time that the shooting took place
A. I was standing there with Mr. Behan and the McLowerys and Clantons.
A. I was there when Behan came up.
A. I was talking to Billy Clanton when he came up

Statement:

The day that this thing happened I went down with Ike Clanton to Doctor Gillingham's office to assist him in getting his head dressed and then I walked up 4th street and met Billy Clanton and Frank McLowery and Billy asked me where was Ike. He said "I want to get him to go out home." He said "I did not come here to fight anyone and no one didn't want to fight me" Then he asked me to go down to Johnny Behan's stable with him and we went down to Johnny Behan's corral and got Billy Clantons horse and went through the OK Corral.

Billy Clanton said he wanted to go to some other Corral to get his brother's horse and then we got down where the McLowery boys and Ike Clanton [were] and he told his brother Ike that he wanted him to go and get his horse and come home to the ranch and his brother told him that he would go directly, and then Mr. Behan the Sheriff came up and was talking to the boys. I did not hear what he said to them. I was talking to Billy and Behan was talking to Ike Clanton, Frank and Tom McLowery.

---

[127] Incorrectly spelled "Clayborn" by the court reporter, which is corrected in this text.

And then, shortly afterwards, Mr. Behan turned his back and walked up the street and the next thing I saw was Morgan Earp his two brothers and Doc Holliday and Marshall Earp said "you sons of bitches you have been looking for a fight and now you can get it". They both said the same thing and at the same time Marshall Earp said "throw up your hands", which Billy Clanton, Ike Clanton and Frank McLowery did and Tom McLowery took hold of the lapels of his coat [and] threw it open and said "I have not got anything".

At that instant the shooting commenced by Doc Holliday and Morgan Earp. The first shot was fired taking Tom McLowery. [It] was fired by Doc Holliday and the next one was fired by Morgan Earp taking Billy Clanton and Billy Clanton was shot with his hands up in this position (showing his hands raised in front and to one side). Billy Clanton said "don't shoot me, I don't want to fight". He said this after the shot was fired and that was the last I saw of Billy Clanton alive. Mr. Behan put me in the photograph gallery out of the way. He said stay there until I get back. I stayed there five or ten minutes.

That was all I saw except I saw the bodies afterwards. I saw the bodies in the presence of the coroner's jury at the house where they were taken to by the undertaker. I recognized the bodies as the bodies of Tom McLowery Frank McLowery and Billy Clanton. I knew them well in their lifetime; have known them about four years. I was sworn that night by the coroner and the statement I made to the Jury at that time was made under oath.

That is all I know. While I was standing talking to the Clantons and Frank McLowery in the presence of Mr. Behan, Ike Clanton and Tom and Frank McLowery were standing on the sidewalk below the photograph gallery about 10 feet facing up the street. I think one of the McLowery boys had a horse, holding it, and Billy and I was standing in the vacant place about half a way between the front and back end of that building, leaning up against the building. Me and Billy were about 4 feet a little more or less from the others. I don't know whether Billy heard the conversation on the part of the Sheriff or not.

Billy was talking with me there about 15 minutes while the Sheriff was there and Billy left me after the Sheriff went away in about 2 or 3 minutes and joined the other boys. When the Earp party came up they had their pistols in their hands. I saw Billy Clanton draw his pistol after he was shot down. I saw also Frank McLowery draw his pistol after about 6 shots had been fired by the Earps. I am positive that the first two shots took effect as I have before stated.

McLowery staggered backwards after the first shot; that was Tom McLowery. I did not see him fall. Tom McLowery did not have a weapon of any kind. I think there was about 16 shots fired before I went to the photograph gallery. I was kind of at one end in a vacant place. I was struck with a bullet through the pants leg. Ike Clanton got away from there after the first 7 or 8 shots. I did not see what Ike Clanton done before he got away. I think that the Sheriff was there about 20 minutes. Behan asked if I was one of the party, I told [him] no, I was not.

The distance between the two parties when they first commenced firing I think was about 4 feet. Doc Holliday fired the first shot with a nickel-plated six shooter. Billy Clanton did not exactly fall at the first shot, but staggered [and] just laid back but I think that he got up afterwards. I was not armed that day. I came into town the day before the shooting and left my arms at Kellogg's saloon. I think I saw the Sheriff when he met the Earp party coming down. I judge it was about twenty feet from the other party where the Sheriff met the Earp party.

I did not see a shotgun in the fight. Ike Clanton threw up his hands at first when the first two shots were fired by Morgan Earp and Holliday. the other two Earps were, I think, behind them or close to the side of them. I did not see the Sheriff at that time I don't remember of seeing him after he went up to meet the Earp boys. Behan put me in the house after the killing.

I think that there was as a couple of shots fired after I got into the house. I think that there was 28 or 30 fired. I think there was 16 or 17 fired before I was put into the house. As I was standing there talking to the Clanton boys, they were talking about going home and were not talking about fighting. I think that it was while Behan was there I saw the other two Earp brothers fire a shot.

I think that Billy Clanton was in town about a half an hour before the shooting. Frank came in with Billy so I understood. I do not know how long Tom McLowery had been in. I cannot exactly tell when the other two Earps commenced to shoot. I don't remember how many shots had been fired before they commenced to fire. I know that the other two Earps commenced firing before Billy Clanton and Frank McLowery commenced firing. I think I saw Wm A. Cuddy pass by while I was standing in a vacant place. I was not talking to anybody.

/s/ Willie Clayborn

TESTIMONY OF MR. JOSEPH "IKE" CLANTON; EARP-HOLLIDAY HEARING; CASE #48 NOVEMBER 1881

TERRITORY OF ARIZONA)
) SS
COUNTY OF COCHISE)

Joseph I. Clanton being duly sworn deposes and says that his name is Joseph I. Clanton and that his occupation is that of a cattle dealer – and that he resides in Cochise County A.T.

I was present in Tombstone on Oct. 26, '81. I am a brother of Wm. Clanton who was killed that day I saw the whole transaction.

Statement:

The night before the shooting I went into the Occidental lunch room for lunch and while in there, Doc Holliday came in and commenced abusing me. He had his hand on his pistol and called me a "da-d son of a b-h" and told me to get my gun out. I told him that I did not have any gun. I looked around to see Morg Earp sitting in the bar behind me with his hand on his gun. Doc Holliday kept on abusing me. I then went out of the door.

Virg Earp and Morg were all out there. Morg Earp told me if I wanted a fight to turn myself loose. They all had their hands on their pistols while they were talking to me. I told them again I was not armed. Doc Holliday said "you son of a bitch, go and arm yourself then". I did go off and heel myself. I came back and played poker with Virg Earp, Tom McLowery and other parties until daylight. Virg Earp played poker with his pistol in his lap all the time. At daylight he got up and quit the game.

We were playing in the Occidental. I followed Virg out when he quit. I told him that I was abused the night before and that I was in town that morning. Then, he told me that he was going to bed. The reason I followed him out [was] because I saw him take his pistol off his lap and stick it into his pants.

When he left the game, I came back and cashed in my chips and stayed around town until about 8 o'clock. I then went and got my Winchester, expecting to meet Doc Holliday on the street but never saw him until after Virg and Morgan Earp slipped up behind me and knocked me down with a six shooter. Shortly afterwards, I met my brother William. He told me to go out of town. I just about that time met the Corral man where my team was. I asked him to harness up the team. We then went to the Dexter

Corral in company with the McLowery brothers to get something my brother had left there. We went direct from there to the corral where my team was. We met the sheriff there. He told us that he would have to arrest us and take our arms off. I told him that we were just going to leave town and he then told Billy, my brother, and Frank McLowery to take their arms up to his office. William told him that we were just leaving town. The Sheriff told Tom and Frank McLowery to take their arms off. Tom opened his coat and showed him and said "Johnny I have no arms on."

Frank McLowery said he would leave town and keep his arms unless the Sheriff disarmed the Earps. He said that if he would disarm them he would lay his off as he had business to attend to in town which he would like to attend before he left. Just at that time I saw Doc Holliday and 3 of the Earps coming down the sidewalk. The Sheriff stepped forward to meet them and told them that he had these parties in charge and to stop that he did not want any trouble. They walked right by the Sheriff. I stopped 2 or 3 steps from the crowd and met Wyatt Earp right at the corner of the building.

He stuck his six shooter at me and said "throw up your hands." The Marshal also told the other boys to throw up their hands. Frank McLowery and Wm. Clanton threw their hands up. Tom McLowery opened his coat and said that he had no arms. They said "you sons of bitches, you ought to make a fight." At the same instant, Doc Holliday and Morg Earp shot. Morg shot Billy Clanton and I don't know which of the other boys that Doc Holliday shot. I saw Virg shooting at the same time. I grabbed Wyatt Earp and pushed him around the corner of the house and jumped into the Gallery.

As I jumped I saw Wm. Clanton falling. I ran through the Gallery and got away. Billy Clanton, Frank McLowery and myself threw up our hands at the order from the Earp party and Tom McLowery threw his coat open and said "I have got no arms". Doc Holliday came into the Occidental saloon and said I had been using his name. I said I had not. I never had any previous trouble with the Earps. They didn't like me.

We had a transaction, I mean myself and the Earps, but it had nothing to do with the killing of these 3 men. There was no threat made by the McLowery boys and Billy Clanton against the Earp boys that day, not that I know of. They had ordered [me to] heel myself and I told them I would be there. Doc Holliday met Billy Clanton about 20 minutes before and [had] shook hands with him and told him he was pleased to meet him. Frank McLowery and Billy Clanton had been in town about a 1/2 hour before the shooting.

The only threats I made was as I have before stated. I might have made other threats but don't remember. However, I made no worse threats against them than they did against me. I did not expect any trouble from Wyatt Earp but I did from Virg and Morg Earp and Doc Holliday. The boys expected no attack until the same body told them just before they were leaving town. I did not have any arms on me when the Earp party came down and ordered us to throw up our hands. Virg Earp had my arms; a Winchester and six shooter.

I had not seen Frank McLowery and Billy Clanton for two days before the shooting. I then saw them on the ranch. I never had a conversation with the McLowery boys or Billy Clanton as to making a fight in my life. I don't know whether any of the Earp party had a shotgun. When the fight commenced, Virg Earp and Doc Holliday were about 6 feet from the McLowery boys and Morg Earp's pistol was about 3 or 4 ft from Billy Clanton when he commenced firing. Wm. Clayborn was there at this time. I did not see my brother or either of the McLowerys fire a shot. I think there was 4 or 5 shots fired before I left.

When the Sheriff and I were talking, Billy Clanton and Clayborn were standing at Billy Clanton's horse talking. Tom McLowery and Frank were standing about 5 or 6 ft to the left of me and the Sheriff. Frank McLowery and Billy Clanton were not sent for that day. They came in from Antelope Springs at the request of Major Fink so I have been told by parties who were out there when they started in. I don't know how near Clayborn was to me when the firing commenced.

I don't know what kind of pistol it was that Doc Holliday fired. One of them, Virg or Doc, had a nickel-plated pistol. I don't know which one had it. They all had their arms in their hands when they passed me after Behan told the party to give up their arms. I did not consider myself under arrest because I was going out of town.

Mr. Behan had this last conversation with Frank McLowery before he started up the street. I do not know exactly what was said between them. I do not know where the Sheriff's office is. We could not have reached the Sheriff's office from where we were before the Earp party arrived. The Sheriff saw the Earp party before we did and told us to stay where we were. [Those were] the last words the Sheriff said to us.

After the Sheriff left us I would not have stayed there if I had not received those orders from the Sheriff. Behan was there 3 or 4 or 5 or 6 minutes, just long enough to say what I have before stated.

/s/ J. I. Clanton

PROBATE OF LOTTA CRABTREE'S ESTATE

Lotta Crabtree

History rarely provides us with answers in real time. Many times, it takes years for conversation, or documents to surface and open a door to unanswered questions. Such is the case with Wyatt Earp. Forty-four years after he left Arizona, he sat for a probate deposition regarding the will of Lotta Crabtree, a prominent nineteenth century actress, and entertainer who passed away on September 25, 1924. The disposition of her will had been challenged by Carlotta Crabtree Cockburn, the daughter of Lotta's brother Jack. As an acquaintance of Jack's while in Tombstone, Wyatt Earp was called to provide witness that he knew Jack Crabtree, his wife, and his daughter. During the deposition, Earp was asked about his time in Arizona, and in an effort to discredit his testimony, was asked specifically about his time in Tombstone. His answers provided a wealth of information regarding that timeframe.

This deposition played a major role in establishing the true identity of the man Wyatt called Johnson, but later became more commonly known as "Turkey Creek" Jack Johnson. It was "Johnson's" determination to have Bud Blount released from jail that revealed him to be John Blount, Bud Blount's brother.

WYATT EARP'S CRABTREE DEPOSITION- APRIL 1926

(Under stipulation, the further hearing of depositions was continued on this day, to no. 1818 Fourth Avenue, Los Angeles, California, at the hour of 3 PM)

Wyatt S. Earp produced as witness on behalf of the Contestant, having been first duly sworn, was examined and testified as follows:

By Mr. Hoy:

Q You live, ordinarily, where?

A. I have been summering in Los Angeles for the last 20 years.

Q In the winter where do you live?

A Down at some mines I have got on the Colorado River.

Q Vidal?

A Yes.

Q Now, Mr. Earp, were in Tombstone in the early days?

A I went to Tombstone in October, 1879.

Q How long did you stay?

A I lived there until the 23rd of March, 1882.

Mr. Chase: May we have the same stipulation as to objections and motions to strike out?

Mr. Hoy: Yes, but I want to add to the stipulation that I have the same objections and motion regarding your cross-examination.

Mr. Chase: Yes.

Mr. Hoy:

Q What position did you hold while you were there, if any?

A I was deputy sheriff from about the 1st of October 1879 up to the latter part of April, just before the election came off in 1880.

Q Then what position did you hold?

A I was Deputy United States Marshal and Wells Fargo private man.

Q Was your brother or brothers or your father any officer there in the early days?

A I had a brother who was chief of police.

Q What was his name?

A Virgil.

Q Was your father down there at all?

A No.

Q Where are you from?

A Do you mean where was I born?

Q Yes.

A Monmouth, Warren County, Illinois

Q When did you strike the West?

A 1864.

Q How old are you now?

A I am in my seventy eighth year. I was 77 the 19th of last month.

Q While you were in Tombstone do you remember any of the people you used to know back there?

A Yes.

Q Who do you remember?

A Well- that is while I was still living in Tombstone?

Q No. Who do you remember among the old timers back there?

A A man by the name of Young, a man by the name of Hunsaker, who is a lawyer here, John P. Clum and his son, and there is a few here- a man named Oscar Roberts- but a lot of them died in the last four or five years.

Q Do you remember anybody down there in the early days by name of Crabtree?

A I did.

Q Will you tell what you know about him, where you met him, how you met him and everything that you know about him?

A Well, I met Crabtree when he first came to Tombstone. He came there with a man named Bullock. Ed Bullock and his wife.

Q Where did you meet him?

A They started a corral in Tombstone and I met him at that corral, but I used to see them often from the street. They were right on the street and passing by I would see them. Of course, I would took see them around the corral and they had been there a time I got acquainted with Crabtree. I went up one time to try

To buy a three seated hack that he had. I had 12 or 15 horses that I had taken to Tombstone with me from Kansas and I had a coach and he had a three seated hack and I thought I could turn that hack into a pretty good coach and I intended to start a stage line from Tombstone to Benson. I went into the corral to try to buy that hack. There is where I first met Mrs. Crabtree to know who she was. Of course, I was satisfied before that that she was the wife of Crabtree but I met her there and I was introduced to her by Crabtree.

Q Later on did you hear of any family coming to them?

A She had a child later on.

Q Do you remember where they were living then?

A They were living east of Fremont. I don't know what the name of the street was that they were living on and I am not positive as to whether it was Fourth or Fifth, but I have always though it was Fifth Street they were living on. I know it was east of Fremont. Those streets east of Fremont, there was no business on those streets at all and they were cut up with washes pretty bad and that made it kind of a residential part of town and I never got down in that part of town very often, very seldom.

Q Was anybody with you when Crabtree introduced you to his wife?

A My brother Virgil. He went with me. We were partners at the time, or had the horses together.

Q How many times in all did you see Mrs. Crabtree in Tombstone, do you think?

A Well, I couldn't say positively, but I have met her afterwards I met her at a family's that I went to see with a man by the name of Johnson. They were friends of his and he asked me to go and visit the family with him.

Q Did you go?

A I went, and I met Mrs. Crabtree there. The first time I made the visit to these people-"I was there probably six or eight times all told.

Q At that time when you went there did they have a baby?

A She had a baby.

Q What kind of a baby was it?

A I don't know that.

Q Don't you remember?

A I don't recollect.

Q When you became acquainted knew him, did you know that he was in any way related to Crabtree, the actress?

A Well, no, I didn't know it at that time.

Q Did you at a later time?

A At that time I didn't know anything about Lotta Crabtree.

Q You are not a Californian, you came from Kansas?

A The first time I heard of Lotta Crabtree was after I left Tombstone and went to San Francisco in the latter part of 1882 and of course there I heard of Lotta Crabtree because they had a fountain there that she had erected, or had had erected in front of the Chronicle Building. That is the first time I ever heard of her.

Q When did you hear of, or did you connect your acquaintance-tip with Crabtree in Tombstone with her, or did you hear anything to lead you to know that there was any connection? A No, I don't think I heard anything.

Q Did you know where the San Jose rooming house was in the early days?

A Yes.

Q Did you ever see Mrs. Crabtree there?

A I have.

Q Did you know the lady who ran that?

A Yes.

Q Who was it?

A Mrs. Falloon. Afterwards she married a man named Taylor. I met Mrs. Crabtree at Mrs. Falloon San Jose rooming house on two or three occasions. I recollect one occasion very well, where there had been a man shot, by the name of Storms, and he had a room at the San Jose rooming house and we took Storms down there to his room. The doctor was going to hold a post mortem and they wanted me to stick around, and being there I met Mrs. Crabtree. She had her baby with her then and I had quite a long talk with her with regard to the shooting and how it came up and what it was about, and all that. On two or three other occasions I met here there. I used to take my prisoners down to the San Jose rooming house. They had no jail in Tombstone at that time. That was before the county was divided. It was all Pima County and we had to take our prisoners to Tucson. In holding them in Tombstone I used to get a room in the San Jose and put a guard over them and in that way, I met Mrs. Crabtree on two or three occasions.

Q How old a woman was she, would you say?

A Oh, I would put her anywhere between 16 and 18 years old at that time, quite young.

Q How old was Crabtree in those days? A Around 25 I should think.

Q What kind of a looking fellow was he?

A Small sized man, a man about the size of - oh, to the best of my knowledge about 5 feet 9 or 9 1/2 and weighed about 135 or 140.

Q Did you hear something about his being in some connection with Ed Bullock?

A He was supposed to be a partner of Bullock.

Q In what?

A In the corral.

Q Who told you that?

A I don't know

Q How did you know it?

A By seeing them together and doing business with each other.

Q Did you do business- did you ever do any business with them or see them doing business with each other?

A Well, you see they were both there at the corral and when I went to buy that hack or try to buy that hack, we all had our talk with Crabtree.

Q Did he talk as if he was the proprietor and interested in it?

A Yes.

Q Someone has said in connection with this case and the taking of these depositions that that was a pretty rough city up there, a very rough town, very little law and order and that law and order was more observed in the breach than in the observance thereof. What have you got to say about that?

A I say it is wrong.

Q What are the facts?

A The facts are there. I arrested pretty nearly every man that done any killing there. I don't think there was only a couple of people that ever got into trouble and killed anyone- just about two outside of what I arrested myself and I can mention all the killings on my fingers.

Q Ten killings?

A Not that many.

Q How many?

A Oh, I will tell you- let's see. The first man killed was Killeen, Mike Killeen.

Q Who killed him?

A Well, I know who killed him.

Q Did Frank Leslie kill him?

A. No.

Q Who was the next one- by the way you were there and saw the shooting?

A I was on the ground not a half a minute afterwards. I arrested Frank Leslie and also this other man.

Q There is one.

A Then City Marshal White. He was killed by Curley Bill. I arrested him and took him to Tucson and put him in jail. Then the next man was killed by a man by the name of Bradshaw. He killed his partner McIntyre. Bradshaw had bought a kind of a funny looking shirt, a red striped shirt and he went up the street and everybody was making fun of it and saying, "Where did you get that shirt?" And he got hot over it and he says, "The next man that kids me about this shirt I am going to kill him." The next man he met was his partner, the man that he was sleeping with and rooming with and of course he said to Bradshaw- we called him "Brad" he said "Where did you get that shirt?" and he jerked his gun out and killed him. That is three. That is Killeen, the Marshal, and McIntyre. The next man killed was Storms and he was killed by Luke Short. That was four. That is all I can recollect outside of the trouble that I had, the Clanton and McLowry boys.

Q Those men were men that were outlaws and you representing law and order, you had to shoot them?

A Yes.

Q By the way, what do you say as to that community's condition regarding law and order and morality and living, according to the ordinary customs of civilization as it was in that mining camp in those days, in 1878 and '83?'

A State that over again.

Q I would like to ask you to state your observation of those times and tell us what the condition of this community was for law and order?

A It was not half as bad as Long Angeles.

Q Tell us whether it was good or bad or whether it was a lawless outpost?

A I called it good.

Q You were in charge?

A I called it good.

Q Did you ever hear a breath of scandal about reputation, ill repute, against the name of Mrs. Crabtree?

A No sir, I did not.

Q I think you have answered this, but I will ask it again. You said that they lived in the residence portion of town?

A They lived on the same street.

Q I never knew the name of those streets up there. They run the same as Fremont, but they lived east of Fremont.

Q Over towards the Dragoons?

A In that direction. It could not have been more than a block away.

Q Did you ever hear it mentioned that Mr. and Mrs. Crabtree were living in any other relationship than as husband and wife?

A No sir.

Q Your understanding was what, as to the relationship?

A That they were man and wife.

Q And you got it from whom?

A I got it from their actions more than

Q And what else?

A From the introduction he gave me.

Q What else?

A And her having a child by him and everything went to show that they were man and wife.

Q Did you ever hear it questioned that the child was Jack Crabtree's child, in Tombstone?

A No.

Q Did you ever hear otherwise?

A No.

Q Did you ever see him with that child on the street or any place else?

A I have seen him with the child on the street several times and then several times I have seen him in the restaurant run by a man by the name of Brown- Doughnut Brown. He had a restaurant there.

Q With that child?

A Yes, and with his wife.

A This Doughnut Brown had a restaurant on Fifth Street between Allen and Fremont. I have seen him there. I used to take my meals there myself.

Q By Mr. Hoy: While you were there and saw him there what was his attitude towards the child? Can you say that it was other than the normal fatherly attitude, or what was it?

A The same as any other father would be. I never did see anything else.

By Mr. Hoy: Your witness, Judge Chase.

Cross Examination by Mr. Chase

Q When did you first see Crabtree?

A Well, I cannot say just what time, but I was under the impression it was along the latter part of 1880. It might have been a little earlier than that, or later.

Q When did you first see Bullock?

A Just about the same rime.

Q You didn't see them come to Tombstone?

A No I didn't see them come to Tombstone but I was under the impression that they both came there together.

Q When did you first see the woman that you have called Mrs. Crabtree?

A Well, the first time that I met the woman, that is just to see her, was around the corral.

Q How long after you saw Bullock and Crabtree was that?

A Oh, they were around the corral the same time.

Q How long after you first saw them at Tombstone was it that you saw her around the corral?

A Why, I saw them all about the same time.

Q Do you remember when the baby was born?

A No.

Q When did you first see the baby?

A I saw the baby at the corral.

Q At the corral?

A Yes.

Q About how long after you first saw Bullock and Crabtree was it that you saw the baby, first?

A Well, it was two or three months after I first saw him.

Q How old was the baby then?

A The first time I saw it?

Q Yes.

A It didn't look to me like it was over a week or ten days old.

Q Do you know where the baby was born?

A No, I do not.

Q Had you heard?

A No, I know it was born in Tombstone, but I don't know at what time.

Q Or where?

A That I could not swear to, but it was supposed to have been born where they were living. I couldn't swear to that.

Q You mean you don't know?

A I don't know.

Q Have you heard that it was born in a carriage at the corral?

A No sir, I never heard that.

Q Do you know Colonel Breckenridge?

A Yes.

Q Has he talked with you about this?

A Yes.

Q Didn't you tell him that you had heard that it was born in a carriage?

A No sir. Breckenridge knows nothing about it except what I told him.

Q Didn't you tell him that you had heard something about it being born in a carriage?

A I told him at one time when he was here, one time, that somehow or other I had got it into my mind that it was born in a carriage.

Q Because you had heard it?

A No.

Q Well, how did you get it in your mind?

A By seeing her around this carriage before, and a short time after.

Q Was that carriage fitted up as a sleeping place?

A Yes.

Q Who fitted it up?

A Crabtree, I suppose.

Q Was that carriage in the corral?

A It was in the front part of the corral.

Q At the time the carriage was there, fitted up as a sleeping place, you say the woman that you called Mrs. Crabtree, you saw her around the corral constantly?

A Yes.

Q Even after the baby was born you saw her around the corral?

A Yes.

Q You understood that she lived there at that time?

A I seen her around the corral quite often after the baby was born, but they were living then down east on Fremont Street.

Q At the time you saw her around the corral she had the little baby with her?

A She had a baby with her. I had seen her there. She would come down quite frequently.

Q You say you saw her in the San Jose house quite also?

A Yes sir.

Q Before or after you saw her around the corral?

A It was afterwards. It was after.

Q She lived there at one time, did she?

A Huh?

Q At the San Jose?

A Not that I know of.

Q Didn't she-

A As I say I have seen her there quite often when I when I would pass by the San Jose rooming house, I would see her there. Several times I saw her there. But whether she lived there or not I don't know.

A It was on Fifth Street, and on one of those streets east of Fremont, about a block from Fremont and half way down the street.

Q Those two streets east of Fremont. Now, who did Johnson go to see?

A The wife of Mahoney, if that was his name?

Q What did you go for?

A Well, I had this Johnson with me and the thing was getting warm between me and the rustlers and Johnson had joined my party, and he had

been identified with this other party for a while and they got on to him. I was using Johnson at that time the same as Chief Heath would use a stool pigeon, but we didn't call them stool pigeons in those days. I was letting him get information for me. They had got on to him and of course it was a little dangerous for a man like that to get out alone and I went with him.

Q Did he go down there to this house?

A I went with him, yes. That is the first time I ever met this family, was this time.

Q Did Johnson go down there to get information as an officer?

A Oh, no.

Q He went to make a call?

A I don't know what he went there for.

Q What did he do?

A There was two rooms to the house, a front room and a back room and a kitchen. I never was in there of course. I sat down in the front part of the room, and they would go into this back room and do the talking.

Q Who was "they?"

A Johnson and this man's wife. They never closed the door.

Q What man's wife? Who are you now referring to?

A Mahoney, or whatever his name was.

Q This lady called Mrs. Crabtree would stay in the other room.

A No sir.

Q What did she do?

A She went off with her child after we came. She was there a few minutes and then went home. She lived just a short ways from there. She went out. So, I was set down there and they went into this back room but they never closed the door. I went there about 6 or 8 times all told inside of 5 or 6

months and that door never was closed, so I know there was nothing wrong
them.

Q Between Johnson and this Mrs. Mahoney?

A Yes

Q You never saw Mrs. Crabtree

A Just once after that.

Q And that is all?

A Yes. I saw her just twice at that house. I met her at other times at an ice
cream parlor.

Q What ice cream parlor?

A On Fourth Street between Allen and Fremont.

Q Whose place?

A A woman named Hinkley. She afterwards married a man named Fay, a
reporter on the Nugget.

Q What was she doing?

A I don't know, I used to go there pretty often. I liked ice cream and I met
her over there. At one time I thought maybe she worked there.

Q Was she behind the counter?

A No, I don't know as they had a counter. They had tables around the room
and another room in back.

Q Did you ever know what her maiden name was, her first name?

A No.

Q Never heard of it?

A I have heard it since this case came up.

Q Did you ever hear that it was Anna Leopold, or Annie'?

A No.

Q Did you ever hear anybody referred to as native daughter?

A No.

Q Nobody in Tombstone?

A No. As a native daughter did you say?

Q Yes.

A No.

Q Was Johnson the man's name?

A That is the name that he was going by but I don't think it was his right name.

Q What was his right name?

A I don't know. I never found out.

Q Why do you think it was not his right name?

A Well, putting two and two together I figured it out. He never told me, and nobody else told me but I figured it out that this man-this man's wife that he was going to see was probably his sister. I knew the family was from Southwest Missouri and I knew that Johnson was from Southwest Missouri and afterwards I met Johnson in Kansas City and he was going by the name of Ritchie. I put it together. I knew there was some parties that had has some trouble in Southwest Missouri, had had a street fight and several people got killed and I knew that he was from that part of the country, so I made up my mind that his name was Blunt. I knew the Blunt boys was in this trouble and I knew they went to Leadville, Colorado, and I also knew that they came to Prescott, Arizona, and Bud Blunt got into some kind of trouble there. Some prizefighter slugged the life out of him one day, pounded him up unmercifully, and he went off and got a gun and killed this fellow. He was sent to the pen for four years. There was Bud Blunt and John Blunt. I never saw him after he went to the Penitentiary. But this fellow Johnson appeared there in Tombstone I got acquainted with him and he got down amongst the rustlers, going into Mexico and picking up a herd of cattle, and he got tired of that and he wanted to quit and I knew that he could give me a lot of information and get a lot of information from the other side so I took him in with my posse. After he had been there awhile he asked me to help get Bud Blunt out of the penitentiary. He said that if I would get up a petition in Tombstone and one in Leadville and one in Prescott he thought that the governor would pardon him. I had heard all about Blunt killing this fellow after he had been pounded up, and I had made up mind that he was about halfway right and I helped him get this petition up and he was pardoned by the governor. He went back to Missouri and I never heard of John Blunt again. I had made up my mind, putting everything together afterwards, that this man Johnson was John Blunt a brother of Bud's, and also a brother of the man's wife.

Q Do I understand that you used Johnson or Blunt or whatever his name was as a stool pigeon because he knew the people that you were after and was familiar with the facts you wanted?

A That was what I wanted.

Q And had been associating with them?

A Yes, I wanted to get information.

Q Was that the reason why you used him?

A Yes,

Q Did he know this Woman that you referred to as Mrs. Crabtree?

A Who?

Q Johnson?

A Did he know' Mrs. Crabtree?

Q Yes.

A He knew her quite well I think.

Q Do you remember when she went away?

A No. She disappeared all at once.

Q Do you know a man named Rabb?

A I do not.

Q Never heard of him?

A No, not until this case came up.

Q Do you know where she went from Tombstone?

A Where who went?

Q This woman who called herself Mrs. Crabtree?

A No, I do not.

Q Never heard?

A Never heard where she went and at that time I didn't know anything about where she went.

Q You said you didn't go down in that part of town very often?

A No, not very.

Q Any particular reason for that?

A Well, there was no business on those streets, there was no business I think at all. It was a residential part of town now that I call to mind- my lawyer lived in that part of town and I went to his place several times and I met Mrs. Crabtree at his house on two or three different occasions. His name was Jones, Harry Jones and he was my lawyer. They lived in that vicinity, but that part of town had no business outside of residential purposes and I had no business down there, much. Of course, the San Jose house, that was on one of the principal streets, on Fremont.

Q You never heard the relations between Mr. Crabtree and this woman discussed, did you?

A Between what?

Q You never heard the relations between them discussed, did you?

A No.

Q It was not a matter of talk about the town was it?

A I never heard it discussed at all, they were supposed to be man and wife.

Q That is your supposition?

A Yes, I never heard anything to the contrary.

Q Or to that point either?

A No sir.

Q You drew your own conclusions to that effect from the fact that you say you saw them together and there was a baby?

A Yes.

Q It was not a matter of gossip about the town, was it?

A Never heard any.

Q You cannot think of anybody you ever heard discussing what they were to each other?

A No.

Q For the most of the time you were there you were deputy marshal, weren't you?

A I was deputy sheriff. I was made deputy sheriff on my way to Tombstone. I stopped off in Tucson. I had some friends in Tucson from Kansas. I had left Dodge City, Kansas, where I had been chief of police of Dodge City for four years before and I went to Tombstone and quite a number of my friends were living in Tucson. I had quite a big outfit and I camped out in the edge of town. I went uptown and met some of those friends and the sheriff there, his name his was Chabelle, I was camped down there and he and another man came down there to see me and the Sheriff prevailed upon me to take the deputyship. I told him I had just got away from that kind of a life at Dodge City and I didn't want to go back to it, but he told me- put it up to me in a glowing way that it would be just the same as being sheriff of the county. He said, "You have got all that country over there and there is money in it." Finally, I accepted the deputyship and I went over there as a deputy sheriff.

SUPPLEMENTAL INFORMATION | 223

Q How long were you deputy sheriff?

A Well, that was in the later part of October, 1879, and I served until 1880.

Q Then you became United States Marshal or Deputy United States Marshal?

A I went to Tucson late in 1880 and put in my resignation to Sheriff Chabelle and he wanted to know why I done that, and I told him that friend of mine was running for sheriff and running on my ticket and that was going to support him and I didn't feel like working for Ball and being his deputy. So, he accepted the resignation.

Q You then became Deputy United States Marshal?

A Then I was appointed Deputy United States Marshal.

Q And were such until you left?

A I was Deputy United States Marshal until I left.

Q After you became Deputy United States Marshal there was not the best of feeling between your office and the office of the sheriff?

A No.

Q The sheriff's name was Behan?

A Yes.

Q You were allied with one faction and he with another?

A Yes.

Q With you was allied Doc Holliday?

A Yes.

Q He was somewhat of a notorious character in those days?

A Well, no. I couldn't say that he was notorious outside of this other faction trying to make him notorious. Of course, he killed a man or two before he went there.

Q Didn't he have the reputation of being a holder-up of stages?

A I never heard of it until I left.

Q With the Behans were allied the Clandens?

A Yes. And the Behan side whenever they got a chance to hurt me over Holliday's shoulders they would do it. They would make a lot of talk about Doc Holliday.

Q Because he was allied with you?

A He never had no trouble in Tombstone outside of being in this street fight with us. Then on one occasion he got in trouble with part of the combination that was against me, Joyce, his partner, and he shot Joyce in the hand and the other fellow in the foot and of course that made them pretty sore against Holliday. But they knew that I was Holliday's friend and they tried to injure me every way they could.

Q Didn't that feud finally culminate in what you have referred to as a street fight?

A No sir.

Q What was that and where did it take place and when?

A It took place in October on Fremont Street.

Q October of what year?

A 1881.

Q How many were killed in that fight?

A Three.

Q Who were they?

A Billy Clandon and the two McLowreys.

Q Was one of your brothers injured at that time?

A I had two brothers wounded in that fight, and Doc Holliday.

Q Was one of them killed?

A No, not then.

Q Was Doc Holliday in that fight?

A Yes.

Q Was one of your brothers subsequently killed?

A Not in that fight.

Q In another fight?

A No other fight. He was killed afterwards by being assassinated, but not in a fight. He was shot through a window.

Q You left after that?

A Yes

Q You said you left Dodge City for Tombstone?

A Yes.

Q what were you going to do in Tombstone?

A I intended to start a stage line when I first started out from Dodge City, but when I got there I found there was two stage lines and so I finally sold my outfit to one of the companies, to a man named Kinnear. But I intended to start this stage line when I went there.

Q What did you do besides being deputy sheriff and marshal?

A What did I do?

Q Yes.

A Well, I dealt awhile in pasteboard and ivory.

Q Well, you are talking to people who don't know what those things are.

A Dealing faro bank.

Q Where was that?

A In Tombstone.

Q What place?

A That was the Oriental.

Q Was that on the main street?

A On the business street.

Q On Allen Street?

A Yes.

Q Was the Bird Cage open while you were there?

A Yes.

Q Do you remember when that was opened?

A Sometime in 1880. I don't recollect just when, just what month. It was about the later part of 1880.

Mr. Chase: I think that is all.

A After this trouble came up, this fellow Behan, he intended to run for sheriff and he knew that I did, and if I do say it myself I was a pretty strong man for the position. He knew that he had to do me some way and he done everything in the world that he could against me. He stood in with this tough element, the cow boys and stage robbers and others, because they were pretty strong and he wanted their vote. Whenever they would get a chance to shoot anything at me over Holliday's shoulders they would do it. So, they made Holliday a bad man. An awful bad man, which was wrong. He was a man that would fight if he had to but-

Q By Mr. Hoy: Do you hear any more or any less about other married people in Tombstone than you heard about Jack Crabtree and his wife?

A I did not.

Q It was just the same- they were treated just the same as married people by everybody?

A Yes

Q And everybody understood that they were married?

A Yes

Q And were according to your understanding?

A Yes?

Q What I am getting at is this. Were there or not many people in Tombstone going as husband and wife that you didn't know whether they were married or not. You had never seen their marriage license, but you took them as man and wife?

A Yes

Q Were Jack and Anna Crabtree taken the same way?

A Yes

Q Were they different than any others?

A No sir, none at all. There was lots of good married people there.

Mr. Hoy: All right, Mr. Earp, that is all. We are very much obliged to you.

ABOUT THE AUTHOR

Kevin Hogge is an old west enthusiast who has ridden the trails of Wyatt Earp, Billy the Kid, Charlie Goodnight, and Col. Ranald Mackenzie. He is part of an elite group of riders and historians who have ridden the back country of Southern Arizona, following the trail of Wyatt Earp and his Vendetta Posse in search of the men who killed his brother, Morgan Earp. He has ridden the trails of Billy the Kid through the mountains of Lincoln New Mexico, where no one had been for a century. With a hard riding group of friends, and horsemen, he has run New Mexico's tough and historic terrain from Santa Fe's Copper Canyon, to the Sangre de Christo Mountains. Add the Palo Duro Canyons in Amarillo Texas where Col. Mackenzie led the final battle to defeat the Comanche, and the Kiowa, he has touched history in a manner which few people have ever attempted.

THANK YOU FOR READING!

If you enjoyed this book, we would appreciate your customer review on your book seller's website or on Goodreads.

Also, we would like for you to know that you can find more great books like this one at www.CreativeTexts.com

CPSIA information can be obtained
at www.ICGtesting.com
Printed in the USA
LVHW011600280420
654634LV00007B/249/J